CW01656501

Adam Robson.

March 2000.

£3

CHURCHES TO VISIT IN SCOTLAND

CRATHIE PARISH CHURCH, ABERDEENSHIRE

This book has
been sponsored by
The Peter Stormonth Darling
Charitable Trust

CHURCHES TO VISIT IN SCOTLAND

Illustrated by John R Hume

ST MICHAEL'S PARISH CHURCH, LINLITHGOW

Published on behalf of Scotland's Churches Scheme
by Saint Andrew Press, Edinburgh

Published on behalf of
SCOTLAND'S CHURCHES SCHEME
by
SAINT ANDREW PRESS
121 George Street, Edinburgh EH2 4YN

Paperback ISBN 0 86153 292 9
Hardback ISBN 0 86153 291 0

British Library Cataloguing in Publication Data
A catalogue record for this book
is available from the British Library.

Designed by Mark Blackadder.
Typeset in Ehrhardt and Gill Sans.

DIRECTOR
Dr Brian Fraser BA PhD FIPD

Office: Dunedin, Holehouse Road, Eaglesham, Glasgow G76 0JF
Telephone: 01355 302416 *Fax*: 01355 303181
E-mail: fraser@dunedin67.freeserve.co.uk
Website: http://churchnet.ucsm.ac.uk/scotchurch/
Registered Charity Number: SC 022868

Printed in Scotland by Bell & Bain Ltd, Glasgow.

HOW TO USE THIS GUIDE

Entries are arranged alphabetically by council and then by locality. The number preceding each entry refers to the map at the beginning of each section. The denomination of the church is shown on the last line of each entry, followed by the relevant symbols:

- Access for partially abled
- Hearing induction loop for the deaf
- Welcomers and guides on duty
- Guidebooks and souvenirs
- Toilet for the disabled
- Features for children/link with schools
- Refreshments
- Toilets on premises
- **A** Category A Listing
- **B** Category B Listing
- **C** Category C Listing

Category A: Buildings of national or more than local importance, either architectural or historic, or fine little-altered examples of some particular period, style or type.
Category B: Buildings of regional or more than local importance, or major examples of some particular period, style or building type which may have been altered.
Category C: Buildings of local importance, or lesser examples of any period style, or building type, as originally constructed or altered; and simple traditional buildings which group well with others.

The information appearing in the gazetteer of this guidebook is supplied by the participating churches. While this is believed to be correct at the time of going to press, Scotland's Churches Scheme cannot accept any responsibility for its accuracy.

PREFACE

From the Chairman, Robin Blair LVO WS

Scotland's Churches Scheme was formed in 1994 as a Charitable Trust with the objective of improving the accessibility of Scotland's ecclesiastical heritage. Our aims and purposes are set out opposite.

The Scheme has grown rapidly since its inception and there are now 647 Churches in membership, operating an 'open doors' policy. As can be seen from this new guidebook, these churches are spread across Scotland and across all the religious denominations. They contain a significant part of the nation's heritage (over 400 are listed buildings, many being Category A).

Having established a permanent means of providing access to the nation's ecclesiastical heritage, with the most significant buildings, large and small, urban and rural, in our Scheme, we are now considering the ways in which we might develop advice and assistance to these member churches in meeting the Scheme's objectives. The Scheme's success to date, over a relatively short period, is hugely encouraging and has the potential of further raising the awareness of our ecclesiastical and spiritual heritage and making it more accessible to a wider audience.

To enable the Scheme to provide greater advice and assistance to member Churches, which has been identified in a recent survey, we have formed a team of Local Representatives and now cover Scotland with a local network of some 20 enthusiastic and knowledgeable volunteers. With the Director, these volunteers will help churches who belong to the Scheme to:

- work together with others to make the Church the focus of the community
- open their doors with a welcoming presence
- tell the story of the Building (however old or new), its purpose, faith and heritage (artistic, architectural and historical),
- provide information and care for visitors, young and old.

At the beginning of this new millennium, the Trustees are confident that the unique nature and purpose of Scotland's Churches Scheme can fulfil the aspirations referred to by Bishop Mario Conti, one of our Trustees, in his Foreword overleaf.

SCOTLAND'S CHURCHES SCHEME

Serving Churches of all denominations in Scotland

AIMS AND PURPOSES

1.

To promote spiritual understanding by enabling the public to appreciate all buildings designed for worship and active as living churches

2.

To advance the education of the public in history, architecture and other environmental subjects through the study of historic church buildings of all denominations in Scotland, their contents and environs

3.

To encourage co-operation among the churches themselves and between them and their local communities

4.

To publish details of churches open to visitors through a handbook *Churches to Visit in Scotland* as a guide for visitors, and to encourage support for the churches visited through donations, especially for specific appeals

5.

To receive donations for churches, in particular or in general, in order to provide when requested advice on the care and reception of visitors and the provision of historical and other information

6.

To promote the common purpose of mission through the ministry of welcome for visitors, tourists and pilgrims

FOREWORD

The Rt Rev Mario Conti DD STL PhL,
Bishop of Aberdeen and SCS Trustee

We entered the new Millennium with a great deal of razzamatazz and with varying degrees of enthusiasm.

For us Christians however the year 2000 has this significance: that it is the two thousandth anniversary of Christ's birth. In Rome the opening of the Holy Door of St. Peter's Basilica signified the entry of the Christian community into a 'year of favour from the Lord' (Isaiah 61,1-2).

The Scottish Churches Scheme started life as a scheme to encourage open churches in Scotland, and it still has that as one of its chief aims.

Up and down the land churches form part of the distinctive profile of our cities and towns. They are among the best of our buildings, a rich heritage to be loved and visited. The publication of this Directory enables visitors to know which churches are open and when.

The Scheme exists above all however to promote an understanding of their social, artistic, and religious significance.

In regard to this latter we do not forget that they constitute more than bricks and mortar. They are treasuries of sacred art and open books of remembrance. Even more they are sacraments of the faithful communities which worship there. We are reminded of the Apostle's words that we are the 'living stones' which are being built into 'a spiritual house' in which the Lord dwells (1 Peter 2,5).

We seek to encourage those who care for our churches to provide a warm welcome to all who want to see where we stay. Andrew, our patron, was one of the first to respond to Christ's invitation 'come and see' and found more than he sought (John 1,39).

Perhaps the words of the psalmist best sums up our desires:

'*Open to me the gates of holiness:*
I will enter and give thanks.
This is the Lord's own gate
Where the just may enter.
I will thank you for you have given answer,
and you are my Saviour'

(Psalm 117,19-21)

+ Mario Conti

SCOTLAND'S CHURCHES SCHEME

SCOTLAND'S CHURCHES SCHEME

LOCAL REPRESENTATIVES

Mrs Elizabeth Beaton *Moray*

Mrs Margaret Beveridge *Lothian*

Mrs Jane Boyd *Glasgow*

Mrs Fiona Cameron *Aberdeen/Press*

Sheriff and Mrs Vincent Canavan *North Lanarkshire*

Mrs Beatrice Fawkes *Aberdeenshire*

Miss Joan Fish *Ayrshire*

Mr Sandy Gilchrist *South Lanarkshire/Tweedale*

Mr Michael Gossip *Argyll & Bute*

Mrs Lyndall Leet *Highland*

Mr Norman McGilvray *Renfrewshire*

Ms Atisha McGregor Auld *Highland/Western Isles*

Mr Alan Naylor *Falkirk*

Mrs Mary Reid *Borders*

Mrs Marion Smith *Dunbartonshire*

Mr Louis Stott *Perthshire/Stirlingshire*

The Rev J W Scott *Dumfriesshire*

The Rev Malcolm Trew *Fife*

The Rev Peter Youngson *Angus*

DIRECTOR

Dr Brian M Fraser

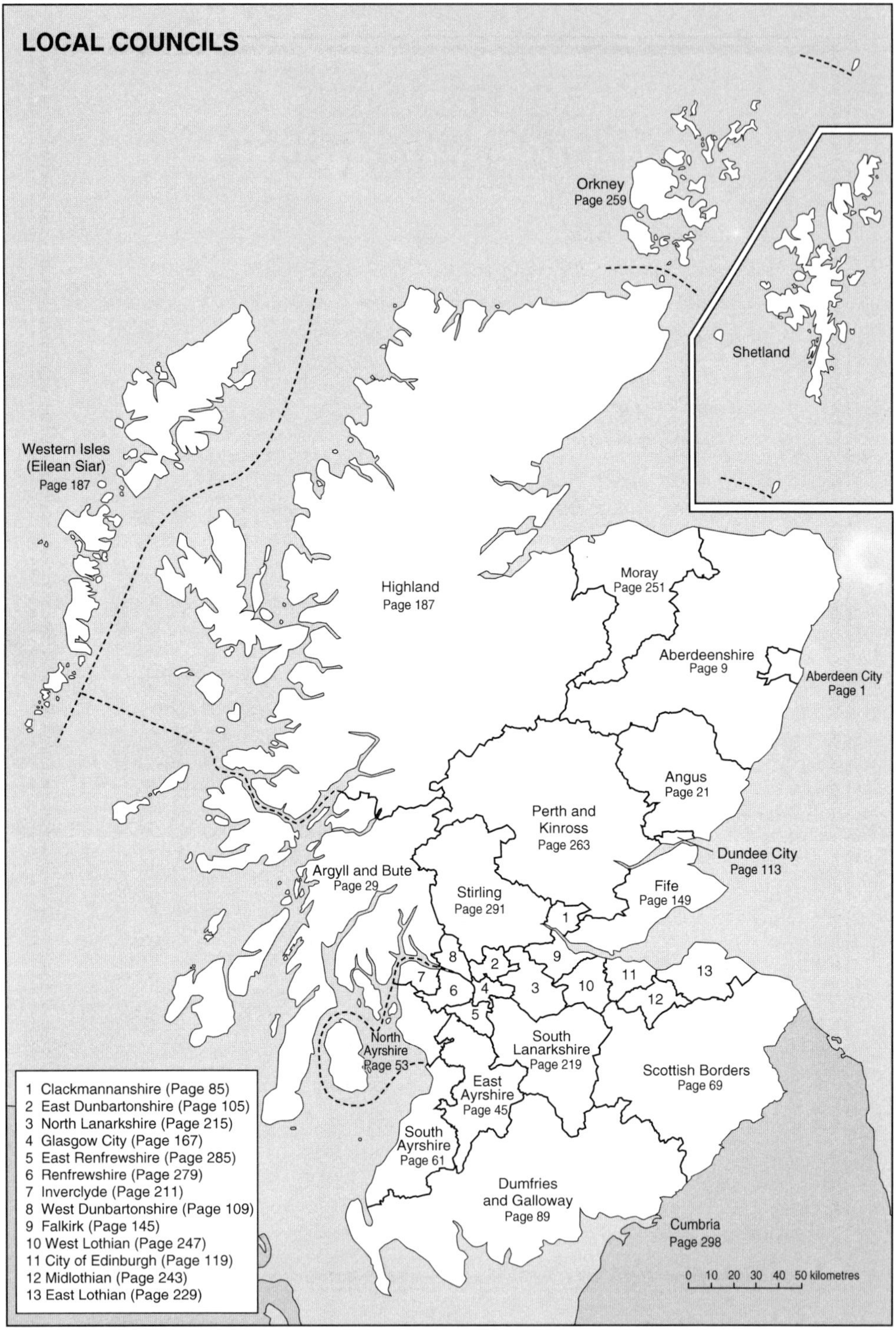
LOCAL COUNCILS
Orkney
Page 259
Shetland
Western Isles
(Eilean Siar)
Page 187
Highland
Page 187
Moray
Page 251
Aberdeenshire
Page 9
Aberdeen City
Page 1
Angus
Page 21
Perth and
Kinross
Page 263
Dundee City
Page 113
Argyll and Bute
Page 29
Stirling
Page 291
Fife
Page 149
North
Ayrshire
Page 53
South
Lanarkshire
Page 219
East
Ayrshire
Page 45
Scottish Borders
Page 69
South
Ayrshire
Page 61
Dumfries
and Galloway
Page 89
Cumbria
Page 298
0 10 20 30 40 50 kilometres
1 Clackmannanshire (Page 85)
2 East Dunbartonshire (Page 105)
3 North Lanarkshire (Page 215)
4 Glasgow City (Page 167)
5 East Renfrewshire (Page 285)
6 Renfrewshire (Page 279)
7 Inverclyde (Page 211)
8 West Dunbartonshire (Page 109)
9 Falkirk (Page 145)
10 West Lothian (Page 247)
11 City of Edinburgh (Page 119)
12 Midlothian (Page 243)
13 East Lothian (Page 229)

CONTENTS

Churches to Visit in Scotland

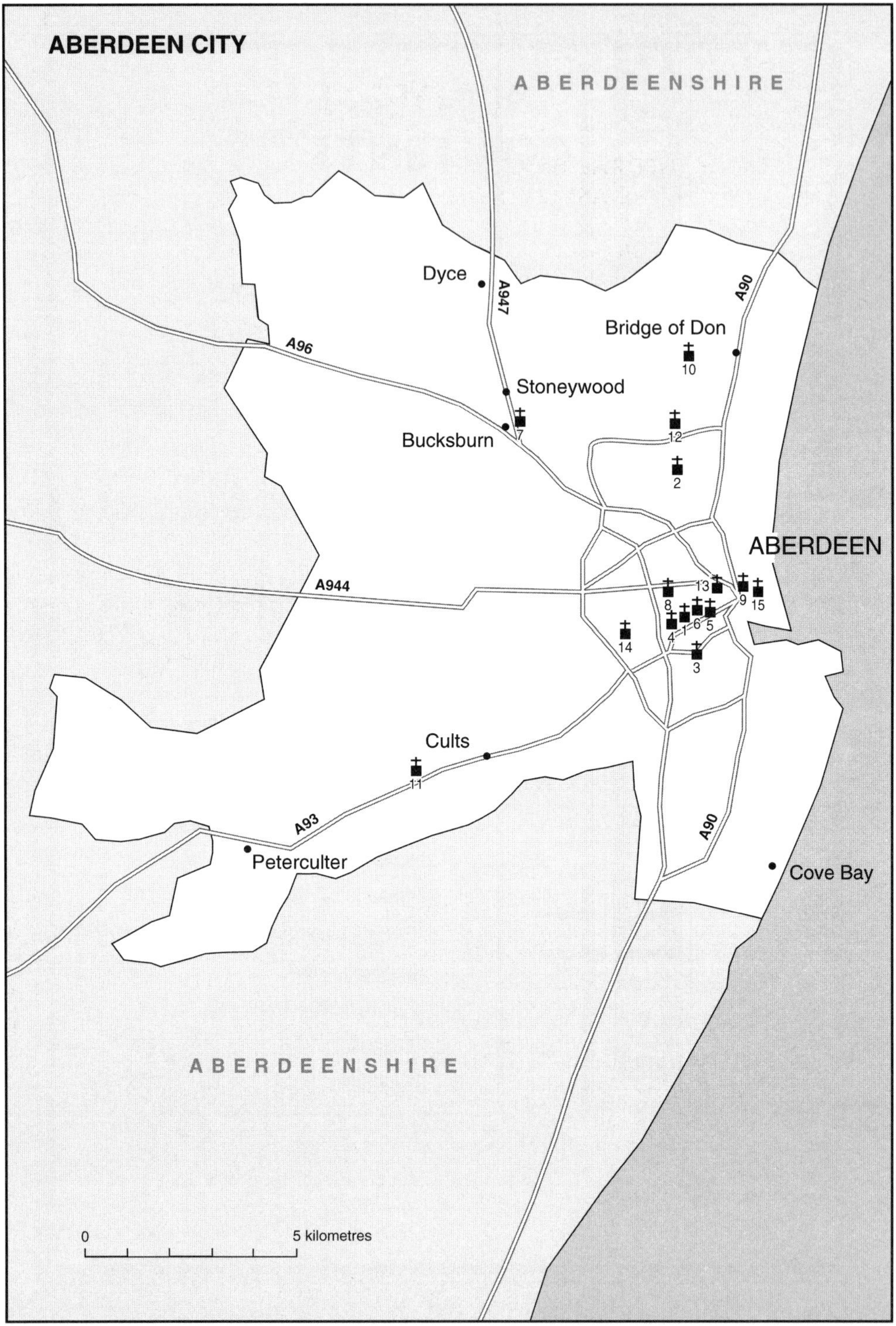

ABERDEEN CITY
ABERDEENSHIRE
Dyce
A947
A90
Bridge of Don
A96
10
Stoneywood
7
12
Bucksburn
2
ABERDEEN
A944
13
9
15
8
6
5
1
4
14
3
Cults
11
A93
A90
Peterculter
Cove Bay
ABERDEENSHIRE
0
5 kilometres

ABERDEEN

1 THE CATHEDRAL OF OUR LADY OF THE ASSUMPTION

NJ 937 061

Huntly Street, Aberdeen

The principal church of the Roman Catholic Diocese of Aberdeen, built in 1860 by Alexander Ellis. Spire and bells added in 1877, designed by R G Wilson. Contains religious artefacts by Charles Blakeman, Gabriel Loire, Ann Davidson, Felix McCullough, David Gulland and Alexander Brodie. The organ is a rare example of the work of James Conacher, Huddersfield, 1887. Off Union Street. Mass Times: Vigil Saturday 7pm; Sunday 8am, 11.15am, 6pm

Open daily, summer 8am-5pm, winter 8am-4pm Also Aberdeen Doors Open Day.

Clergy House at 20 Huntly Street

ROMAN CATHOLIC WC **B**

THE CATHEDRAL OF OUR LADY OF THE ASSUMPTION

2 THE CHAPEL OF THE CONVENT OF ST MARGARET OF SCOTLAND

NJ 941 074

17 Spital, Aberdeen

The chapel, built in 1892, is one of the earliest works of Sir Ninian Comper, son of the Rev John Comper, Rector of St John's Church in Aberdeen, who in 1863 had invited sisters from St Margaret's Convent, East Grinstead to work with him. The furnishings, fittings and windows were also designed by Sir Ninian, and executed in his workshop. The oak panelling over the stalls was a thank offering after the Second World War. On left hand side of road from Mounthooly roundabout to the Old Town. Services: Vespers 5.30pm (Thursdays, 5pm); Daily Eucharist at varying times. Please telephone 01224 632648 for exact information

Open by arrangement. Apply at front door of convent. Chapel may be viewed through grille in west porch

SCOTTISH EPISCOPAL **A**

3 FERRYHILL PARISH CHURCH

FERRYHILL PARISH CHURCH

NJ 939 054

Junction of Fonthill Road and Polmuir Road, Aberdeen

Designed by Duncan McMillan for the Free Church 1874 in Early Gothic style with a tall square bell tower with octagonal spire. Side galleries added in 1896. The building was known as Ferryhill South Church from 1929 to 1990. Now contains several fine windows (by James McLundie and others) removed from the former Ferryhill North Church. The sanctuary was re-ordered 1994 by Oliver Humphries and further developments, mainly at the entrances to the church and the halls, are due to be completed early in 2000. The memorial Chapel incorporates the 51st (Highland) Divisional Signals War Memorial, the Piper Alpha window by Jane Bayliss and the Steele memorial window by the same artist. Allan organ. Sunday Service 11am. See notice board for other services and musical events

Open weekday mornings during school term times. Extended opening hours and refreshment facilities likely to be introduced in 2000. To visit at other times telephone 01224 589465 or 01224 584176

CHURCH OF SCOTLAND WC WC **B**

4 GILCOMSTON SOUTH CHURCH

NJ 935 059

Union Street, Aberdeen

Sandstone and granite building by William Smith 1868. Spire added in 1875 and rebuilt in 1995. Stained glass by David Gauld, Douglas Strachan and Jane Bayliss. Oak screen and choir stalls. Binns pipe organ 1902. A hundred yards from west end of Union Street. Sunday Services 11am and 6.30pm; Wednesday 7.30pm; Saturday Prayer Meeting 7pm

Open Aberdeen Doors Open Day.

Other times, telephone Mr John Glibborn 01224 873919

CHURCH OF SCOTLAND WC **C**

5 GREYFRIARS JOHN KNOX CHURCH

NJ 943 044

Broad Street, Aberdeen

Striking Gothic building, designed to complement the impressive granite front of Marischal College. Both designed by architect A Marshall Mackenzie. Light and airy interior. Great window from original 1532 Franciscan church, moved here 1903. Stained glass in this and six side windows by C E Kempe. Organ, 1903, by Willis. Chancel panelled with pew ends c.1690. Sunday Service: 11am

Open 10.30am-12.30pm Thursday, Friday and Saturday mid-June to mid-September

CHURCH OF SCOTLAND A

6 KIRK OF ST NICHOLAS

NJ 941 063

Back Wynd, Aberdeen

The 'Mither Kirk' of Aberdeen dates from the 12th century. The present building is largely 18th and 19th century. The west end 1755, by James Gibbs, the east end by Archibald Simpson 1837. The church contains the Chapel of the Oil Industry, and the 15th-century St Mary's Chapel. The carillon of 48 bells is the largest in Great Britain. Seventeenth century embroidered wall hangings. Situated in Aberdeen city centre. Sunday Service 11am, also July and August 9.30am; Daily Prayers Monday to Friday 1.05pm. The World of Worship Exhibition (RCAHMS) from 19 June to 8 July 2000

Open 1 May to 30 September, Monday to Friday 12 noon-4pm, Saturday 1-3pm. Other times, on application to the Church Office 10am-1pm

CHURCH OF SCOTLAND WC WC A

7 NEWHILLS CHURCH

NJ 876 095

Bucksburn, Aberdeen

The present church was built in 1830 to a design by Archibald Simpson, near to the site of the original 17th-century church (now part of the graveyard). Painted coat of arms of the patron, Lord James Hay of Easton, Earl of Fife and several modern banners add colour to the interior. Sunday Services 10.30am and 6pm (not July and August)

Open Monday to Friday 9am-1pm

CHURCH OF SCOTLAND (by arrangement) WC C

8 ROSEMOUNT CHURCH

NJ 933 069

120 Rosemount Place, Aberdeen

Traditional church, 1870, converted to multi-purpose Celebration Centre in 1984. Ground floor accommodates Sunday worship, weekday activities and coffee lounge. Gallery houses 'Jonah's Journey' – children's museum. Situated close to two municipal parks. By road or by bus 22 from lower end of Union Street. Sunday Service 11am

Open all year (not public holidays), Monday to Saturday 10am–12 noon, Sunday 2.30–4.30pm (except July)

CHURCH OF SCOTLAND WC C

9 ST ANDREW'S CATHEDRAL

NJ 945 065

King Street, Aberdeen

Built by Archibald Simpson 1817 and altered and enhanced by Sir Ninian Comper 1939–45. Gold burnished baldacchino over the high altar. National memorial to Samuel Seabury, first Bishop of America consecrated in Aberdeen in 1784. Interesting roof heraldry depicting American states and Jacobite supporters of the '45 rebellion. Stained glass. Sir John Betjeman described it as one of Aberdeen's best modern buildings. Three-manual organ by Hill, Norman & Beard, recently restored. Services: Holy Communion 8am; Sung Eucharist 10.15am; Evensong 6.30pm

Open May to September, Monday to Saturday 10am–4pm

SCOTTISH EPISCOPAL WC A

ST ANDREW'S CATHEDRAL

ST COLUMBA'S PARISH CHURCH

10 ST COLUMBA'S PARISH CHURCH

NJ 1094

Braehead Way, Bridge of Don

St Columba's Parish Church is shared with the local Roman Catholic congregation. The most notable feature is a steel cross at rear of the church. Sunday Services 10am and 6.30pm

Open by arrangement, telephone Mr Thompson 01224 703753

CHURCH OF SCOTLAND

11 ST DEVENICK'S BIELDSIDE

NJ 882 025

North Deeside Road, Bieldside

Pink and grey granite church, designed by Arthur Clyne and opened in 1903. Organ (Wadsworth) installed in 1910 'best specimen of its kind by Wadsworth ever placed in Aberdeen or for a considerable distance round about'. North transept completed in 1959 by building of Lady Chapel, which seats 24. Sunday Services: 8.30 and 10.30am; Thursday 10.30

Open by arrangement, telephone the Rector 01224 861552

SCOTTISH EPISCOPAL B

ST DEVENICK'S BIELDSIDE

ST MACHAR'S CATHEDRAL

12 ST MACHAR'S CATHEDRAL

NJ 939 008

The Chanonry, Aberdeen

Fourteenth to 16th-century nave with unique heraldic ceiling and fortified west front. Interesting monuments, stained glass. Ruined transepts. Peal of eight bells. Sunday Services 11am and 6pm

Open daily 9am–5pm

Recitals programme information, telephone 01224 485988.

E-mail: stmachar@ifb.co.uk *Website:* www.ifb.net/stmachar

CHURCH OF SCOTLAND **A**

13 ST MARGARET OF SCOTLAND

NJ 942 067

Gallowgate, Aberdeen

Completed in 1869, the spacious sanctuary includes many fine examples of the work of Sir Ninian Comper, including the chapel of St Nicholas, the first building he designed and with the original stained glass. His style is mainly Early English with elements of Byzantine and Renaissance. Memorial garden. Just north of Marischal College. Sunday Services: Low Mass 9.15am, Parish Mass 10.30am, Evensong 6pm, Folk Mass 7.30pm

Open Tuesday mornings. Other times, telephone Canon Nimmo 01224 644969, or A Allan 01224 872960. Gallowgate Festival Saturday in early August

SCOTTISH EPISCOPAL **B**

14 ST MARY'S CHURCH

NJ 929 060

Carden Place, Aberdeen

The variety of granites and patterned roof tiles earned it the nickname 'The Tartan Kirkie'. To a design by Alexander Ellis and the Rev George Lee, dating from 1864. The east end sustained severe damage during an air raid in April 1943. Reconstructed 1952. The church is home to a Samuel Green chamber organ, built in 1778. On the left between Skene Street and Queen's Road. Sunday Services: 8am and 10.15am; Tuesday 7pm; Wednesday 11am

Open by arrangement, telephone the Rector 01224 584123

SCOTTISH EPISCOPAL WC **A**

15 ST PETER'S CHURCH

NJ 942 065

Chapel Court, Justice Street (off the Castlegate), Aberdeen

1803-4, by James Massie, gallery added 1815 and façade finished 1817, by Harry Leith. Within the courtyard is the residence occupied since 1774, including, in the 18th century, the Vicars Apostolic of the Lowland district: Bishop James Grant and Bishop John Geddes. Services: Saturday Vigil 6pm (5pm in winter), Sunday 11am, Weekdays as announced

Open Monday, Wednesday, Friday 10.30am-2pm or by arrangement

ROMAN CATHOLIC WC **B**

ABERDEENSHIRE
0
10
20
30
40
50 kilometres
Portsoy
Banff
Macduff
Rosehearty
Fraserburgh
Crimond
St Fergus
Cornhill
Turriff
New Deer
Mintlaw
PETERHEAD
Boddam
Huntly
Fyvie
Cruden Bay
Ellon
Oldmeldrum
Newburgh
Rhynie
Inverurie
Balmedie
Kildrummy
Alford
Strathdon
Sauchen
ABERDEEN CITY
Lumphanan
Banchory
Crathie
Ballater
Braemar
Portlethen
Newtonhill
Stonehaven
Drumlithie
Laurencekirk
Inverbervie
Johnshaven
St Cyrus
Montrose
Arbroath
Dundee
Perth
MORAY
HIGHLAND
ANGUS
PERTH & KINROSS
FIFE
A96
A98
A942
A97
A95
A941
A940
A939
A920
A981
A950
A952
A947
A948
A975
A938
A944
A980
A93
A957
A90
A937
A92
A924
A935
A926
A923
A9
A826
A94
A822
A914
M90
A823
A91
19
35
28
31
44
24
25
37
38
43
27
32
39
42
20
23
18
26
41
21
36
40
17
30
29
16
22
33-34

ABERDEENSHIRE

Local Representatives: Mrs Beatrice Fawkes, The Manse, Lonmay, Fraserburgh (*telephone* 01346 532227); Mrs Fiona Cameron, The Newk, Monboddo Road, Torphins (*telephone* 013398 82405)

16 ST TERNAN'S CHURCH, ARBUTHNOTT

NO 801 746

Almost certainly a St Ternan cult church long before it became a parish church by the late twelfth century. The chancel dates from the early 13th century, the Arbuthnott family aisle and the bell-tower from the late 15th century and the nave is medieval or earlier but has been much altered. The church was gutted by fire in 1889 and reopened in 1890 with the nave and chancel restored as at the time of consecration in 1242; the architect for the restoration was A Marshall Mackenzie. The unique Arbuthnott Missal, Psalter and Prayer Book (now in Paisley Museum) were transcribed and illuminated in the Priest's Room above the Arbuthnott Aisle between 1497 and 1500. On the B967, Three miles from Inverbervie. For Services, see local paper and notice board

ST TERNAN'S CHURCH, ARBUTHNOTT

Open all year. Refreshments in Grassic Gibbon Centre in village

CHURCH OF SCOTLAND ♿ A

17 ST PALLADIUS or AUCHENBLAE PARISH CHURCH

NO 726 784

Auchenblae, near Laurencekirk

Built by John Smith 1829 as Fordoun Parish Church on a site known as Kirkton of Fordoun. Religious site since seventh century. St Palladius died and reputedly buried here. Celtic stone in vestibule. Memorial to first Protestant martyr George Wishart (born at Mains of Pittarrow in old parish of Fordoun) in graveyard. Seating in nave replaced 1990. Stained glass rose window. Sunday Service 11am, excluding first Sunday of month

Open by arrangement, telephone Rev David Jack 01561 340203

CHURCH OF SCOTLAND ♿ B

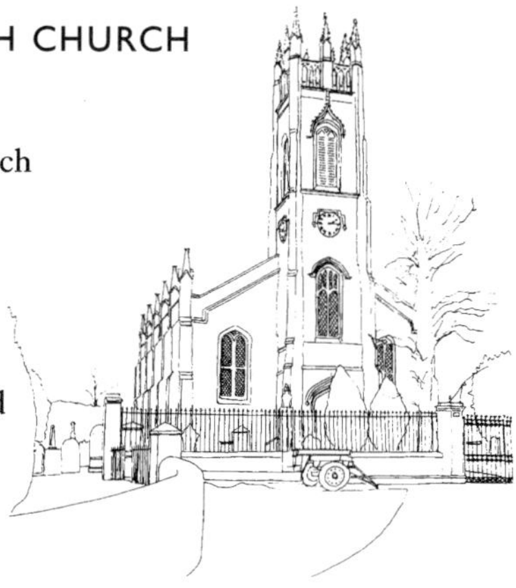

ST PALLADIUS or AUCHENBLAE PARISH CHURCH

18 BIRSE AND FEUGHSIDE PARISH CHURCH, BALLOGIE

NO 554 973

Ballogie, near Banchory

Dates from twelfth century. Link with Crusades. 17th-century graveyard. United with Finzean and Strachan. Sunday Service: 11am, July

Open May to September, Monday to Friday 10am-4pm

CHURCH OF SCOTLAND ♿ WC **B**

BIRSE AND FEUGHSIDE PARISH CHURCH, BALLOGIE

19 BANFF PARISH CHURCH

NJ 689 638

High Street, Banff

Built in 1789, Andrew Wilson architect and builder, with tower added in 1849, William Robertson. Chancel added and interior altered in 1929. Stained glass. Small chapel created at rear of church in 1994. Pulpit, font, communion table and stained glass in chancel all gifted in 1929. Other furnishings from Trinity & Alvah Church, united in 1994. Beside St Mary's car park. Sunday Services: 11am and 6.30pm

Open mid June to August, 2-4pm. Also Doors Open Day, September

CHURCH OF SCOTLAND ♿ WC **A**

20 ST MARY'S CHAPEL, BLAIRS

NJ 883 009

The building, designed by Richard Curran of Warrington, was opened in 1901 and follows the neo-Gothic style, while the unusual interior design is due to the fact that it is a former collegiate chapel. The walls originally had painted decoration but in 1911 were lined with marble. At the same time were added the reredos and baldacchino in carved wood with its figures of the Scottish patron saints, Andrew and Margaret. The church also has fine stained glass windows. Four miles south of Aberdeen on B9077. Sunday Service 9.00am

Open Monday, Tuesday and Thursday 10.30am-2pm. Saturday/Sunday by arrangement, telephone 01224 869424

ROMAN CATHOLIC ♿ **A**

ST MARY'S CHAPEL, BLAIRS

21 BRAEMAR CHURCH

NO 1591

behind the Braemar Mews

The inspiration for the building of this former Free Church in 1870 was the Rev Hugh Cobban. Unusually, he was buried in the church, behind the pulpit. Four lancet stained glass windows with lilies, a branch with fruit and a tree with palms. Some interesting tapestry banners, described as 'living pictures'. Sunday Service 10am

Open 9am-9pm April-October

CHURCH OF SCOTLAND **C**

22 ST PHILIP'S, CATTERLINE

NO 869 789

St Ninian was reputed to have landed at Catterline. The present building, designed by Charles Brand, dates from 1848 and was built on the site of an earlier church, retaining its historic graveyard. The style is Early English. The interior has been recently refurbished. Off A9 between Montrose and Stonehaven and near Dunottar Castle. Sunday Services 9.30am; Holy Communion second and last Sundays in month

ST PHILIP'S, CATTERLINE

Open by arrangement, telephone Mr Reid 01569 750360

SCOTTISH EPISCOPAL **C**

23 CRATHIE PARISH CHURCH

NO 265 949

on A93 Ballater-Braemar

Queen Victoria laid the foundation stone in 1893, the church opened 1895. Cruciform design by A Marshall Mackenzie. The church stands on a hill overlooking the ruins of the 14th century church and the River Dee. Memorial stones, plaques and stained glass commemorate royalty and ministers. Fine Iona marble communion table and 17th century oak reredos. Sunday Service 11.30am

Open April-October Monday to Saturday 9.30am-5pm Sunday 12.45pm-5pm

CHURCH OF SCOTLAND **B**

CRATHIE PARISH CHURCH

24 ST JAMES'S CHURCH, CRUDEN BAY

NK 069 356

Chapel Hill, Cruden Bay

The tall spire of St James's can be seen from miles around. Designed by William Hay in 1842. The font is from the chantry chapel, built after the battle between the Scots and the Danes in 1012. One and a half miles from Cruden Bay. Sunday Service Family Communion 9.30am

Open daily 10am-dusk

SCOTTISH EPISCOPAL **B**

25 ST MARY ON THE ROCK, ELLON

NJ 958 301

Craighall, Ellon

A superb example of the work of George Edmund Street, built in 1871 to incorporate chancel, nave, narthex and spire. Floor tiles by Minton. Good glass, including windows by Clayton & Bell on the north side of the nave, Lavers & Barreau on the south side, all dating from the 1880s, and by Jane Bayliss 1996. On the A90/A948, at the south end of the town. Sunday Service: Eucharist 9.30am, Parish Eucharist 11.15am

Open daily 10am-dusk

SCOTTISH EPISCOPAL **A**

26 FINZEAN CHURCH

NO 617 924

Finzean, near Banchory

Small mission church. United with Birse and Strachan. Between Banchory and Aboyne on South Deeside Road. Sunday Service 11am, June and September

Open May to September, Monday to Friday 10am-4pm

CHURCH OF SCOTLAND **B**

27 FOVERAN PARISH CHURCH

NJ 985 241

1 mile south of Newburgh on A975

Built 1794, organ apse added 1900, interior refurbished 1934 with pews and fittings from the demolished Foveran United Free Church. Number of items from medieval church (since disappeared): early 15th-century Turin Stone, 17th-century bust of Sir John Turing, Queen Anne hour glass attached to pulpit and font using carved medieval column. Various monuments including bronze plaque to painter and etcher James McBey, born nearby. Sunday Service: 11am (shared with Holyrood Chapel, Newburgh)

Open by arrangement, key available from the Manse, or from Newburgh Post Office during opening hours

CHURCH OF SCOTLAND **B**

FOVERAN PARISH CHURCH

28 FRASERBURGH OLD PARISH CHURCH

NJ 998 671

The Square, Fraserburgh

Present building dates from 1801, with a church on this site since 1572. The pulpit is one of the highest in Scotland and the superb memorial window designed by Douglas Strachan 1906, was gifted by Sir George Anderson, Treasurer of the Bank of Scotland, in memory of his parents. A front pew in the south gallery is marked as the place where Marconi, pioneer of wireless telegraphy, worshipped during his stay in Fraserburgh. Sunday Services 11am and 6pm

Open daily June-September

CHURCH OF SCOTLAND WC **C**

FRASERBURGH OLD PARISH CHURCH

29 FETTERCAIRN PARISH CHURCH

N0 651 735

Fettercairn, near Laurencekirk

Built in 1803 and with a steeple added in 1860, the building was completely refurbished and extended in 1926. The interior has interesting stained glass and locally made furnishings. Sunday Service 9.30am

Open by arrangement, telephone the Minister 01561 340203

CHURCH OF SCOTLAND WC **B**

30 GLENBERVIE PARISH CHURCH

N0 766 807

Glenbervie, near Stonehaven

Built 1826 and preserving original design and features. Oil lamps electrified. Stones preserved and sheltered. Grandparents of Robert Burns buried in old kirkyard. Sunday Service 11am first Sunday of month

Open by arrangement, telephone Rev David Jack 01561 340203

CHURCH OF SCOTLAND **B**

31 ST MARGARET'S CHURCH, HUNTLY

NJ 528 402

Chapel Street, Huntly

Octagonal church with impressive classical front façade built 1834. The architect was Bishop James Kyle in collaboration with William Robertson. Eighty ft spire with fine toned bell. Altar piece and other paintings from the Gordon family of Xeres, Spain 1840. Restored 1990 by Doric Construction, Aberdeen. Sunday Service 9.45am

Open by arrangement, telephone Mr W McKay 01466 792409

ROMAN CATHOLIC WC **A**

ST MARGARET'S CHURCH, HUNTLY

32 ST DROSTAN, INSCH

NJ 630 281

Commerce Street, Insch

Alexander Ross, 1894. Agreeable rustic Gothic in red granite with sandstone dressings. Red-tiled roof with broach-spired wooden bellcote. Font 1892, and screen 1904. Church is on road from Insch railway station to town centre. B992 off A96. Service second and fourth Sundays Sung Eucharist 10am

Open by arrangement, telephone Mrs Mitchell, Greenhaugh, Rannes Street, Insch 01464 820276

SCOTTISH EPISCOPAL **C**

33 BERVIE PARISH CHURCH, INVERBERVIE

NO 830 727

43 King Street, Inverbervie

Built in 1836 with elegant clock and bell tower. Two stained glass windows originally from United Free Church. Hammond organ 1904. In centre of town. Sunday Service 11.30am

Open by arrangement, telephone Mr W Beattie, 39 King Street 01561 361256, or 9 Farquhar Street 01561 362728

CHURCH OF SCOTLAND WC **B**

BERVIE PARISH CHURCH, INVERBERVIE

34 KING DAVID OF SCOTLAND EPISCOPAL CHURCH, INVERBERVIE

NO 828 733

Victoria Terrace, Inverbervie

Small, simple church with very pretty interior. Shared with the local Roman Catholic community. Sunday Service 9.30am Holy Communion; Roman Catholic Mass Saturday 6.30pm

Open daily 9am-4.30pm

SCOTTISH EPISCOPAL

35 MACDUFF PARISH CHURCH

NJ 701 643

Church Street, Macduff

Once used to guide boats to safe haven, this white box kirk of 1805 high on the bluff above the harbour was transformed in 1865 by architect James Matthews of Aberdeen into a magnificent Italianate landmark, with notable stained glass windows and a lovely three-storey tower with a lead-domed roof and cupola above. Galleried interior, most of the fittings dating from 1865. Magnificent views. Nearby stand the town cross and an anchor, symbolic of the message of the church. Sunday Services 11am and 6pm

Open by arrangement, telephone 01261 833905

CHURCH OF SCOTLAND ♿ 👂 WC **B**

MACDUFF PARISH CHURCH

36 ST TERNAN'S, MUCHALLS

NO 891 921

Muchalls, by Stonehaven

Simple country church with attractive chancel. The oldest church building in the Diocese of Brechin, built 1831-1870. Sunday Service 10.30am Holy Communion

Open during daylight hours

SCOTTISH EPISCOPAL

37 HOLYROOD CHAPEL, NEWBURGH

NJ 999 253

Main Street, Newburgh

Built in 1838 as the original Newburgh Mathers school; converted as Chapel of Ease for Foveran Parish Church 1882. Clock Tower added 1892, interior refurbished 1907, including pitch pine roof in imitation of St Laurence, Forres. Named in honour of the original medieval chapel of the Holy Rood and St Thomas the Martyr in Inch Road, Newburgh – all that remains of this is the Udny Family Mausoleum in the Holyrood Cemetery. Sunday Service 11am (shared with Foveran Church)

Open by arrangement, key available from the Manse,
or from Newburgh Post Office during opening hours

CHURCH OF SCOTLAND **B**

HOLYROOD CHAPEL, NEWBURGH

38 ST MATTHEW & ST GEORGE, OLDMELDRUM

NJ 812 279

Ross & Joass, 1863. Pleasing granite Early Decorated with striking chequered voussoirs to west window. Octagonal spire alongside the simple nave and chancel. Tendril-like freestone tracery is carved with real freedom. Stained glass by Hardman records the Life of Our Lord. Intricate Arts & Crafts monument to Beauchamp Colclough Urquhart of Meldrum. Church is at the north end of the village on A947. Sung Eucharist 11.30am

Open by arrangement, telephone the Rector 01651 872208

SCOTTISH EPISCOPAL ♿ B

ST MATTHEW & ST GEORGE, OLDMELDRUM

39 SKENE PARISH CHURCH, KIRKTON OF SKENE

NJ 803 077

¼ mile off A944 Aberdeen-Alford Road, 9 miles from Aberdeen city centre

The church was built in 1801 and contains stained glass by Blair & Blyth. Sunday Service 11.15am

Open by arrangement, telephone the Minister 01224 743277 or the Beadle 01224 743534

CHURCH OF SCOTLAND ♿ WC 👂 B

SKENE PARISH CHURCH, KIRKTON OF SKENE

ST JAMES THE GREAT, STONEHAVEN

40 ST JAMES THE GREAT, STONEHAVEN

NO 873 857

Arbuthnott Street, Stonehaven

The nave was built by Sir R Rowand Anderson in 1877 in Norman/Early English style. The chancel was added in 1885 and the narthex and baptistry in 1906 by Arthur Clyne. Baptistry glass by Sir Ninian Comper 1929. Elaborately sculptured reredos by Gambier-Parry of London. Off south side of Market Square in Stonehaven. Sunday Services 8.30 and 10.30am, Thursday 10.30am

Open Easter to end September, Monday to Friday 2-4pm

SCOTTISH EPISCOPAL **A**

41 STRACHAN CHURCH

NO 674 923

Strachan, near Banchory

Situated on old drove road. Ancient graveyard. United with Birse and Finzean. Between Banchory and Aboyne on South Deeside Road. Sunday Service 11am, May and August

Open May to September, Monday to Friday 10am-4pm

CHURCH OF SCOTLAND **C**

42 TRINITY CHURCH, WESTHILL

NJ 8307

Westhill Drive, Westhill (off A944 Aberdeen-Alford Road)

Built 1981 by Stock Brothers. Ecumenical and multi-purpose. Plans for an extension of the building during 2000. Services: Roman Catholic: 9am, Church of Scotland: 10am, Scottish Episcopal 11.15am.

Open most of week, check with Minister, telephone 01224 743277

INTERDENOMINATIONAL

TRINITY CHURCH, WESTHILL

43 ALL SAINTS', WHITERASHES

NJ 855 235

Gothic style nave and chancel built by James Matthews in 1858. Windows by Sir Ninian Comper of saints chosen for the Christian names of the Irvines of Drum and Straloch. On A947, three miles south of Oldmeldrum. Service first Sunday, Evensong 3pm

Open by arrangement, telephone the Rector 01651 872208

SCOTTISH EPISCOPAL ♿ (one step) **B**

44 ALL SAINTS', WOODHEAD OF FETTERLETTER

NJ 790 385

Early English aisleless nave and chancel by John Henderson 1849. The fine tower with the slated broach spire was added in 1870. Described by Pratt in Buchan as 'one of the finest examples of a Scottish village church'. Crosses and a sheaf of arrows from Fyvie Priory are incorporated in the walls. The altar and reredos are from St Margaret's, Forgue. One and a half miles east of Fyvie. Sunday Service 10.15am

Open by arrangement, telephone Mrs Cleaver, Gowanlea, Woodhead 01651 891513

SCOTTISH EPISCOPAL ♿ **B**

ANGUS
A939
A93
A980
A93
ABERDEENSHIRE
52
A937
Marykirk
Hillside
A90
Brechin
48
A935
60
Montrose
62
Ferryden
Kirriemuir
58
Rescobie
A926
55-57
A932
PERTH
&
KINROSS
49-50
Forfar
Friockheim
Inverkeilor
Glamis
51
54
53
A90
St Vigeans
A94
45-46
ARBROATH
A92
Muirdrum
47
Muirhead
A923
61
Dundee
Carnoustie
Monifieth
59
A90
Perth
A914
M90
0
10 kilometres
A915

ANGUS

Local Representatives: The Rev Peter Youngson, 'Correen', Northmuir, Kirriemuir (*telephone 01575 572832)*

45 ST JOHN'S, ARBROATH

NN 645 411

Ponderlaw Street, Arbroath

Opened for worship by the Rev John Wesley on 6 May 1772. Built in the octagonal style favoured by Wesley, this is the only one of these churches left in Scotland. Known as the 'Totum Kirkie'. Vestibule added 1883. The Lifeboat Window is a memorial to the loss of the Lifeboat *Robert L Lindsay* and six crew members in 1953. Old manse adjacent to church. Sunday Service 11am

Open by arrangement telephone Mr Nicoll 01241 875172

METHODIST

46 ST VIGEAN'S CHURCH, ARBROATH

NO 583 446

St Vigean's, Arbroath

Dedicated to St Vigean (or Fechin), Irish saint, died 664. Church rebuilt in twelfth century, but not dedicated until 1242. Some 15th-century alterations. 19th-century restoration with lovely stained glass windows. Largely unaltered since. Sunday Service 11.30am

Key available from house opposite church main gate. St Vigean's Museum also open

CHURCH OF SCOTLAND **A**

ST VIGEAN'S CHURCH, ARBROATH

47 AUCHTERHOUSE CHURCH

N0 342 381

Kirkton of Auchterhouse

Built 1630 with stone from earlier churches of 1275 and 1426. Partially rebuilt 1775. Chancel and nave with tower at west end. Burial vault at east end. Interior completely renovated 1910. Gothic chancel arch lends character and dignity. Three impressive stained glass windows, medieval octagonal font, stool of repentance and 18th-century clock. Linked with Murroes and Tealing. Situated on south side of Sidlaw Hills one mile east of B954 Dundee to Meigle, six miles from Meigle. Sunday Service 11.30am

Open by arrangement, telephone John Skea 01382 320257, or Elizabeth Adams 01382 320302

CHURCH OF SCOTLAND **B**

48 BRECHIN CATHEDRAL

N0 595 601

Church Lane, Brechin

Founded in the eleventh century, the round tower of that date is of Irish inspiration. 13th, 14th and 15th-century medieval architecture underwent major restoration in 1900-02 supervised by J Honeyman (Honeyman, Keppie & Mackintosh). Special features include the twelfth-century font and a collection of Pictish sculptures. Stunning 20th-century stained glass by Henry Holiday, Gordon Webster, Douglas Strachan, Herbert Hendrie, William Gauld, Hugh Easton and the firm of William Morris. The cathedral also contains the largest group of William Wilson windows in Scotland.

BRECHIN CATHEDRAL

Sunday Service 11am

Open most days all year 9am-4pm. With guides in summer months only (and by special arrangement outwith these times). Afternoon teas in church hall, alternate Tuesdays 2pm. Brechin Caledonian Railway nearby. Historical artefacts in Brechin Library. Pictavia

CHURCH OF SCOTLAND WC (100 yards) A

49 LOWSON MEMORIAL CHURCH, FORFAR

NO 465 509

Jameson Street, Forfar

A gem of a church designed by A Marshall Mackenzie 1914. In the style of late Scots Gothic, cruciform in shape with five-bay nave, aisleless transepts and a one-bay chancel. Built of a ruddy-hued local stone. Low central tower and squat spire. Wooden wagon roof. Excellent stained glass, Douglas Strachan. At east end of Forfar off Montrose Road. Sunday Service 11am

Open Monday to Friday 9.30am-4.30pm all year

CHURCH OF SCOTLAND

WC A

LOWSON MEMORIAL CHURCH, FORFAR

50 ST JOHN THE EVANGELIST, FORFAR

N0 458 507

71 East High Street, Forfar

Built on the site of an earlier church, the present building was designed in Early English style by Sir R Rowand Anderson and consecrated in 1881. The broach spire intended for the tower was never built. Panelling and redecoration of the roof by Sir Matthew Ochterlony, late 1940s. Altered in 1975 by Dr F R Stevenson to provide Lady Chapel and vestries. The font has traditionally been associated with St Margaret and Restenneth Priory. Three-manual pipe organ by Conacher of Huddersfield. Stained glass by Charles E Kempe and Septimus Waugh. Queen Elizabeth The Queen Mother was confirmed in the church. Historic graveyard predates present church. Sunday Services 8.30 and 11am, weekdays as announced

Open daily, summer months 9am-4pm, winter months 9am-2pm

SCOTTISH EPISCOPAL WC **B**

51 ST FERGUS CHURCH, GLAMIS

N0 386 469

Kirk Wynd, Glamis

Present church built 1792 on site of church dedicated to St Fergus 1242. Substantially altered and beautified 1933. Classic bell tower and spire. seventh-century Celtic stone in manse garden and Well of St Fergus nearby. Category B kirkyard with interesting stones. Strathmore Aisle (category A) built in 1459 by Isabella Ogilvy on death of her husband Patrick Lyon, first Lord Glamis. United with Inverarity and Kinnettles. Sunday Service 11.30am

Open daily

CHURCH OF SCOTLAND WC **A/B**

ST FERGUS CHURCH, GLAMIS

52 GLEN PROSEN CHURCH

N0 328 657

Glen Prosen, by Pitcarity, Kirriemuir

Present church built 1802, paid for by local inhabitants, ensuring continuous worship in the glen for nearly 400 years. Special features include wood carvings by Sir Robert Lorimer and war memorial porch with rare slated cross. Sunday Service second and fourth Sundays 12.15pm; summer months Holy Communion (Scottish Episcopal) fourth Sunday 8.30am; Songs of Praise for Guide Dogs for the Blind April to September first Sunday of month 6pm

Open daily, access via vestry door. Teas available from Old School Restaurant, 400 yards, April to September

CHURCH OF SCOTLAND **B**

53 INVERARITY CHURCH

NO 460 440

Inverarity

Church built 1754 with recent impressive renovation. Kirk Bell by Peter van dem Heim dated 1614, cast in Holland. Gable porches added 1854. Modern church/community hall next to church. Situated at eastern boundary of village on triangle of ground at division of B9127. Sunday Service 10am

INVERARITY CHURCH

Open by arrangement, telephone Mr A L Ingram 01307 840223

CHURCH OF SCOTLAND B

54 KINNETTLES CHURCH

NO 426 460

Kirkton, Kinnettles

Built 1812, architect Samuel Bell, in Gothic style with belfry. Late 19th-century additions. Typically rural and unspoiled. Said to be an excellent example of an 'auld Scottish kirk'. Beautiful stained glass and original precentor's box. United with Glamis and Inverarity. Sunday service 6pm second Sunday of month

Open by arrangement, telephone Norman Knight 01307 820348

CHURCH OF SCOTLAND B

KINNETTLES CHURCH

55 KIRRIEMUIR OLD PARISH CHURCH

NO 386 539

Bank Street, Kirriemuir

Ninth-century stones were found when the church was rebuilt on this earlier Christian site in 1788 to a design by James Playfair, father of William Henry Playfair. The steeple was completed in 1790. Stained glass includes the triple window of The Last Supper, a Violet Jacobs window, and windows by William Wilson. Interesting kirkyard, the earliest stone dating from 1613. In centre of the town, behind Bank Street's shops. Sunday Services 9am and 11am

Open June to August daily 10am–12 noon, 2–4pm

CHURCH OF SCOTLAND B

56 ST ANDREW'S CHURCH, KIRRIEMUIR

N0 386 535

Glamis Road, Kirriemuir

Late Gothic style church (originally the South United Free Church) with a 60 ft tower by Patrick Thoms 1903. It replaced an earlier church (the South Free Church) built in 1843 for those who left the South Church (across the road) at the 'Disruption'. In the grounds are the headstones of the Rev Daniel Cormick, first minister of the South Free Church and of the Rev A Duff, minister of the South Church. Linked with Oathlaw and Tannadice. Sunday Service 11.15am

Open daily 9am-5pm

CHURCH OF SCOTLAND

ST ANDREW'S CHURCH, KIRRIEMUIR

57 ST MARY'S CHURCH, KIRRIEMUIR

NO 383 544

West Hillbank, Kirriemuir

Gothic revival church by Sir Ninian Comper, 1903 built to replace classical church of 1797 destroyed by fire. Stained glass by Comper and William Wilson. Two-manual tracker organ, Hamilton of Edinburgh 1906. Sanctus bell 1741. Conspicuous red sandstone bell tower. Sign-posted to north side of the town. Sunday Services 9.30am Said Eucharist, 11am Sung Eucharist (except Fourth Sunday Matins)

Open daily 10am-4pm. Otherwise key at Rectory, 128 Glengate, Kirriemuir

SCOTTISH EPISCOPAL **A**

ST MARY'S CHURCH, KIRRIEMUIR

58 ST MARGARET'S CHURCH, LUNANHEAD

N0 476 522

Carsebarracks, Lunanhead

Built in the planned village of Carsebarracks on the site of an earlier chapel in 1907 by the builder/architect William L McLean of Forfar as a gift of Mrs Susan Helen Gray of Bankhead House in memory of her husband. Stained glass window of the Crucifixion 1913, by A D Fleming of London. Mural 1909 by Miss W M Watson of Edinburgh. On the B9134, one mile east of Forfar. Service first and third Sundays, excluding July and August 2pm

Open by arrangement, telephone Mr Orrock 01307 468156

SCOTTISH EPISCOPAL

HOLY TRINITY CHURCH, MONIFIETH

59 HOLY TRINITY CHURCH, MONIFIETH

NO 499 327

High Street, Monifieth

Black and white half-timbered style building by Mills & Shepherd 1909. Originally intended as church hall, adapted to church. Pleasant sheltered garden. Buses from Dundee to Monifieth, Carnoustie and Arbroath stop outside. Sunday Services 8am, 10.30am

Open daily

SCOTTISH EPISCOPAL **B**

60 MONTROSE OLD CHURCH

NO 715 778

High Street, Montrose

Built 1793 by John Gibson with a 'lovely flying-buttressed spire (J Gillespie Graham 1832) which is Montrose's town-mark' (Colin McWilliam, *Scottish Townscape*). By rail Intercity London to Aberdeen. Sunday Service 11am, also last Sunday 6.30pm

Open June to August, Monday to Friday 2pm-4.30pm

CHURCH OF SCOTLAND **A**

61 MURROES AND TEALING CHURCH

N0 461 351

Murroes, near Broughty Ferry

T-plan church by William Smith 1848 on a site occupied by a church for 750 years. Church records from 1202. Interesting gravestones and coping on churchyard wall carved with texts in English, Latin and Greek. Interior is simple and relatively original. Pews with doors, four impressive stained glass windows in south wall and small pipe organ in gallery recently restored. Former coach house and stables restored to provide hall, chapel, kitchen and toilet facilities. Linked with Auchterhouse. Sunday Service 10am

Open by arrangement, telephone Gordon Laird 01382 350242

CHURCH OF SCOTLAND

MURROES AND TEALING CHURCH

62 TANNADICE CHURCH

NO 475 581

Tannadice

Present church by John Carver built 1866 on site of previous buildings. Place of Christian worship since seventh century. Monastery recorded in 1187 and Kirk of Tanatheys consecrated by the Bishop of St Andrew's 1242. Union with Oathlaw 1982. St Columba and St Francis windows at west end of church 1976 in memory of second Lord Forres of Glenogil. Former Oathlaw war memorial windows on north wall, by James Ballantine 1923 and Neil Hamilton 1949. Linked with St Andrew's, Kirriemuir four miles north of Forfar on B957, A90 from Dundee.

Sunday Service 9.45am

Key available at Post Office 9.30-11.30am.

Or by arrangement, telephone Mrs Davidson 01307 850345

CHURCH OF SCOTLAND

WC C

TANNADICE CHURCH

ARGYLL AND BUTE

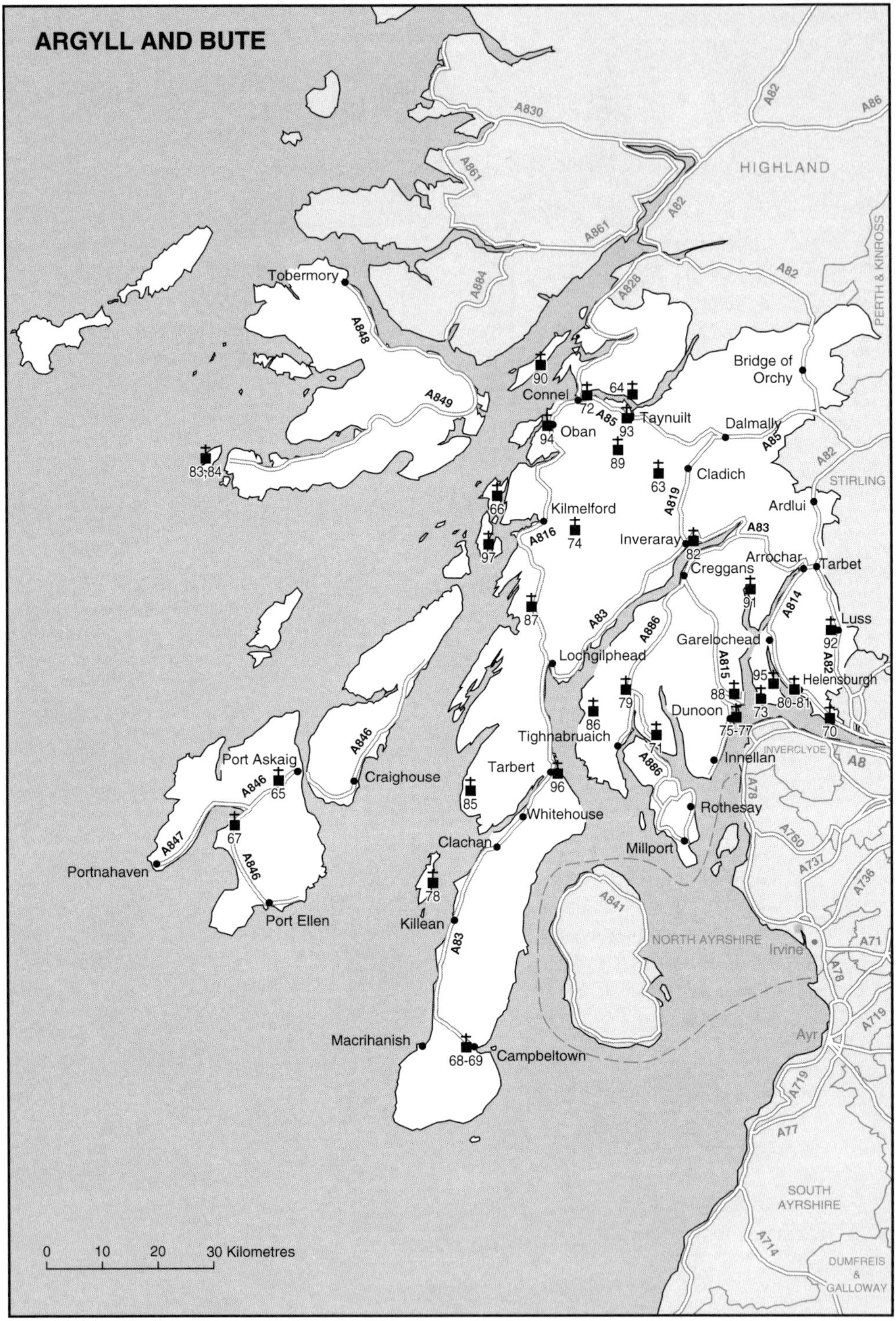

ARGYLL & BUTE

Local Representative: Mr Michael Gossip, Tigh-na-Coille, Ardrishaig (*telephone 01546 603454)*

63 ST JAMES' CHURCH, ARDBRECKNISH

NN 072 212

Ardbrecknish

Built 1891, stone interior with fine series of monuments and excellent windows. Bells rehung 1991. Grass churchyard overlooking Loch Awe. Sunday Service in summer 11am. Linked with St John's Cathedral, Oban

Open daylight hours in summer

SCOTTISH EPISCOPAL

64 CHURCH OF THE HOLY SPIRIT, ARDCHATTAN

NM 971 349

Ardchattan

Built 1886. Fine First World War memorial incorporating the three banners of Scotland, England and Ireland. Ardchattan crucifix on south wall. Stone pedestal font and ancient stone stoup. One mile west of Bonawe Quarry, beside Loch Etive. Sunday Service 2nd Sunday, times vary. Linked with St John's Cathedral, Oban

Open by arrangement, contact Mrs Colquhoun, The Ferry House, Ardchattan

SCOTTISH EPISCOPAL

65 KILMENY PARISH CHURCH, BALLYGRANT

NR 353 636

Ballygrant, Isle of Islay

Kilmeny Parish Church is situated in sheltered wooded grounds. The present church was remodelled in the 1820s to plans by Thomas Telford on the site of the original church of 1790. There is evidence of a number of early Celtic Church foundations within the parish boundary, and nearby is the Finlaggan site, administrative centre of the Lords of the Isles. The church has received lovely gifts, most recently a new organ, gifted by the Caol Ila Distillery Company on the occasion of their 125th anniversary in 1996. Linked with Kilarrow. Situated above the main Port Askaig/Bowmore road. Sunday Service 12.30pm, 9.30 July and August

Open July to August, Thursday 10.30am-12.30pm and 2-4pm

CHURCH OF SCOTLAND WC **B**

66 KILBRANDON KIRK, BALVICAR

NM 758 155

Balvicar, Isle of Seil

Kilbrandon Kirk was built in 1866 and contains a beautiful set of five stained glass windows – the work of Douglas Strachan. The windows were commissioned by Miss Mackinnon of Ardmaddy Castle in 1937 in memory of her friend the Marchioness of Breadalbane. On the B8003, one mile south of the Balvicar turn-off. Sunday Service 10am, except last Sunday 11am

Open all year

CHURCH OF SCOTLAND ♿ (two steps) 🦻 WC **C**

67 KILARROW PARISH CHURCH, BOWMORE

NR 312 596

Bowmore, Isle of Islay

This 18th-century church, known as 'The Round Church', was built by Daniel Campbell of Shawfield and Islay in 1767. A year after the building commenced, the village of Bowmore came into being as a 'planned village' to rehouse those of the village of Kilarrow who were not directly involved in the work of Islay Estate, mainly agricultural workers and weavers. The two-storey circular body of the church has a main central pillar 19 inches in diameter, possibly of hemlock oak, harled and plastered. Above the coved ceiling is a radial king-post roof truss into which eight major beams are jointed. The gallery was added in 1830, increasing its capacity to 500. Extensive renovation has been carried out in recent years. At the top of Main Street. Linked with Kilmeny. Sunday Service 11am

Open daily all year, 9am-6pm

CHURCH OF SCOTLAND ♿ 🚻 (during summer months) 🦻 📖 **A**

KILARROW PARISH CHURCH, BOWMORE

HIGHLAND PARISH CHURCH, CAMPBELTOWN

68 HIGHLAND PARISH CHURCH, CAMPBELTOWN

NR 720 201

New Quay Street, Campbeltown

'To be causewayed with whinstone and paved with hewn flags. The lock on the front door to be of 20/- value and the rest to have snecks and wooden bolts': the instruction of the architect George Dempster of Greenock, for a new church, built for the Highland, Gaelic-speaking, congregation of the area, and completed in 1807. Harled rubble with red sandstone dressings, an oblong with rectangular stair towers at each end of the front. Three galleries. The planned belfry was not large enough for the heritors, so a steeple was built; twice since it has been rebuilt, the casualty of lightning strikes. The pipe organ, Harrison & Harrison, Durham 1954, is a memorial to the fallen of the Second World War. Sunday Services 11.15am and 6.30pm

Open daily

CHURCH OF SCOTLAND **B**

69 LORNE AND LOWLAND CHURCH, CAMPBELTOWN

NR 718 206

Longrow, Campbeltown

Built in 1872 to the design of John Burnet, historically called The Longrow Church. Classical, influenced by Italian Renaissance style. Its bell tower is a well-known landmark. Two stairways lead from the entrance foyer to a horse-shoe gallery. Fine plaster ceiling. Pulpit 1895. Sunday Services 11.15am, 7pm (fortnightly)

Open July to August, Monday to Friday 11am-4pm. Other times, telephone Mr J Gill 01586 552781

CHURCH OF SCOTLAND WC **C**

LORNE AND LOWLAND CHURCH, CAMPBELTOWN

70 CARDROSS PARISH CHURCH

NS 345 775

Station Road, Cardross

Church founded 1225 on west bank of River Leven and rebuilt in village 1640. Present building 1872. Stained glass windows, Sadie McLennan 1972, embroidered panels, Hannah Frew Paterson 1981, woven silk hangings, Sarah Sumsion 1990, and engraved glass windows, John Lawrie 1992. Peal of six bells augmented to eight for the Millennium. A82 from Glasgow; half hourly train service from Glasgow Queen Street. Sunday Services 9.30am and 11am; June, July, August 11am only; also September to Easter second Sunday 7pm

CARDROSS PARISH CHURCH

Open Monday, Wednesday, Friday mornings.
Or by arrangement, telephone Mrs S McLatchie 01389 841509

CHURCH OF SCOTLAND **B**

71 COLINTRAIVE CHURCH

NS 045 735

Colintraive

Erected 1840 by Mrs Campbell of Southhall as a chapel of ease, part of Inverchaolain parish. Became a Free Church in 1843, United Free in 1900 and returned to the Church of Scotland in 1929. United with Kilmodan Church. Spectacular views over Kyles of Bute. Sunday Service 10am or 11.30am alternating monthly with Kilmodan

Open daily

CHURCH OF SCOTLAND

72 ST ORAN'S CHURCH, CONNEL

NM 914 343

Gothic Revival cruciform church of 1888 with lancet and pointed traceried windows, gabled porch and a central tower with corbelled parapet. Good interior with open timbered ceiling. Twentieth-century glass by various artists. Beautiful views up Loch Etive from garden. On A85.

Sunday Service 11am

Open during daylight hours

CHURCH OF SCOTLAND

B

ST ORAN'S CHURCH, CONNEL

73 CRAIGROWNIE CHURCH, COVE

NS 224 810

Church Road, Cove, near Helensburgh

Daughter Church of Rosneath, opened 1851. Architect David Cousins, enlarged by Honeyman & Keppie 1889. Organ by James J Binns of Leeds. Various examples of stained glass including J Benson, S Adam, Mayer & Co. Frescoes by the sisters Doris and Anna Zinkeisen of the four Evangelists. Nearby Church Hall in a former church designed by Hugh Barclay, 1858, with windows by F Hase-Hayden, A Webster, A McW Webster and others. Sunday Service 10am in 2000, 11.30am in 2001

Open by arrangement with the Minister, telephone 01436 842274

CHURCH OF SCOTLAND **B**

74 DALAVICH CHURCH

NM 968 124

15 miles from Taynuilt

The building dates from about 1770. Linked with Muckairn and Kilchrenan. A small bell tower is being built on the gable to celebrate the Millennium. Sunday Services 10.00am on the 2nd and 4th Sundays of the month

Open by arrangement, telephone MacIntosh, 1 Dalavich, by Taynuilt

CHURCH OF SCOTLAND

DALAVICH CHURCH

75 DUNOON BAPTIST CHURCH CENTRE

NS 171 770

9 Alexandra Parade, Dunoon

Formerly the American servicemen's YMCA. The centre welcomes all visitors to the beautiful Cowal Peninsula. Browse in the well-stocked Christian book and gift shop. Sample excellent coffee and home baking with a splendid view of the Clyde estuary. Next to Tourist Information Centre and five minutes from the pier. Sunday Services 11am and 6.30pm

Open Monday to Saturday 10am–4pm

BAPTIST **A**

76 DUNOON OLD AND ST CUTHBERT'S CHURCH

NS 173 769

Church Square, Dunoon

The present building probably stands on the site of a much earlier church which until 1688 was the Cathedral Church of both the Roman Catholic and Episcopalian Bishops of Argyll. Towards the end of the 18th century the building became dilapidated and was demolished, the stone being used to build Gillespie Graham's Late Decorated Gothic Revival church of 1816. The belfry tower was added in 1839 and the church was lengthened and widened by Andrew Balfour in 1909. Chancel window 1939 by Douglas Hamilton. Gravestones of the 13th and 17th century in the kirkyard. Sunday Service October to May 11am, June to September 10.30am

June to July inclusive: exhibition (history and memorabilia), Monday to Saturday 10.30am-12.30pm and 2pm-4pm. Open by arrangement, telephone the Rev P Lang, 1 Royal Crescent, Dunoon 01369 701291

CHURCH OF SCOTLAND WC **B**

77 ST JOHN'S CHURCH, DUNOON

NS 172 769

Argyll Street, Dunoon

A magnificent nave and aisles kirk by R A Bryden 1877 built to supersede the original Free Church of 1843. Normandy Gothic spired tower. Galleried 'concert hall' interior. Raised choir behind central pulpit. Three-manual pipe organ by Brook & Co 1895. Interesting stained glass including windows by Stephen Adam and Gordon Webster, also Lauder Memorial. Sunday Services 10.15am and 6.30pm

Open June, July, August and September: Monday to Friday 10am-12pm. September Sunday concerts at 3.00pm (last 3 Sundays in September), includes organ recitals, visiting choirs etc. 01369 830639

CHURCH OF SCOTLAND WC **B**

78 GIGHA AND CARA PARISH CHURCH

NR 643 481

Isle of Gigha

Built 1923. Windows by Gordon Webster. First minister Dr Kenneth MacLeod author of 'The Road to the Isles'. Gigha Gardens and nine-hole golf course ten minutes walk from church. Ferry from Tayinloan/Kintyre 20 minutes.
Sunday Service 12 noon

Open daily

CHURCH OF SCOTLAND WC at village shop

KILMODAN CHURCH, GLENDARUEL

79 KILMODAN CHURCH, GLENDARUEL

NR 995 842

Clachan of Glendaruel

A Georgian T-plan church of 1783 on site of an earlier church of 1610. Completely restored in 1983. Segmental-arched windows; lofts in the three arms. Two long narrow communion tables. Memorial to Rev John MacLaurin and his two famous sons (Colin, author of MacLaurin's Mathematical Theorem). Bus and post bus from Dunoon. On A886. United with Colintraive. Sunday Services 10am or 11.30am alternating monthly with Colintraive

Open daily

CHURCH OF SCOTLAND ♿ WC (nearby)

80 ST MICHAEL AND ALL ANGELS, HELENSBURGH

NS 292 825

William Street, Helensburgh

Built by Sir R Rowand Anderson in 1868 in French Gothic style. Tower with peal of eight bells added in 1930. Richly decorated interior with oak chancel screen, elaborately carved Austrian oak north porch screen. West porch screen (1996) of light oak and engraved glass by James Anderson. Alabaster and mosaic reredos against encaustic tiling. Organ by August Gern, foreman to Cavaille-Coll. Fine sculpted west portal nave and chancel capitals. Good stained glass; light by Clayton & Bell, Shrigley & Hunt, Adam & Small, and Barraud & Westlake, with five windows by C E Kempe including fine rose window in west facade. 800m west of Central railway station, off Clyde Street. Services: Sunday 8am, 10.15am and 6.30pm; Tuesdays 10.30am; Wednesdays 7.30pm

Open daily 9am-5pm

SCOTTISH EPISCOPAL WC **A**

81 THE WEST KIRK OF HELENSBURGH

NS 295 825

Colquhoun Square, Helensburgh

Victorian Gothic building of 1853 J, W H & J M Hay, restored after disastrous fire in 1924 by Robert Wemyss, with a porch by William Leiper. Impressive panelled interior, with fine woodwork and half-timbered ceiling. Exceptionally fine stained glass including memorial windows to Andrew Bonar Law, one time Prime Minister, and to John Logie Baird, inventor of television and son of the Manse in Helensburgh. Hill House (Charles Rennie Mackintosh) is one mile away. Sunday Service 10am April to September, 11am October to March

Open daily all year 9am-5pm; and with guides June to August, Monday, Wednesday and Friday 2-4pm. Exhibition summer months

CHURCH OF SCOTLAND WC **B**

82 GLENARAY & INVERARAY PARISH CHURCH, IN INVERARAY

NN 096 084

Church Square, Inveraray

Designed by Robert Mylne in 1792 to house two congregations, English and Gaelic. A solid wall separated the two. Gaelic portion converted to church hall 1957. Sunday Service 11.15am

Open July and August on request at Church exhibition and sale in Church Hall at rear of Church

CHURCH OF SCOTLAND **A**

GLENARAY & INVERARAY PARISH CHURCH, IN INVERARAY

83 IONA ABBEY

NM 287 245

Isle of Iona

On the original site of St Columba's monastery c.563. St Columba's Shrine dates from the ninth century, most of the present buildings from around 1200. The massive restoration of the Abbey Church was undertaken by the Iona Cathedral Trust, who own the buildings, and was completed in 1910. The Iona Community now occupy the monastic buildings which they restored under the leadership of the Rev Dr George MacLeod. Historic Scotland now have the resposibility to care for the Abbey and associated monuments. Beautiful Augustinian nunnery, twelfth-century ruin, Reilig Odhrain (Royal burial ground), 'Street of the Dead', imposing standing crosses and one of the largest collections of early Christian carved stones in Europe. Ferry from Oban to Mull, by bus/car to Fionnphort, pedestrian ferry to Iona. Services: Sunday 10.30am and Monday to Saturday 2.00pm March to October. Also Monday to Saturday 9.00am all year

Open at all times

INTER-DENOMINATIONAL WC **A**

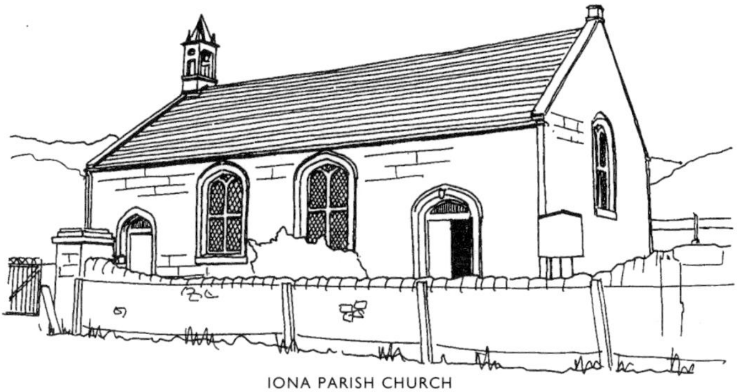

IONA PARISH CHURCH

84 IONA PARISH CHURCH

NM 285 243

Isle of Iona

A Thomas Telford church of 1828. Pews, pulpit and communion table realigned in 1939. Former manse of same date now a heritage centre with picnic area adjacent. Ferry from Oban to Mull. Bus/car to Fionnphort for ferry to Iona. Sunday Service 12 noon. Short Service Tuesday 1pm and each weekday in high summer

Open daily

CHURCH OF SCOTLAND **B**

85 KILBERRY PARISH CHURCH

NR 741 620

The church was built in 1821. A plain oblong building, galleries on three sides, later alterations provided an internal stair and removed the original external access. At Lergnahension, twelve miles from Tarbert on the B8024. Sunday Services fortnightly, summer 10am, winter 2pm

Open all year during daylight hours

CHURCH OF SCOTLAND **B**

KILBERRY PARISH CHURCH

86 KILFINAN PARISH CHURCH

NR 934 789

Kilfinan

A place of worship since 1235. Gothic 1759, including the earlier Lamont Vault of 1633. Stones of interest. B8000 from Tighnabruaich or Strachur. Sunday Service 12 noon

Open all year

CHURCH OF SCOTLAND **B**

87 KILMARTIN PARISH CHURCH

NR 836 993

Kilmartin, by Lochgilphead

On the site of earlier churches, the present building opened in 1835. The architect was James Gordon Davis. Three interesting memorial panels from the 18th and 19th centuries to members of the family of Campbell of Duntroon. The church has two outstanding crosses, with explanatory panels provided by Historic Scotland. The kirkyard contains the mausoleum of Bishop Neil Campbell and medieval tomb slabs. Extensive views over Bronze Age burial cairns. For services, see local paper and notice board

Open April to October, 9.30am-6pm

CHURCH OF SCOTLAND **B**

KILMARTIN PARISH CHURCH

88 KILMUN PARISH CHURCH, ST MUNN'S

NS 166 821

Kilmun, by Dunoon

On the site of a Celtic monastery, overlooking Holy Loch. Tower of 15th-century collegiate church. Present building dates from 1841, by Thomas Burns with interior remodelled by P MacGregor Chalmers in 1899. Important stained glass by Stephen Adam and Alfred Webster. Water-powered organ. Ancient graveyard with fine 18th-century carved stones. Mausoleum of Dukes of Argyll, Douglas vault. Grave of Elizabeth Blackwell, first lady doctor. On A880, 6 miles from Dunoon. Sunday Service 12 noon

Open May to end September, Tuesday to Thursday and holiday Mondays 1.30-4.30pm (last tour 4pm). Other times, including coach parties by arrangement, telephone Valerie Gilles 01369 840342.

Younger Botanic Gardens, 2 miles, open April to October

CHURCH OF SCOTLAND WC **B**

KILMUN PARISH CHURCH, ST MUNN'S

89 KILCHRENAN PARISH CHURCH

NN 037 229

Kilchrenan

The building was built in 1770 on the site of an earlier church dating back to the twelfth century. Some stones from that church have been incorporated into the present building. There are interesting tombstones in the graveyard including that of Cailean Mor in 1294. Linked with Muckairn and Dalavich. Sunday Services 10.00am on the first, third and fifth Sundays of the month

Open during daylight hours

CHURCH OF SCOTLAND

KILCHRENAN PARISH CHURCH

90 ST MOLUAG, ISLE OF LISMORE

NN 007 573

Kentallen, Lismore

'The Cathedral of Argyll' was built in late 14th to early 15th century and attributed locally to 'The Roman' or '*An Roimhanach*'. Six stained glass windows, two modern by Mitton. Eight medieval carved slab-stones, said to be of the 'Loch Awe' school and recumbent carved stone within the building. Traditional Baptismal font is carved in a natural rock surface. Exhibition on 800 years of Christianity on Lismore

Open at all times

CHURCH OF SCOTLAND WC (by arrangement)

LOCHGOILHEAD & KILMORICH PARISH CHURCH

91 LOCHGOILHEAD & KILMORICH PARISH CHURCH

NN 198 015

Lochgoilhead

Dedicated to the Three Holy Brethren, the church is first mentioned in papal letters of 1379. It was rebuilt in the 18th century incorporating the medieval walls. Many features of interest. A83 Arrochar–Inveraray, top of Rest and Be Thankful, B828 and B839 into village. Sunday Service 10.30am

Open by arrangement, telephone Mr W Workman 013013 280

Church Fair in August. Coffee mornings depending on local weather conditions

CHURCH OF SCOTLAND **B**

92 LUSS PARISH CHURCH

NS 361 929

This picturesque church, the third built on this site on the banks of Loch Lomond, with its beautiful stained glass windows and uniquely timbered roof, features frequently in 'Take the High Road'. The ancient graveyard has 15 listed ancient monuments. Luss Village, off A82. Sunday Service 11.45am

Open daily from 10am

CHURCH OF SCOTLAND **B**

93 MUCKAIRN PARISH CHURCH, TAYNUILT

NN 005 310

Taynuilt

Built in 1829 the church stands adjacent to the ruins (1228) of Killespickerill once the seat of the Bishop of Argyll. Two stones of antiquity are built into the walls of the present Church. Tombstones from the 14th century can be seen in the graveyard. Linked with Kilchrenan and Dalavich. Sunday Service 11.45am

Open during daylight hours

CHURCH OF SCOTLAND WC

MUCKAIRN PARISH CHURCH, TAYNUILT

94 CATHEDRAL CHURCH OF ST JOHN THE DIVINE, OBAN

NM 859 304

George Street, Oban

The cathedral is a small part of the projected building, consisting of chancel, crossing, nave of one bay and one transept James Chalmers, 1908 attached at right angles to existing church by Charles Wilson and David Thomson, giving an extraordinary building internally. Tall reredos on a Scottish theme with painting of Ascension set in the West Highlands by Norman Macdougall. Vast hovering bronze eagle. Choir stalls in form of Celtic graveyard. Much Iona marble and terrazzo. Sunday Services 8am, 10.15am, 11.30am and 5pm. Weekdays 9.30am or 11am

Open daily

SCOTTISH EPISCOPAL WC **C**

95 ST MODAN'S PARISH CHURCH, ROSNEATH

NS 2583

A814 to Garelochhead, then B833 to Rosneath

There has been a church at Rosneath since the time of St Modan c.600-650 AD, the present building, 1853, is by architect David Cousins. The bell, made by Ian Burgerhuis in 1610, is re-used from the older church, and was used as a summons to arms during the 1715 Jacobite rebellion. Two-manual organ by Hill, 1875. Reredos of ten commandments by W A Muirhead and The Last Supper by Meredith Williams, carved by Thomas Wood. Mural of St Modan by Mary Ainsworth, 1995. Stained glass by Clayton & Bell, Douglas Strachan, Stephen Adam & Co, Gordon Webster, Crear McCartney. Sunday Service: 11.30am (10 am in 2001)

Open by arrangement, telephone the Minister 01436 842274

CHURCH OF SCOTLAND WC (by arrangement) **A**

ST MODAN'S PARISH CHURCH, ROSNEATH

96 TARBERT PARISH CHURCH

NR 863 686

Campbeltown Road, Tarbert

Built in 1886 on the site of an earlier mission church dating from 1775 and granted *quoad sacra* status in 1864. Architects J McKissack and W G Rowan of Glasgow. The building features an imposing square tower rising over 100 ft, surmounted by a crown and lantern. Stained glass windows and unusual roof decoration. Eighteenth-century graveyard within walking distance. Sunday Service 11.30am

Open April to September, 10am–5.30pm

CHURCH OF SCOTLAND **B**

TARBERT PARISH CHURCH

97 KILCHATTAN KIRK, TOBERONOCHY

NM 743 104

Toberonochy, Isle of Luing

Kilchattan Kirk was built in 1936 and houses a beautifully carved, floor-standing, wooden lectern and two wooden offering plates donated by Latvian ship owners to mark the rescue efforts of the islanders when one of their ships foundered in a storm on the island of Belnahua in 1938. Just beyond the school on the road to Toberonochy. Sunday Service 11am, except last Sunday in month 3.15pm

Open all year

CHURCH OF SCOTLAND

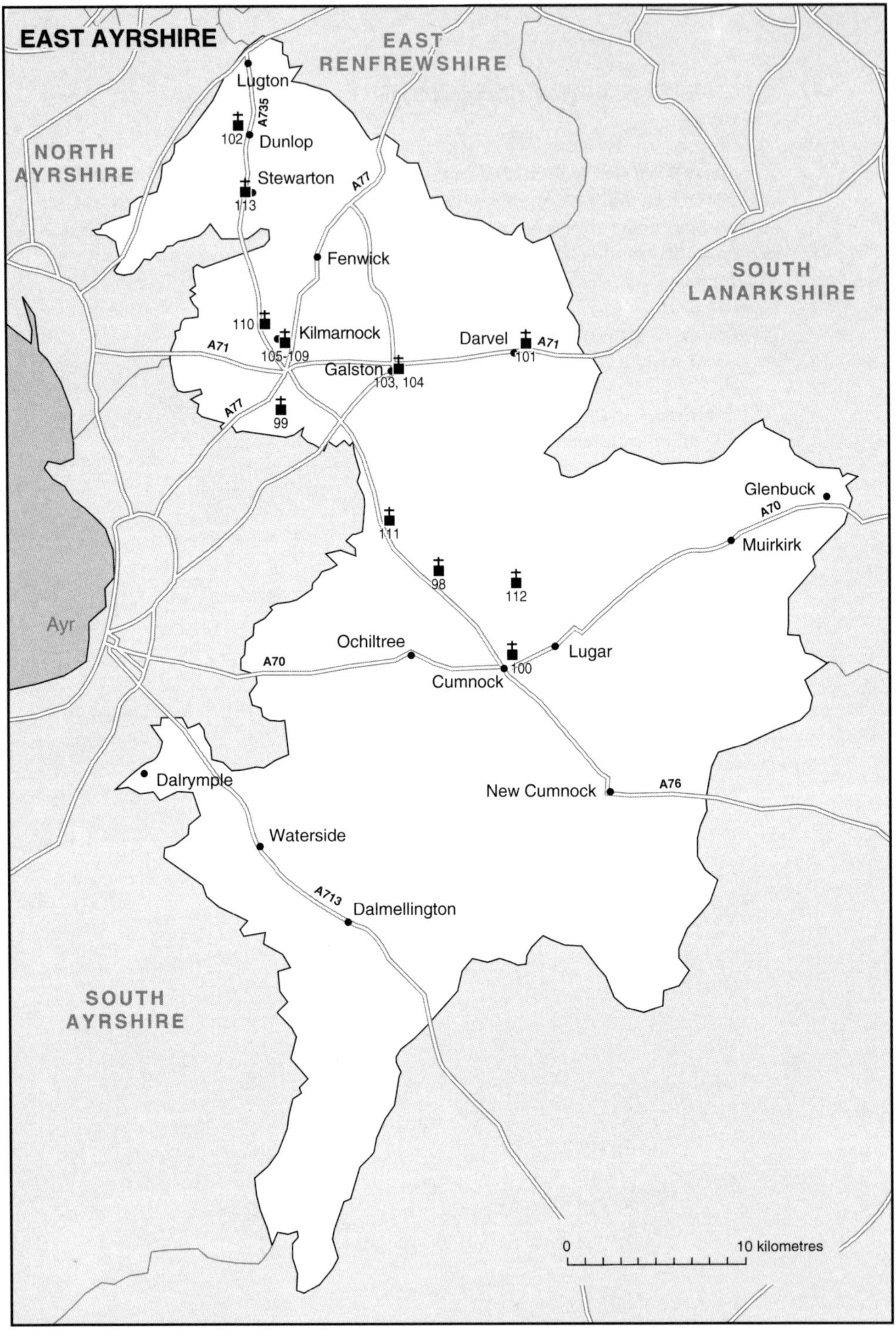

EAST AYRSHIRE
EAST RENFREWSHIRE
NORTH AYRSHIRE
SOUTH LANARKSHIRE
SOUTH AYRSHIRE
Lugton
A735
102
Dunlop
Stewarton
113
A77
Fenwick
110
Kilmarnock
105-109
A71
Darvel
101
Galston
103, 104
A77
99
Glenbuck
A70
Muirkirk
111
98
112
Ayr
Ochiltree
A70
100
Lugar
Cumnock
Dalrymple
New Cumnock
A76
Waterside
A713
Dalmellington
0
10 kilometres

EAST AYRSHIRE

Local Representative: Miss Joan Fish, 31 Oaklands Avenue, Irvine (*telephone* 01294 272654)

98 CATRINE PARISH CHURCH

NS 528 260

Chapel Brae, Catrine

Charming church, built as a chapel of ease in 1792, financed by Sir Claud Alexander of Ballochmyle. It was established as a parish church when Catrine was made a *quoad sacra* parish in 1871. Major renovations in 1874, 1960 and 1992. Stained glass. Harrison & Harrison pipe organ 1874. Overlooking Catrine in the river Ayr valley. B713, off A76 Dumfries–Kilmarnock, between Mauchline and Auchinleck. Sunday Service 12 noon

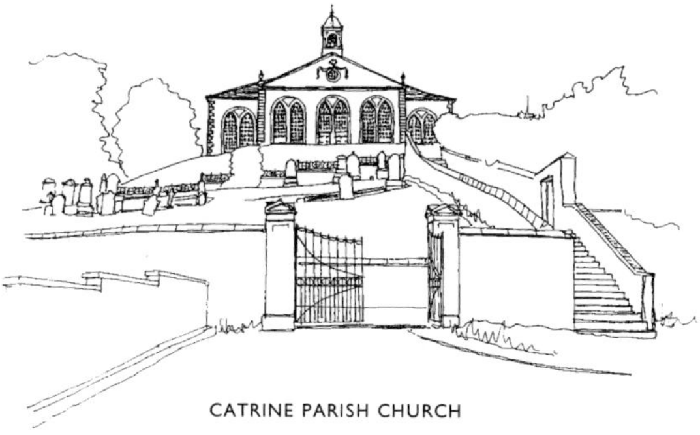

CATRINE PARISH CHURCH

Open by arrangement, telephone Mr Holland 01290 551718

CHURCH OF SCOTLAND **A**

99 CRAIGIE PARISH CHURCH

NS 427 323

Craigie

Pleasant traditional country kirk built 1776. Remains of previous church c.1580 but the site was occupied by a church from medieval times. Three miles from Prestwick Airport off A77 (two miles along Tarbolton Road).
Sunday Service 12 noon first and third Sundays

Open by arrangement, telephone Mrs E MacLeod 01563 860249

CHURCH OF SCOTLAND

CRAIGIE PARISH CHURCH

100 OLD CUMNOCK OLD CHURCH

NS 508 202

The Square, Cumnock

Commanding a prominent position in the square of this old market town, the church was built in 1866 through the patronage of the Marquess of Bute and the Bute family seats remain in the Memorial Chapel. Organ 1966. Mosaic of Jesus walking on the water by James Harrigan. Bell in vestibule was cast in 1697 by Quinus de Vesscher of Rotterdam, and was used in the two churches which preceded the present building. Services: Sunday 11.30am, days of opening: 12.30pm, plus Tuesday and Friday: 12.30pm

Open July and August Tuesday and Fridays 12noon-4pm, Thursdays 10am-2pm

CHURCH OF SCOTLAND (at Words of Wisdom opposite church) **B**

101 OUR LADY OF THE VALLEY, DARVEL

NS 5637

4 West Donington Street, Darvel

Church built by seceders in 1874 and closed in 1927. Various users of the building, e.g. Girl Guides, until early 1950s when it again lay empty. Purchased in mid-1960s by Darvel Parish Church and used as a Church Hall before being sold to the Catholic community and opened by Bishop Maurice Taylor on 25 November 1984. Sunday Service 10am

Open by arrangement, contact Mr A Dougherty telephone 01560 320346

ROMAN CATHOLIC WC

102 DUNLOP PARISH CHURCH

NS 405 494

Main Street, Dunlop

A Christian site since the13th century, the present church dates from 1835, though the sculptured stonework of the Dunlop Aisle, 1641, was preserved. Magnificent collection of stained glass by Gordon Webster. Beside the church is Clandeboyes Hall, 1641, built as a school. Built on to the back of Clandeboyes is the early 17th century monumental tomb of Hans Hamilton, first Protestant minister of Dunlop. Sunday Service 11am

Open 2-4 pm June-September

CHURCH OF SCOTLAND WC **B** (church) **A** (tomb and hall)

103 GALSTON PARISH CHURCH

NS 500 367

Cross Street, Galston

Present church, designed by John Brash of Glasgow, erected 1809 on site of Christian worship since 1252. Third church since Reformation. 120 ft spire. Chancel added 1912 and three-manual pipe organ by J J Binns 1913. Ministers include Dr George Smith, great-grandfather of Robert Louis Stevenson and mentioned by Robert Burns in 'The Holy Fair' (grave on north side of church). Gravestone of Andrew Richmond, killed by Graham of Claverhouse, on south porch and Covenanters' memorial on north side.

Sunday Service 11am

Open by arrangement, telephone Mrs May McHoull 01563 820890

CHURCH OF SCOTLAND **B**

GALSTON PARISH CHURCH

104 ST SOPHIA, GALSTON

NS 504 365

Bentinck Street, Galston

Constructed 1885-86, architect Sir R Rowand Anderson, the church is a distinctive building freely based on Haghia Sophia in Istanbul. At the behest of Lord Bute, who commissioned the church, Anderson, and possibly Weir Schultz brought to Galston this dark brick echo of the Byzantine Empire. Re-opening after restoration scheduled for early in 2000. Services: Saturday 6.00pm, Sunday 11.30am, daily Mass as announced

Open by arrangement, telephone Mr T Heggan 01563 821587

ROMAN CATHOLIC (disabled access available on request) WC

105 HENDERSON PARISH CHURCH, KILMARNOCK

NS 431 380

London Road, Kilmarnock

Brilliantly individual Arts & Crafts treatment of Gothic motifs by Thomas Smellie, Kilmarnock, completed in 1907. Very tall tower above tall church built on rising ground, with halls below. Carillon of bells 1950. Fine Norman & Beard three-manual organ restored in 1987. Stained glass windows by Gordon Webster 1907, and, in side chapel, by Wendy Robertson 1987. On Burns Heritage Trail, leading to Dean Castle Country Park (open all year). Church in town centre, adjacent to Grand Hall, Palace Theatre and bus station. Sunday Services 9.45am and 11am

Open by arrangement, telephone Mr J Neil 01563 528212

CHURCH OF SCOTLAND WC **B**

HENDERSON PARISH CHURCH, KILMARNOCK

106 HOLY TRINITY CHURCH, KILMARNOCK

NS 426 377

Portland Road, Kilmarnock

The nave to a design by James Wallace 1857 with chancel and sanctuary by Sir George Gilbert Scott 1876. Wall and ceiling murals in the chancel, stained glass. At the junction of Portland Road with Dundonald Road, 200 yards from King Street. Sunday Services: 9.15am Holy Communion, 11am Sung Eucharist, 6pm Evensong. Matins 11am, first Sunday if not a festival

Open daily

SCOTTISH EPISCOPAL **B**

HOLY TRINITY CHURCH, KILMARNOCK

LAIGH KIRK, KILMARNOCK

107 LAIGH KIRK, KILMARNOCK

NS 428 379

John Dickie Street, Kilmarnock

Body of the church by Robert Johnstone 1802. Enlarged 1831 with later 19th-century session room. Major refurbishment 1996 by W I Munro Architects, winning 1997 Civic Trust Award for part of town centre regeneration. Interesting monuments and stained glass. Covenanters' graves in adjacent kirkyard. Close to bus and rail stations. Sunday Services 11am, also 9.30am June to August

Open Tuesday, Thursday and Friday morning. Other times, telephone 01563 528051

CHURCH OF SCOTLAND WC **A**

108 OLD HIGH KIRK, KILMARNOCK

NS 430 382

Soulis Street, Kilmarnock

Kilmarnock's oldest church, built 1732 of local stone by the Hunter Brothers to a design adapted from St Martin's-in-the-Fields London. Austere exterior contrasts with pleasing interior enhanced by unique set of 23 stained glass windows by W & J J Keir, glaziers to Glasgow Cathedral. Graveyard with tombs including John Wilson, publisher of Robert Burns' first book of poems, and Tam Samson. Sunday Service 11am

Open by arrangement, telephone Mr G Thomson 01563 526064, or during business hours contact 'Pet Shop', 53 Foregate

CHURCH OF SCOTLAND WC **A**

109 ST MARNOCK'S PARISH CHURCH, KILMARNOCK

NS 427 377

St Marnock's Street, Kilmarnock

Perpendicular Gothic, rectangular plan six-bay church with centrally placed tower on north gable end, by John Ingram 1839. Fine carillon of bells. Three-manual pipe organ 1872, painted organ screen. Extensive restoration programme completed in 1997. In centre of town with easy access from bus and railway station. Sunday Service 11am

Open first Sunday in September each year 12 noon–4pm. Or by arrangement, telephone the Session Clerk 01563 523951. E-mail: jwrca@globalnet.co.uk

CHURCH OF SCOTLAND (free) WC **B**

110 ST MAUR'S GLENCAIRN PARISH CHURCH, KILMAURS

NS 415 408

The church at Kilmaurs was in the possession of Kelso Abbey as early as 1170. In 1413 the present foundation was endowed by Sir William Cunninghame as a collegiate church. Rebuilt by Robert S Ingram 1888 in a cruciform shape. Twentieth-century stained glass, including a window by Roland Mitton of Livingston, and three rose windows. The clock tower holds the original bell inscribed 'Michael Burgerhuys Me Fecit 1618'. Glencairn Aisle adjacent to the church with sculptured mural 1600 commissioned by James, seventh Earl of Glencairn, in memory of the Earl and Countess of Glencairn, and worked by David Scougal, mason and burgess. On A735. Sunday Service 11am

Open by arrangement, telephone the Rev John Urquhart 01563 538289

CHURCH OF SCOTLAND **B**

111 MAUCHLINE PARISH CHURCH

NS 498 272

Loudoun Street, Mauchline

Present church by William Alexander 1829 stands on site of St Michael's Church founded in 13th century. Single bell cast in 1742. Willis pipe organ 1888 rebuilt in 1980. Associations with Covenanters and Robert Burns, many of whose contemporaries are buried here. At junction of B743 with A76. Sunday Service 11am

Open June to August, Tuesday and Wednesday 2–4pm.

Also Ayrshire Doors Open Day (date to be announced)

CHURCH OF SCOTLAND WC **B**

112 SORN PARISH CHURCH

NS 550 268

Main Street, Sorn

A rather splendid edifice, quietly assured, built in 1656 and much reconstructed in 1826. Outside stairs to three galleries. Jougs on the west wall. East wall memorial to George Wood, last Covenanter to die 1688. Sunday Service 10.30am

Open by arrangement, telephone Miss McKerrow 01290 551256

CHURCH OF SCOTLAND WC **B**

SORN PARISH CHURCH

113 ST COLUMBA'S PARISH CHURCH, STEWARTON

NS 419 457

1 Kirk Glebe, Stewarton

Built in 1696, renovated in 1775 and widened in 1825 with later additions. Bell tower. Lainshaw Loft used for smaller services. New and restored windows installed for tercentenary in 1996. Beside the mini-roundabout at the south end of Stewarton. Sunday Service 11am

Open by arrangement, telephone the Minister 01560 482453

CHURCH OF SCOTLAND WC **B**

ST COLUMBA'S PARISH CHURCH, STEWARTON

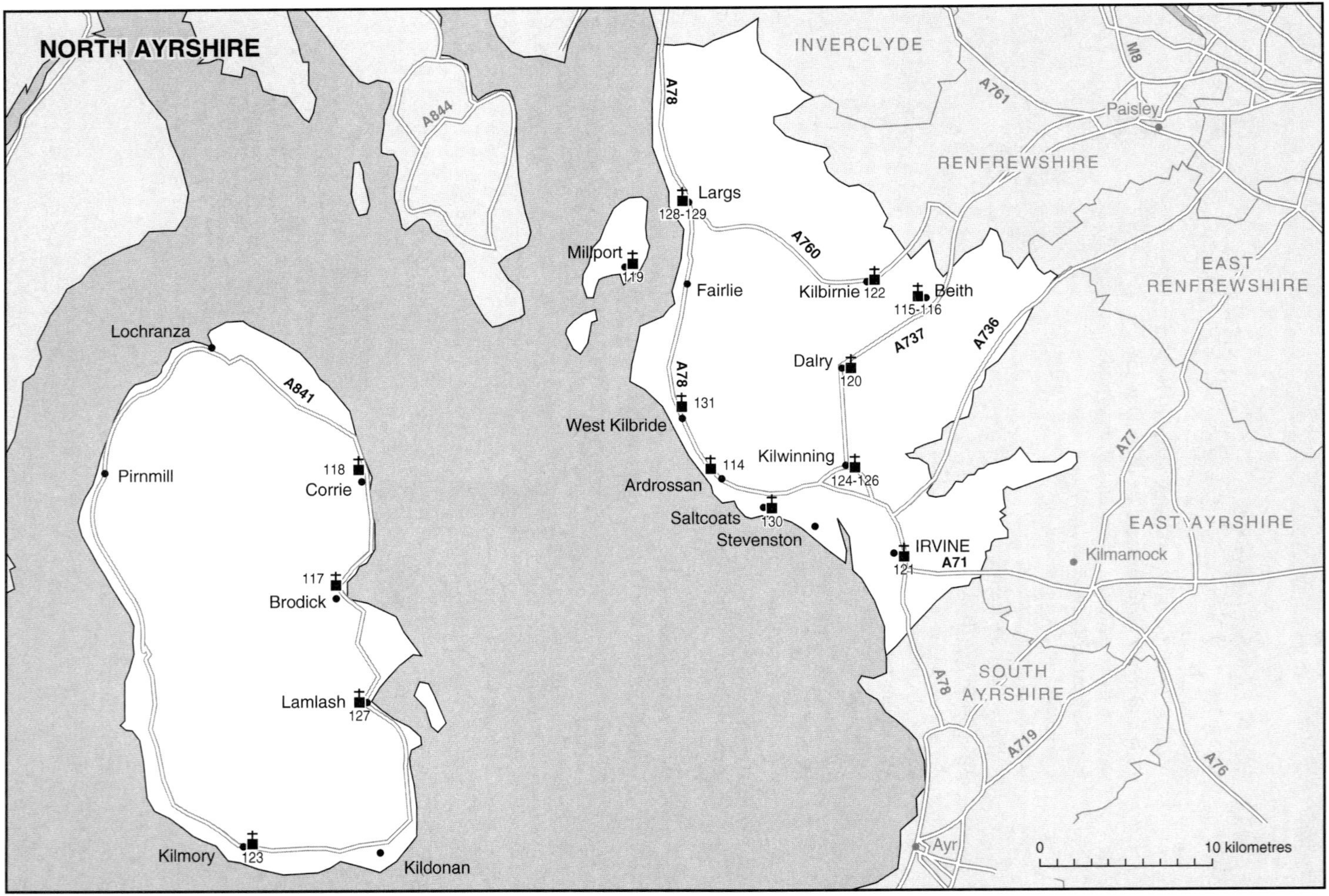
NORTH AYRSHIRE
INVERCLYDE
RENFREWSHIRE
EAST RENFREWSHIRE
EAST AYRSHIRE
SOUTH AYRSHIRE
Paisley
Kilmarnock
Ayr
M8
A761
A844
A78
A760
A737
A736
A77
A71
A719
A76
A841
Largs
128-129
Millport
119
Fairlie
Kilbirnie
122
Beith
115-116
Dalry
120
131
West Kilbride
Kilwinning
124-126
114
Ardrossan
Saltcoats
130
Stevenston
IRVINE
121
Lochranza
Pirnmill
118
Corrie
117
Brodick
Lamlash
127
Kilmory
123
Kildonan
0
10 kilometres

NORTH AYRSHIRE

Local Representative: Miss Joan Fish, 31 Oaklands Avenue, Irvine (*telephone* 01294 272654)

114 ST PETER IN CHAINS, ARDROSSAN

NS 233 421

1 South Crescent, Ardrossan

Designed by Jack Coia and opened in 1938, St Peter in Chains is probably the most academic of this period. The church, in reddish facing brick, has a high west gable as at St Columba, Hopehill Road, Glasgow and a tower to the right reminiscent of Stockholm Town Hall. Striking brick main doorway with stone keystone; the door feature continues to the gable roof and ends in a small well-detailed cross. Services: Monday-Saturday Mass 9.30am, 7pm, Saturday Vigil Mass 6.30pm, Sunday 10am 12noon and 6.30pm

Open daily 9am-7.30pm

ROMAN CATHOLIC **A**

ST PETER IN CHAINS, ARDROSSAN

115 BEITH HIGH CHURCH

NS 350 539

Kirk Road, Beith

Built in 1807 and extended in 1885. Gothic T-plan kirk dominated by the tall five-stage tower. Stained glass by Gordon Webster. Harrison & Harrison pipe organ 1885. From Beith bypass along Barrmill Road to Kirk Road.

Sunday Services 10 and 11.30am

Open by arrangement, telephone The Rev Andrew Black 01505 502686

CHURCH OF SCOTLAND WC **B**

BEITH HIGH CHURCH

116 BEITH TRINITY CHURCH

NS 351 544

Wilson Street, Beith

Built 1883, architect Robert Baldie. The chief external feature is a graceful octagonal tower. Interior destroyed by fire 1917, rebuilt 1926. Gothic style, with rectangular navem Gothic arched chancel and one transept on the east side. Stained glass by John C Hall & Co. Organ 1937 by Hill, Norman & Beard. Sunday Services: 11.30am, July. 10am and 11.30am, August in High Church.

Opening by arrangement telephone 01505 502131

CHURCH OF SCOTLAND WC

117 BRODICK CHURCH, ISLE OF ARRAN

NS 012 359

Knowe Road, Brodick (1 mile north of pier, turn left at sports park)

The present church was built in 1910 from local red sandstone. The pulpit, built by local craftsmen, is an exact replica of John Knox's pulpit. Two stained glass windows are in memory of church member Bethia Torrance who died in 1958. Sunday Service 10.45am

Open by arrangement, telephone Mr Hannah 01770 302248. Flower Festival Easter 2000

CHURCH OF SCOTLAND WC **B**

118 CORRIE CHURCH, ISLE OF ARRAN

NS 024 437

6 miles north of Brodick

Designed by J J Burnet, 1887, as 'one of a family of long, low friendly churches'. Constructed in red sandstone in an early Gothic style with a simple stone belfry and wooden porch. An unusual baptismal font is set into the arch and church wall and rush-bottomed chairs take the place of pews. Lit by circular candelabra. Two tapestries by Mrs Sandeman and two recently installed stained glass windows designed by Richard Leclerc. Sunday Service 12noon

Open by arrangement, telephone the Session Clerk 01770 810675 or Mr McConnachie 01770 810246 or Mrs Pringle 01770 810210

CHURCH OF SCOTLAND WC **B**

CORRIE CHURCH, ISLE OF ARRAN

119 THE CATHEDRAL OF THE ISLES, ISLE OF CUMBRAE

NS 165 561

College Street, Millport, Isle of Cumbrae

Cathedral, college and cloister by William Butterfield 1851. A Tractarian church built by sixth Earl of Glasgow. Peal of bells, organ, stained glass by William Wailes and Hardman. Visitors welcome to picnic in the grounds. Ferry from Largs and bus to Millport. Sunday Service 11am Sung Eucharist; other times see notice board in porch

Open daily

SCOTTISH EPISCOPAL WC **A**

120 ST MARGARET'S PARISH CHURCH, DALRY

NS 291 496

The Cross, Dalry

David Thomson architect of a landmark Victorian Gothic building (1871-73) on a 1604 or earlier site. Inventive 159ft broach spire 'worthy of the many tasks thrust upon it'; the whole building is a 'powerful, carefully handled composition'. The restored interior (with good acoustics) of the early 1950s presents 'a space of deep solemnity enhanced' by Beith-made pulpit, table, lectern and stained glass by Guthrie & Wells, Charles Payne, C L Davidson, plus the only decent amount of Munich glass and only Francis Hemony bell (1661) in a UK church. Three-manual Blackett & Howden organ (1899). Communion silver of 1618. Bronze sundial and some interesting stones in Kirkyard. Kirk bears the name of the original medieval dedication: St Margaret of Antioch (see modern Rona Moody window) the only such in Scotland. Cunninghame Choir Concert in the Kirk: Saturday 20 May 2000. In the vicinity – Blair House may be viewed from outside; Cleeves Cove (interesting limestone cave system).

Sunday Services 11.30am all year, 6.30pm September to April (except first of month), 10.30am May to August, and 1 November to April

Open by arrangement, telephone 01294 833135/832234.

Also Ayrshire Doors Open Day

CHURCH OF SCOTLAND WC **B**

ST ANDREW'S PARISH CHURCH (FERGUSON MEMORIAL), IRVINE

121 ST ANDREW'S PARISH CHURCH (FERGUSON MEMORIAL), IRVINE

NS 3239

Caldon Road x Oaklands Avenue, Irvine

St Andrew's was gifted in 1957 to commemorate the centenary of the death of John Ferguson, founder of the Ferguson bequest. Architect Rennie & Bramble of Saltcoats. Stained glass windows by Mary Wood 1957 and Ann Marie Docherty 1998. The congregation has shared the church with the local Scottish Episcopalian congregation who built on a chapel/meeting room, containing tapestry by Vampboulles, and coffee lounge in 1981. Architect, R L Dunlop of Troon. Sunday Services: Scottish Episcopal 9.30am; Church of Scotland 11.15am

Open Tuesdays 10–10.45am. Tuesday Morning Club for Senior Citizens, with tea and coffee in coffee lounge, October to May

CHURCH OF SCOTLAND WC WC

122 THE AULD KIRK OF KILBIRNIE

NS 315 536

Dalry Road, Kilbirnie

A pre-Reformation church on or near the site of sixth-century Christian settlement of St Brendan of Clonfert. The nave dates from 1470 and the tower from 1490. Glengarnock aisle added 1597. Crawfurd aisle with Laird's loft and splendid Italian Renaissance-style carving 1642. Pulpit c.1620. Signed from B737 Irvine–Paisley. By bus to Kilbirnie, by rail to Glengarnock. Sunday Services September to May 11am and 6.30pm, June to August 9.30am and 11am

Open July to August, weekdays 2–4pm except Mondays; and Ayrshire Doors Open Day September.

Other times, telephone Mr J Lauchland 01505 683459

CHURCH OF SCOTLAND WC A

THE AULD KIRK OF KILBIRNIE

123 KILMORY PARISH CHURCH

NR 700 449

Kilmory, Isle of Arran

Present church built 1880 over previous building 1765. Small, delightful church with plain windows surrounded by red-coloured stained glass, providing a warm ambience. Linked with Lamlash. Situated in village of Kilmory, turn right after Creamery on road from Whiting Bay. Sunday Service 10am

Open by arrangement, telephone Mrs Mairi Duff 01770 870305

CHURCH OF SCOTLAND **B**

124 THE ABBEY CHURCH, KILWINNING

NS 303 433

Main Street, Kilwinning

Built in 1774 by John Garland and John Wright. The church is on the site of the ruined Abbey, founded in 1188, and replaced a second church of 1590. Visitor Centre in Abbey tower. Abbey ruins. Sunday Services 9.15am and 11am September to June, 10am July and August

Open Ayrshire Doors Open Day.

Or by arrangement, telephone Mr J Muir, 30 Underwood, Kilwinning 01294 552929

CHURCH OF SCOTLAND

125 ERSKINE CHURCH, KILWINNING

NS 303 434

Main Street, Kilwinning

Simple UP-style building, 1838, down a lane from Main Street. Pedimented open bellcote flanked by ancones. Gable finials. Pleasant restored interior with gallery. Sunday Service 11.30am

Open by arrangement, telephone Mr Welsh 01294 554376

CHURCH OF SCOTLAND **C**

FERGUSHILL CHURCH, KILWINNING

126 FERGUSHILL CHURCH, KILWINNING

NS 337 430

Benslie Village, Kilwinning

Church extension for the mining community from Kilwinning Parish Church in 1879 to a plan prepared by William Railton of Kilmarnock. Attractive church with bell tower. Fine views to Arran. Sunday Service 10am

Open by arrangement, telephone Mrs Borland 01294 850257

CHURCH OF SCOTLAND WC

127 LAMLASH PARISH CHURCH

NS 026 309

Shore Road, Lamlash, Isle of Arran

A massive campanile tower over 90 ft high sits above this Gothic-style, red sandstone building by H & D Barclay 1886. The church was built by twelfth Duke of Hamilton to replace an earlier building of 1773. Boarded, barrel-vaulted ceiling and carved, wooden tripartite Gothic sedilia. Seven stained glass windows by Meiklejohn, Gordon Webster and Christian Shaw; all other windows are hand painted, German cathedral glass. Pipe organ, William Hill, Norman and Beard 1934. In the front grounds are an ancient cross and baptismal font from the old monastery on Holy Isle in Lamlash Bay. Major restoration programme begun 1997. Sunday Service 11.30am

Open by arrangement. See Church notice board for information, or contact Captain J L Davidson, Rock Cottage, Cordon, Lamlash, telephone 01770 600787

CHURCH OF SCOTLAND WC A

128 CLARK MEMORIAL CHURCH, LARGS

NS 202 593

Bath Street, Largs

Gifted by John Clark of the Anchor Thread Mills, Paisley, and designed by William Kerr of T G Abercrombie, Paisley 1892. Red sandstone from Locharbriggs and Corsehill in Early English Gothic style. Superb stained glass, all manufactured in Glasgow at height of Arts and Crafts movement. Hammer-beam roof. Views of the Clyde and Cumbraes. Sunday Services 9.30 and 11am, Thursday 10.30am

Open by arrangement (not Thursdays), telephone Church Officer 01475 675186. Viking Festival one week each September

CHURCH OF SCOTLAND WC A

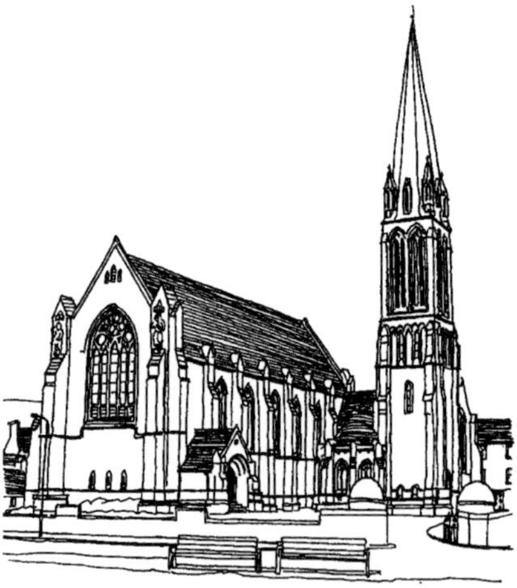

CLARK MEMORIAL CHURCH, LARGS

129 ST COLUMBA'S PARISH CHURCH, LARGS

NS 203 596

Gallowgate, Largs

The old parish church was replaced by the present building in 1892. It is a handsome structure, architects Henry Steele and Andrew Balfour, of red stone with a three-stage tower with spire and clock. Interesting carved octagonal oak pulpit and notable windows. 'Father' Willis organ. Memorial to General Sir Thomas MacDougall Brisbane, astronomer, soldier and Governor of NSW. Sunday Service 11am

Open 10am-noon, Monday to Friday

CHURCH OF SCOTLAND (by arrangement) (Saturdays June–September) WC B

ST COLUMBA'S PARISH CHURCH, LARGS

130 ST CUTHBERT'S PARISH CHURCH, SALTCOATS

NS 244 418

Caledonia Road, Saltcoats

Designed by Peter MacGregor Chalmers and dedicated in 1908, the fourth building of the congregation of Ardrossan Parish. The chancel displays a marble reredos of the Last Supper. Sixteen stained glass windows the Life of Christ by William Wilson 1947; two windows by Gordon Webster 1976. Model of a French frigate of 1804, by a sailor William Dunlop, hangs in the church. He made it as a thanksgiving for his surviving the Napoleonic wars when a canonball narrowly missed his hammock! Sunday Service 11.15am

Open by arrangement, telephone Mrs Hanlon 01294 466636

CHURCH OF SCOTLAND WC B

131 OVERTON CHURCH, WEST KILBRIDE

NS 203 481

Ritchie Street, West Kilbride

Just over 100 years old, designed by Mr Le Blanc (of Glasgow Baths fame). Very good stained glass with two recent modern additions. Two manual Binns Organ – tubular pneumatic. Unusual hipped wooden ceiling to nave. Sunday Service 11am, all year, 6.30pm during autumn and winter.

Open Thursday 10am–12noon or by arrangement, telephone Mr Leahy 01294 823140

CHURCH OF SCOTLAND (2 steps to the hall) WC (by arrangement) (Thursdays)

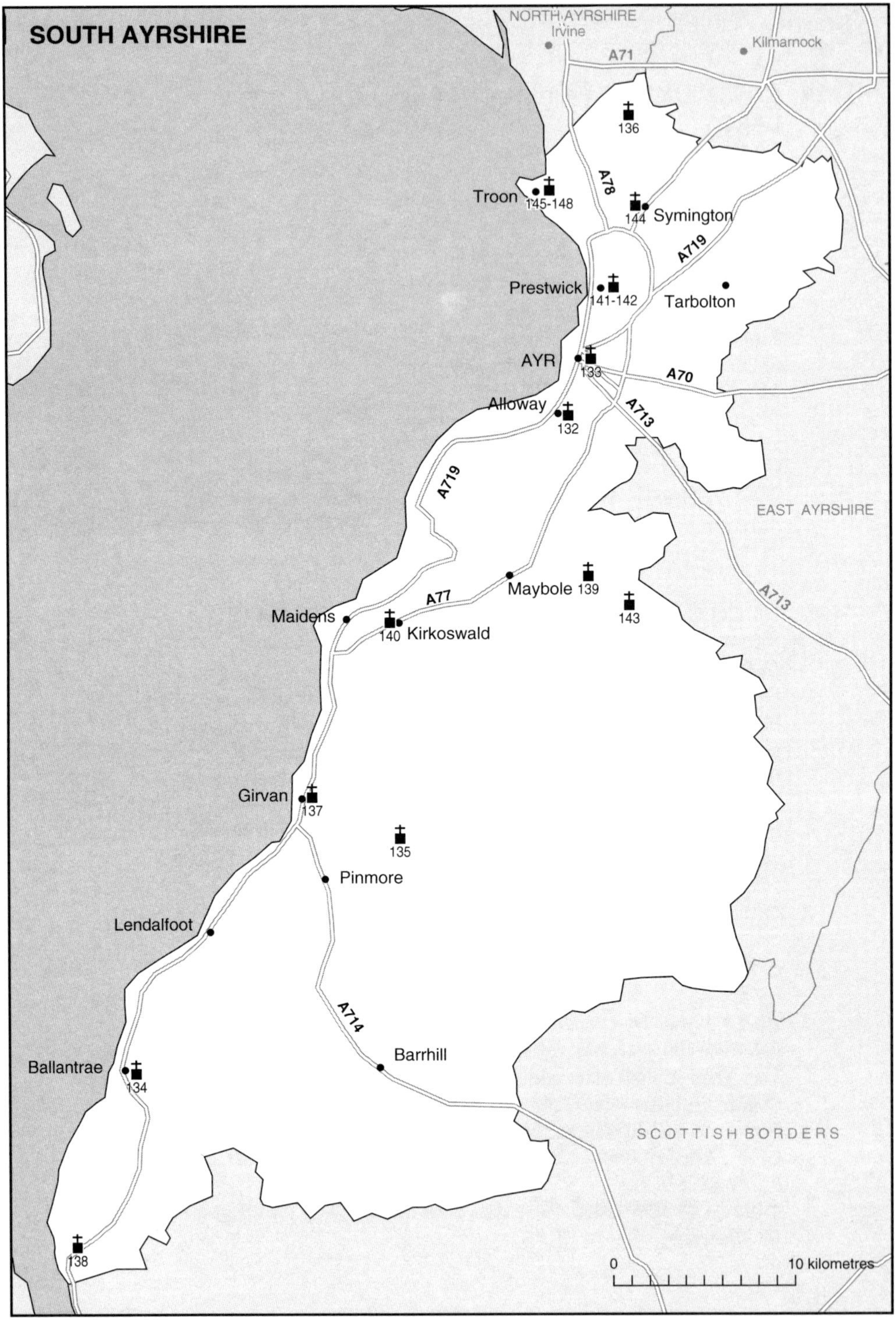
SOUTH AYRSHIRE
NORTH AYRSHIRE
Irvine
Kilmarnock
A71
136
A78
Troon
145-148
144
Symington
A719
Prestwick
141-142
Tarbolton
AYR
133
A70
Alloway
132
A713
A719
EAST AYRSHIRE
Maybole
139
A77
143
A713
Maidens
140
Kirkoswald
Girvan
137
135
Pinmore
Lendalfoot
A714
Barrhill
Ballantrae
134
SCOTTISH BORDERS
138
0
10 kilometres

SOUTH AYRSHIRE

Local Representative: Miss Joan Fish, 31 Oaklands Avenue, Irvine (*telephone* 01294 272654)

132 ALLOWAY PARISH CHURCH

NS 332 181

Alloway

Built in 1858, Campbell Douglas. South transept added in 1877, chancel built and nave extended in 1890. Excellent stained glass including Stephen Adam, Clayton & Bell, Gordon Webster, W & J J Keir. Douglas McLundie's memorial window to D F McIntyre, pilot on first flight over Mount Everest in 1933. Two windows by Susan Bradbury were installed in 1996, one depicting the four seasons, the other in memory of Robert Burns. B7024 south of Burns' cottage.

Sunday Services 9.45am and 11.15am

Open June to September, Monday to Friday 10am-4pm.

Conducted tours, contact local tourist office

CHURCH OF SCOTLAND **B**

133 HOLY TRINITY CHURCH, AYR

NS 336 218

Fullarton Street, Ayr

Dedicated in 1888. Scotland's major example of the work of J L Pearson, designer of Truro Cathedral. Pulpit of Caen stone and very fine stained glass windows by, among others, Clayton & Bell. Next to Ayr bus station, walking distance from railway station.

Sunday Services 8am, 10.30am and 6.30pm; Wednesday Eucharist 11am

Open mornings in summer. Concert series

SCOTTISH EPISCOPAL

(for visiting groups by arrangement) WC **A**

HOLY TRINITY CHURCH, AYR

134 BALLANTRAE PARISH CHURCH

NX 084 825

Main Street, Ballantrae

Built in 1819. Memorial to Lord Ballantrae. Regency pulpit. Nephew of Robert Burns was minister 1826-30. Kennedy tomb beside church. Ruins of Ardstinchar Castle. A77. Railway station at Girvan, 13 miles. Buses from Glasgow. United with Glenapp.

Sunday Service 11am

Open daily, May to September 10am-sunset

CHURCH OF SCOTLAND WC (in village) **B**

BALLANTRAE PARISH CHURCH

135 BARR PARISH CHURCH

NX 275 941

Main Street, Barr, by Girvan

Dating from 1878, built to a design by A Stevenson. Early Gothic gabled chapel. Slate roof, skew gables, rubble walls, freestone dressings. Picturesque south east bellcote. Fine wooden ceiling. Restored in 1978 P J Lorimer, London. B734 from Girvan. Occasional buses from Girvan. Sunday Service 12 noon

Open all year, 9am-7pm. Teas in July and August; Monday, Friday and Saturday 2.30-5pm

CHURCH OF SCOTLAND WC **C**

BARR PARISH CHURCH

136 DUNDONALD PARISH CHURCH

NS 366 343

Main Street, Dundonald

Tranquil setting for this traditional stone church of 1804, built on the site of an earlier building. The clock tower was added in 1841, and the chancel in 1906. Some fine stained glass, particularly Henry Dearle's unique 'Last Supper'. Pipe organ, Norman & Beard 1906. Interesting grave stones in the tidy graveyard. Sunday Service 11am

Open by arrangement, telephone Rev Robert Mayes 01563 850243

CHURCH OF SCOTLAND WC **B**

137 SACRED HEARTS OF JESUS AND MARY, GIRVAN

NS 183 979

Harbour Lane, Girvan

A plain Gothic structure of 1860 with a huge prow-like porch added in 1959 by Stevenson & Ferguson. Stained glass windows of 1860. Services 7pm Saturday, 9am and 11am Sunday

Open during daylight hours

ROMAN CATHOLIC

138 GLENAPP CHURCH

NX 075 746

Glenapp

Memorial window to Elsie Mackay, third daughter of Earl of Inchcape. She was killed in 1928 attempting to fly the Atlantic. Modern stained glass window above door, 'The Stilling of the Tempest', in memory of first Earl. Graveyard contains tombs of the three Earls of Inchcape. Seven miles south of Ballantrae on A77, ten miles north of Stranraer. United with Ballantrae. Sunday Service occasional

Open summer and autumn

CHURCH OF SCOTLAND

GLENAPP CHURCH

139 KIRKMICHAEL PARISH CHURCH

NY 005 884

80 Patna Road, Kirkmichael, near Maybole

Believed to stand on the site of a 13th-century church under the care of the monks of Whithorn, the present church was built in 1787 by Hugh Cairncross, and the belfry rebuilt in 1887. Stone pulpit of 1919 depicting St Michael, St George, St Andrew and St Patrick incorporates the war memorial. The oldest building is the lychgate, the bell inside is dated 1702 and is still rung when a bride leaves the church after her wedding. Interesting stones in surrounding graveyard including Covenanter's memorial. Two miles east of Maybole. Sunday Service 10.30am

Open by arrangement, telephone the Minister 01655 750286

CHURCH OF SCOTLAND

(in village) WC **B**

KIRKMICHAEL PARISH CHURCH

140 KIRKOSWALD PARISH CHURCH

NS 240 074

Robert Adam 1777 contemporary with Culzean Castle. It is suggested that Adam, touring with Lord Cassillis, his client at Culzean, came across the church during construction and recommended some changes, giving the building fine Palladian details. The church was visited by Robert Burns and President Eisenhower. Burns' characters, Tam o' Shanter, Souter Johnnie and Kirkton Jean, are buried in the old graveyard. On the A77, five miles from Maybole. Sunday Service 11am

Open during daylight hours

CHURCH OF SCOTLAND **A**

BARR PARISH CHURCH

141 KINGCASE PARISH CHURCH, PRESTWICK

NS 348 244

Waterloo Road, Prestwick (behind Safeway store)

The church was built in 1912, extended 1956, in attractive red sandstone with three small but beautiful stained glass windows. Fairly small building in excellent state of repair. Sunday Services 9.45am and 11.15am, 7pm (9pm in July and August). Large-print hymn books available.

CHURCH OF SCOTLAND WC

142 ST QUIVOX, PRESTWICK

NS 352 257

St Quivox Road, Prestwick

The building was completed in 1933 and is built of Accrington brick in Romanesque style. The church was extended in 1969 and incorporates the old building to form a rectangular shaped church. Inside are a sanctuary mosaic panel and the Stations of the Cross. Sunday Services
10am, 11.30am and 6pm

Open daily 10am-5pm

ROMAN CATHOLIC

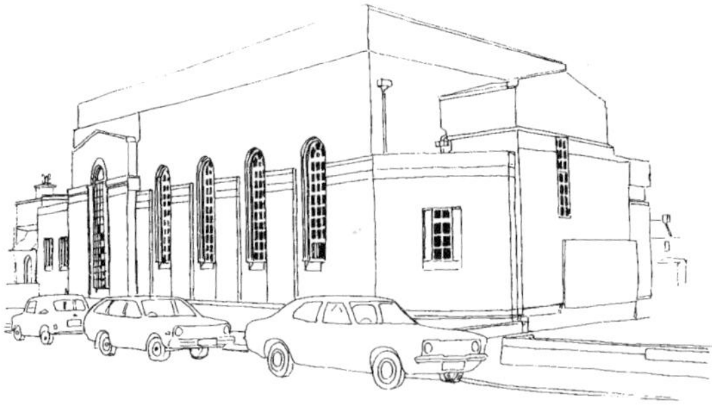

ST QUIVOX, PRESTWICK

143 STRAITON PARISH CHURCH (ST CUTHBERT'S)

NS 380 049

STRAITON PARISH CHURCH (ST CUTHBERT'S)

The main part of the church dates from 1758. The piscina of the original church is still visible on the east wall. Chantry chapel of late 15th century containing various memorial plaques to members of the Hunter Blair family. In 1901 the church was renovated by John Kinross and the bell tower was added to the design of John Murdoch. The interior is noted for its beautiful carvings, especially on the ceiling and pulpit. Tapestry cushions 1993 depict themes from the life and work of the community. The stone font is the gift of the Fergusson family. Splendid stained glass. Covenanter's memorial in graveyard. Of special interest is the artwork undertaken by the ladies of the local Sewing Guild to commemorate 1997 as 'The Year of Faith'; 1998 as 'The Year of Hope'; and 1999 as 'The Year of Love'. Straiton is four miles east of Kirkmichael. Sunday Service noon

Open by arrangement, telephone the Minister 01655 750286

CHURCH OF SCOTLAND WC (nearby) **A**

144 SYMINGTON CHURCH

NS 999 352

Symington

Known as Ayrshire's Norman church, the rectangular building with three ft thick walls was founded c.1160 by Symon de Loccard whose own story in itself makes a visit worthwhile. Restored 1919 by P MacGregor Chalmers. Norman arched windows, piscina and ancient oak-beamed ceiling. The stained glass, much of it by Douglas Strachan, is glorious in creation and colour. Though small in size, its stones breathe the atmosphere of prayer and praise of all the saints over 800 years. Two miles from Prestwick Airport on A77. Sunday Service 10.30am

Open by arrangement, telephone Rae Mitchell 01563 830441, or Jim Knox 01563 830043

CHURCH OF SCOTLAND

A

SYMINGTON CHURCH

145 TROON OLD CHURCH

NS 321 309

Ayr Street, Troon

Neo-Gothic building in red sandstone by Hippolyte Blanc and dedicated in 1895. The stained glass of the Ascension window is by the Morris Studio, other windows by Gordon Webster. Alabaster reredos depicting Moses, St Paul and the Last Supper has a finely carved canopy and stands above a mosaic pavement of the Paschal Lamb. Richly carved pulpit, communion table and font. Various memorials. Sunday Service 10.30am, Wednesday 11.15am

Open Tuesday-Sunday 10am-12 noon

CHURCH OF SCOTLAND WC (by arrangement), (Saturday and Sunday) **B**

146 OUR LADY AND ST MEDDAN CHURCH, TROON

NS 327 311

4 Cessnock Road, Troon

Built to a design by Reginald Fairlie 1910, this church is a mixture of architectural styles and also copies the rear view of Holyrood Church in Stirling. The church has undergone major restoration funded by Historic Scotland. Two minutes from railway station, Glasgow–Ayr, half hourly train service. Sunday Mass 9am and 11.15am, Saturday Vigil Mass 6pm

Open daily until 4pm; and Ayrshire Doors Open Day, September

ROMAN CATHOLIC WC WC **A**

OUR LADY AND ST MEDDAN CHURCH, TROON

147 PORTLAND PARISH CHURCH, TROON

NS 323 309

St Meddan's Street, Troon

Opened in 1914 as a United Free Church by H E Clifford & Lunan. Perpendicular Gothic in white sandstone with fine tracery in the great north window which is repeated in the nave windows. Interior has exposed stone with blonde Austrian oak pews and fittings. The stained glass chancel window was donated in 1920 as a war memorial by Mr A F Steven. Harrison & Harrison two-manual organ, rebuilt 1970. Halls extension added 1964. Two minutes walk from railway station. Sunday Service 11.15am

Open July and August, Sunday and Thursday 2-4.30pm, and Ayrshire Doors Open Day, September

CHURCH OF SCOTLAND WC **B**

PORTLAND PARISH CHURCH, TROON

148 ST MEDDAN'S, TROON

NS 323 309

corner of Church Street and St Meddan's Street, Troon

Built 1888–89 for the United Presbyterian Church, architect J B Wilson, St Meddan's has many noteworthy features. The tall and stately spire houses a clock which was originally part of the University of Glasgow's Old College in High Street, Glasgow. Many beautiful stained glass windows, the largest, opposite the pulpit, depicts the healing of Jairus's daughter. Sunday Services 9.30am and 11.15am

Open Monday, Tuesday and Thursday 9am–2pm

CHURCH OF SCOTLAND ♿ WC 🦻 **B**

ST MEDDAN'S, TROON

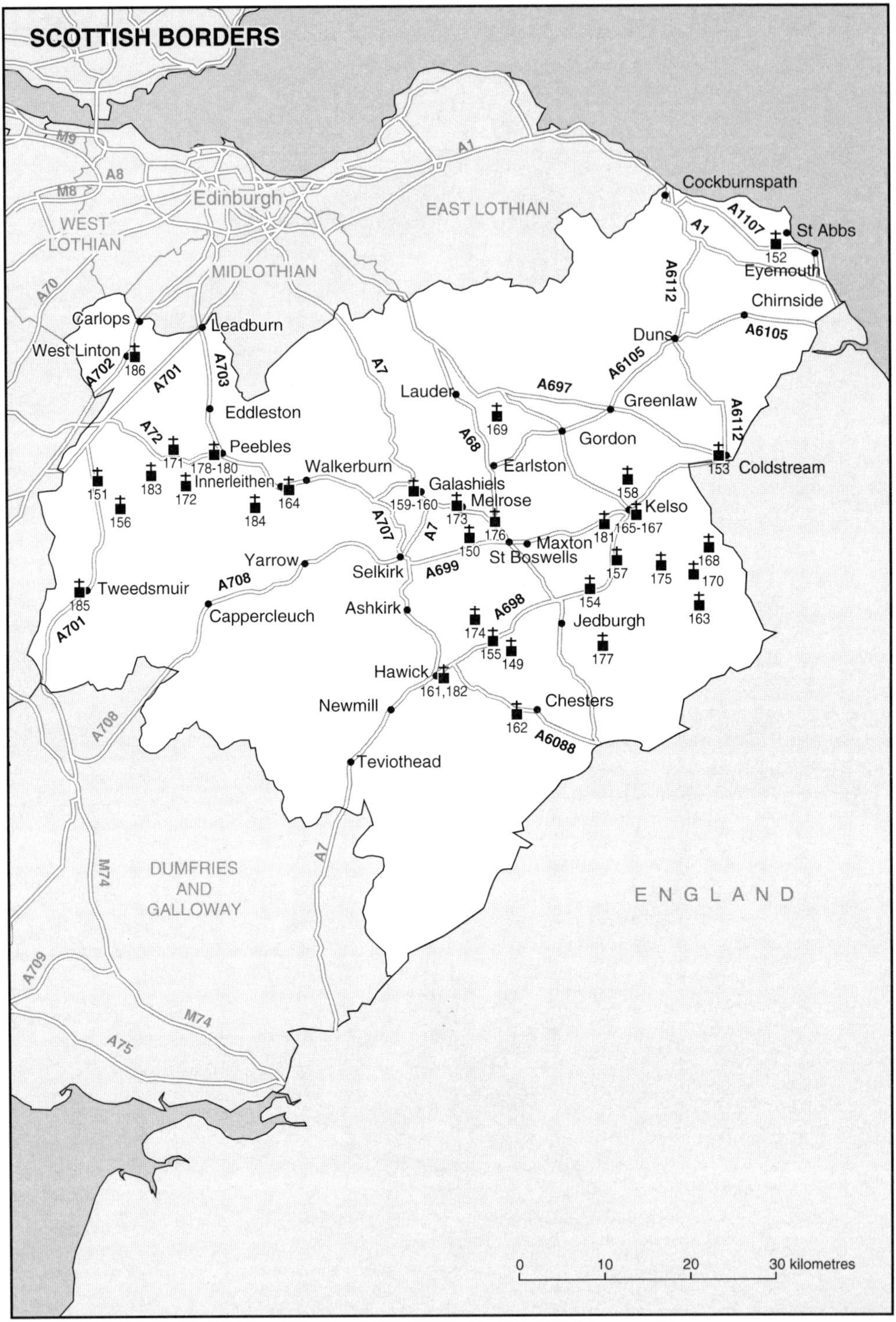
SCOTTISH BORDERS
M9
A8
M8
Edinburgh
WEST LOTHIAN
MIDLOTHIAN
EAST LOTHIAN
A1
A70
Cockburnspath
A1107
A1
St Abbs
152
Eyemouth
A6112
Chirnside
Duns
A6105
A6105
Carlops
Leadburn
West Linton
186
A702
A701
A703
A7
Lauder
A697
Greenlaw
A6112
Eddleston
169
A68
Gordon
A72
171
178-180
Peebles
Earlston
153
Coldstream
151
183
172
Innerleithen
Walkerburn
Galashiels
158
156
184
164
159-160
173
Melrose
Kelso
A707
176
181
165-167
150
A7
Maxton
Yarrow
Selkirk
A699
St Boswells
157
175
168
170
185
Tweedsmuir
A708
154
163
A701
Cappercleuch
Ashkirk
174
A698
Jedburgh
155
149
177
Hawick
161,182
Newmill
162
Chesters
A708
A6088
Teviothead
A7
M74
DUMFRIES AND GALLOWAY
ENGLAND
A709
M74
A75
0
10
20
30 kilometres

BORDERS

Local Representatives: Mrs Mary Reid, 2 Crookhaugh, by Biggar (*telephone* 01899 880258) and Mr Sandy Gilchrist, 11 Mercat Loan, Biggar (*telephone* 01899 221350) – Tweedale

149 BEDRULE CHURCH

NT 599 179

Bedrule, by Jedburgh

Beautifully rebuilt in 1914 by T Greenshields Leadbetter, the church has a plaque commemorating Bishop Turnbull, founder of Glasgow University in 1451. Stained glass, including Guild centenary window 1992 and windows by Douglas Strachan 1922. Memorial with interesting link to war-time 'Enigma' decoding project. Fine views over Rule Valley to Ruberslaw. Linked with Denholm and Minto. Time of fortnightly Sunday Service, which alternates with Minto changes every four months; 11.30am February to May 2000, 10am June to September; 11.30am October to January

BEDRULE CHURCH

Open during daylight hours.

CHURCH OF SCOTLAND (free) **B**

150 BOWDEN KIRK

NT 554 301

Sitting by St Cuthbert's Way, the pilgrim route from Melrose to Lindisfarne, the church has a wealth of architectural history. It was founded in 1128, part of the north wall is possibly 15th century, east end from 1644, cross aisle from 1661, west gable and doorway at west end of north wall 17th century. Repaired in 1794 and with major alterations in 1909 by P MacGregor Chalmers. Carved wooden 17th-century laird's loft for Riddell-Carre family. Burial vaults of Riddell-Carre of Cavers-Carre and Dukes of Roxburghe. Memorials, including one to Lady Grizell Baillie, first Deaconess of the Church of Scotland. Many notable tombstones in graveyard. Sunday Service 11am

Open during daylight hours

CHURCH OF SCOTLAND

(from Post Office) WC **A**

BOWDEN KIRK

151 BROUGHTON, GLENHOLM AND KILBUCHO PARISH CHURCH

NT 111 368

Broughton, Biggar

Built in 1804 and extended by Robert Bryden of Broughton and Glasgow 1886 to whom there is a memorial stained glass window in the north wall. Roof lights above the communion table are based on originals in Copenhagen Museum. Linked with Tweedsmuir, Skirling and Stobo with Drumelzier. Sunday Service 10am

Open by arrangement, telephone Mr Donald Strathairn 01899 830226

CHURCH OF SCOTLAND WC

152 THE PRIORY CHURCH, COLDINGHAM

NT 904 659

Coldingham, Berwickshire

Influential centre of Christian witness in Scottish Borders since seventh century. Present church formed from the choir and sanctuary area which comprised the eastern arm of the early 13th-century cruciform-plan Priory Church of St Mary. Splendid free-standing arch of original church to the east of the main building. South and west walls rebuilt 1662 and extensive renovation in 1850s. Interior renovation 1950 providing present chancel and its furnishings. Nine modern stained glass windows. Detailed scale model of the Priory on exhibition. Sunday Service 12 noon

Open Wednesdays, May to October 2-4pm, and by arrangement, telephone Mr A M Scott 018907 71280

CHURCH OF SCOTLAND **A**

153 COLDSTREAM PARISH CHURCH

NT 844 400

High Street, Coldstream

The square church tower with its four stages, clocks and octagonal stone roofed bell tower and weathervane is a distinctive feature of the outline of Coldstream. It and the west entrance are part of the original church built in 1718. The rest of the church was rebuilt in 1905 to a design by J M Dick Peddie. A classical nave and aisles church with barrel-vaulted roof supported by eight Tuscan columns. A fine stone pulpit sits in front of the semi-circular arch which leads into the chancel. The church contains many reminders of its close association, along with the town, with the Coldstream Guards. The King's and Regimental Colours hang in the chancel. Plaque to the Rev Adam Thomson who formed the Coldstream Free Bible Press in 1845, thus breaking the monopoly held by Oxford and Cambridge Universities and the King's printers in Scotland. Sunday Service 11.15am

Open June to August, Thursday 2-4.30pm.

Other times by arrangement, telephone Dr B J Sproule 01890 882271

CHURCH OF SCOTLAND WC **B**

CRAILING KIRK

154 CRAILING KIRK

NT 682 250

Built c.1775 on an ancient site of worship; the bell is dated 1702. Aisle added in the early 19th century and further alterations and additions 1892. Restoration by P Macgregor Chalmers 1907. On A698 Jedburgh–Kelso. Services second and fourth Sunday 10.30am

Open by arrangement, telephone Mrs Rose, The Braeheids, Crailing 01835 850268

CHURCH OF SCOTLAND **B**

155 DENHOLM CHURCH

NT 569 186

Denholm, by Hawick

Dates from 1845. Interior much altered 1957. 150th anniversary wall hangings. Situated in a beautiful conservation village. Best small village in 'Beautiful Scotland in Bloom 1999'. A698 Jedburgh–Hawick. Time of weekly Sunday Services changes every four months: 10am February to May 2000, 11.30am, June to September 10am, October to January

Key from the Manse in Leyden's Road or Robert L Brown, Marybank, Douglas Drive, Denholm 01450 870218

CHURCH OF SCOTLAND (free) WC **C**

156 DRUMELZIER KIRK

NT 135 343

Drumelzier, by Broughton

A simple rectangular building. The original date is uncertain, but it owes its present appearance largely to major alterations carried out in 1872. Seventeenth-century bellcote on the west gable. Burial vault 1617 for Sir James Tweedie of Drumelzier. United with Stobo and linked with Broughton, Tweedsmuir, Skirling. One hundred yards off B712 in Drumelzier village. Sunday Service first and third of the month 6.30pm (except July and August)

Open for guided tours, telephone The Rev Rachel Dobie 01899 830331

CHURCH OF SCOTLAND **B**

157 ECKFORD KIRK

NT 706 270

Eckford, by Kelso

Built 1771 on an ancient site of worship, incorporating fragments of the 1668 building and the north aisle of 1724. Very sweet interior with rich turn-of-the-century furnishings in the sanctuary. Jougs 1718, mort bell and 19th-century watch-tower. Many fine 17th-century gravestones. On A698 Jedburgh–Kelso. Services irregularly throughout the year

Open by arrangement, telephone Mrs Fish, Eckford House, Kelso 01835 850397

CHURCH OF SCOTLAND **B**

ECKFORD KIRK

158 EDNAM PARISH CHURCH

NT 737 372

Ednam, by Kelso

Church built 1800 and recast 1902. Situated in the village of Ednam where hymnwriter Henry Francis Lyte was born. In union with Kelso North. Sunday Service 10am

Open daily 10am-4pm, July and August

CHURCH OF SCOTLAND ♿ 🦻 📖 WC

159 GALASHIELS OLD PARISH CHURCH & ST PAUL'S

NT 490 362

Scott Crescent, Galashiels

Built in 1881 to plans in the Gothic Revival style by George Henderson, the main feature is the 190 ft spire. Front porch added 1922. Good glass, including some by Douglas Strachan. Stone carvings by John Rhind and wood carving by Francis Lynn. Willis organ. Sunday Services 11am and 6.30pm

Open by arrangement, telephone Dr Borthwick 01896 752221

CHURCH OF SCOTLAND

♿ (via hall) 🦻 WC **B**

GALASHIELS OLD PARISH CHURCH & ST PAUL'S

160 ST PETER'S CHURCH, GALASHIELS

NT 496 356

Abbotsford Road, Galashiels

Gothic Revival style Hay & Henderson 1853. Reredos Sir Robert Lorimer 1914. Stained glass, memorial brasses. Setting of church with lawns, graveyard, hall and rectory encapsulated the Tractarian ideal. Quarter mile south of town centre on Selkirk road. Sunday Services Holy Communion 8am, Sung Eucharist 10.30am

Open by arrangement. Key from the Rectory, Parsonage Road, Galashiels, telephone 01896 753118, or contact Mr R Brown, 52 Croft Street, Galashiels, telephone 01896 754657

SCOTTISH EPISCOPAL **C**

161 ST CUTHBERT'S CHURCH, HAWICK

NT 491 361

Slitrig Crescent, Hawick

A Sir George Gilbert Scott building of 1858. Reredos J Oldrid Scott 1905. Chancel screen Robert Lorimer. Some fine stained glass including two contemporary windows of 1995. Sunday Services Holy Communion 9.30am, Family Eucharist 10.30am, Friday 12 noon Holy Hour

Open Monday and Tuesday, 10am-12 noon, Wednesday 7am-12 noon, Thursday and Friday 2-4pm

SCOTTISH EPISCOPAL **B**

162 HOBKIRK PARISH CHURCH

NT 587 109

Hobkirk, Bonchester Bridge, by Hawick

A Christian site for over 900 years. The present church was built in 1862. Stones from the earlier churches are incorporated in the font. The bell is inscribed 'I was made for Hobkirk in 1745'. One mile west of Bonchester Bridge on the A6088 Hawick to Newcastle (off A68). United with Southdean. Sunday Service 11.15am

Open daily all year

CHURCH OF SCOTLAND

HOBKIRK PARISH CHURCH

163 HOWNAM PARISH CHURCH

NT 778 193

Hownam, Morebattle, Kelso

In an idyllic situation on the haugh by the Kale Water. The original building appears to have been cruciform, but was remodelled in 1752 as a rectangle, and substantially modernised in 1844. The interior was refurbished in 1986. From the original church there remains a round-headed doorway in the south wall, dating from the turn of the 15th and 16th centuries. Linked with Linton, Morebattle and Yetholm. Sunday Service second and fourth of every month 12.30pm

Open all year during daylight hours

CHURCH OF SCOTLAND **B**

164 ST JAMES CHURCH, INNERLEITHEN

NT 329 366

High Street, Innerleithen

Built in 1881 to a design by John Biggar, a church with some interesting works of art including a large icon of Our Lady of Czestochowa, Poland. This is by K Kryska 1944, the captain of Polish Forces based in Peebleshire. Other monuments include ones dating from 1861 and a copy of the bust of John Ogilvie. The sanctuary is being brought back into use, and a rood screen division is under construction within the church to provide a gathering and social space towards the rear of the nave. Sunday Service 11.15am; Holy Days 7pm

ST JAMES CHURCH, INNERLEITHEN

Open summer 10.00am-4.00pm, and by arrangement, telephone Mrs Helen Garrett 01896 830025, or Mrs Anne Tait 01896 831184

ROMAN CATHOLIC **B**

165 KELSO NORTH CHURCH

NT 727 341

Roxburgh Street, Kelso

Erected 1866 for the congregation of Kelso North Free Church, architect Frederick T Pilkington. The front of the church is very ornate, being designed in the Gothic style, with the tower and spire rising to some 180 ft. Extensively renovated in 1934 and 1984-89. Although the exterior is quite massive, in contrast the interior is fairly neat and compact. Sunday Service 11.30am, Evening Worship 6.30pm first Sunday October-June

Open July and August, Monday to Friday 10am-12 noon, 2-4pm. Also Saturdays all year for coffee mornings

CHURCH OF SCOTLAND WC **A**

KELSO NORTH CHURCH

166 KELSO OLD PARISH CHURCH

NT 729 339

The Butts, Kelso

Octagonal plan church, James Nisbet, dating from 1773, and altered by William Elliot in 1823. Built to continue worship begun in Kelso Abbey in 1128. Recently extensively restored. Banners of Blues & Royals, presented to the church by the Duke of Roxburghe 1927. Off Market Square, by Knowes car park and adjacent to Kelso Abbey. Sunday Service 10am (not July and August) and 11.30am

Open Easter to September, Monday to Friday 10am-4pm

CHURCH OF SCOTLAND **A**

KELSO OLD PARISH CHURCH

167 ST ANDREW'S CHURCH, KELSO

NT 728 337

Belmont Place, Kelso

Situated close to the banks of the River Tweed, built 1868 by Sir Robert Rowand Anderson. Altar, reredos, font and Robertson memorial sculpted in marble and Caen stone. Decorative wooden chancel roof and decorated pulpit. Stained glass. Small garden to rear (including Garden Room for meetings and Junior Church). Opposite Kelso Abbey on B6089. Sunday Services 8.30am and 10.30am; Wednesday Eucharist 10.30am: Thursday Eucharist 7.00pm

Open daily 8.30am-5pm

SCOTTISH EPISCOPAL **B**

ST ANDREW'S CHURCH, KELSO

168 THE KIRK OF YETHOLM

NT 826 281

Kirk Yetholm, Kelso

The church for the delightful twin villages and parish of Yetholm stands on a site in use since David I's apportionment of parishes. Built by Robert Brown 1837 to replace a small dank thatched affair, it is a rectangular plan Gothic church of local whinstone with cream sandstone dressings, and a tower to the south. A remodelling in 1935, and the creation of an upper room out of the gallery in the 1970s, gives the interior a lightness belied by the sombre imposing exterior. Stained glass by Ballantine & Son, Edinburgh. The medieval bell is still in use. As the nearest burial ground to Flodden, the graveyard is believed to have interred officers fallen in that battle (1513). Seventeenth-century gravestones. Linked with Linton, Morebattle and Hownam. Sunday Service 10am

Open daily during daylight hours

CHURCH OF SCOTLAND ♿ **B**

169 LEGERWOOD PARISH CHURCH

NT 594 434

Legerwood, Berwickshire

The church dates from 1127. Repaired in 1717 and 1804. Its chancel has a fine Norman arch. Sunday Service 11.45am first Sunday of each month

Open daily

CHURCH OF SCOTLAND ♿ **B**

170 LINTON KIRK & HOSELAW CHAPEL

NT 773 262 and NT 802 318

near Morebattle, Kelso

On a sandy knoll, a twelfth-century church much altered in 1616, 1774, 1813 and finally restored to an approximation of its Romanesque appearance in 1912 by P MacGregor Chalmers. It retains its Norman feel and today the visitor enters under a unique stone tympanum to discover an attractive nave and substantial chancel, the arch richly carved (1912). A Norman font and chancel stalls are of particular interest. Linton Kirk is most noted for the stone above the porch said to depict a knight on horseback lancing two creatures – the stone is Norman and unique in Scotland, and legend suggests that this is the first known Somerville killing a worm. The Leishman father and son ministries completed most of the present improvements; the son Thomas also had a small chapel built in the district of Hoselaw (seven miles away) to serve the cottagers, architect P MacGregor Chalmers. Linked with Morebattle, Hownam and Yetholm. Sunday Service first, third and fifth of every month, and fifth Sunday at Hoselaw Chapel (except December and January) 12.15pm

Open daily during daylight hours

CHURCH OF SCOTLAND **B**

171 LYNE KIRK

NT 192 405

on A72 from Peebles

Located on the site of a twelfth-century church, the present church was built between 1640 and 1645 by John Hay of Yester (later first Earl of Tweeddale). The porch was added in the 19th century. The church interior remains substantially unaltered; of particular interest are the Dutch pulpit and canopied pews dated 1644. Pre-Reformation font. The earliest stone in the graveyard is dated 1707, the Adam and Eve stone dated 1712 is uncommon. Roman fort of Lyne immediately to the west. Service: 11am first Sunday of each month

Open daily

CHURCH OF SCOTLAND **B**

172 MANOR KIRK

NT 220 380

Kirkton Manor, by Peebles

First referred to in 1186 as 'the chapel of Maineure'. Tradition speaks of an earlier chapel of the fourth century dedicated to St Gordian, a martyred Roman soldier. The present building was completed in 1874. The bell, rung before every service, is inscribed *In honore Santi Gordiani MCCCCLXXVIII* and is one of the oldest bells in use in Scotland. Pewter baptismal basin, inscribed *Manner Kirk 1703*. Services second, third and fourth Sundays of each month 11am, fifth Sunday 6.30pm

Open daily

CHURCH OF SCOTLAND ♿ (ramp) 📖

HOLY TRINITY, MELROSE

173 HOLY TRINITY, MELROSE

NT 540 342

High Cross Avenue, Melrose

Built in the Early English style by Benjamin Ferrey 1846-50. Decorated chancel and transepts by Hay & Henderson 1900. The chancel floor is mosaic. Open timber roof carried on mask corbels. Stained glass windows in transept 1900, by Kempe, other commemorative glass by Mayer & Co and W Wilson 1963. Quarter mile from Melrose centre, on road to Darnick. Services Sunday 8.30 and 11am; Wednesday 10.30am; Evensong first Sunday of month 6.30pm

Open by arrangement, telephone the Rector 01896 822626. Occasional concerts

SCOTTISH EPISCOPAL ♿ 🦻 WC **B**

174 MINTO CHURCH

NT 557 201

Minto, by Hawick

Designed by William Playfair, the church dates from 1830, the interior recast in 1934. Fine external war memorial. Panoramic views of Teviotdale and Minto Hill. Linked with Bedrule and Denholm. Time of fortnightly Sunday Service which alternates with Bedrule, changes every four months; February to May 11.30am, June to September 10am, October to January 11.30am, and so on

Key from Mrs Marjorie Walton, Kirk View, Minto, Hawick 01450 870351

CHURCH OF SCOTLAND 🦻 **C**

175 MOREBATTLE PARISH CHURCH

NT 772 250

Morebattle, Kelso

The church of 'Mereboda' is recorded as belonging to the Diocese of Glasgow from about 1116. The building was burnt down in 1544 and rebuilt; the present structure dates substantially from 1757, extensions having been made in 1899 and 1903. It is oblong in plan, with chancel, porch and vestry which seem to be additions. The bellcote at the west end is currently being rebuilt. Look for the plan in the porch which shows the archaeological work carried out in the early 1900s, and inscriptions painted on fabric on the west wall. Linked with Hownam, Yetholm and Linton. Sunday Service 11.15am

Open all year during daylight hours

CHURCH OF SCOTLAND B

176 NEWTOWN CHURCH

NT 315 693

St Boswells Road, Newtown St Boswells

Church opened in 1868. Contains memorials to past ministers. On bus routes between Jedburgh to Edinburgh and Galashiels. Sunday Service 9.45am

Open by arrangement, telephone the Minister 01835 822106

CHURCH OF SCOTLAND WC

NEWTOWN CHURCH

177 OXNAM KIRK

NT 701 190

Oxnam, by Jedburgh

OXNAM KIRK

On the site of a medieval church dating from before 1153. The present church was built in 1738 and enlarged to form a T-plan in 1874. A characteristic Scottish 18th-century church with plain glass and white-washed walls. Many fine 17th and 18th-century gravestones. Continuo pipe organ by Lammermuir Pipe Organs 1990. Signposted from A68 at Jedburgh. Services first and third Sundays, Christmas and Easter, 10.30am

Open by arrangement, telephone Patrick Wood, Ladfield 01835 840358. Pennymuir Fair, ancient Border hill sheep fair, 1st Saturday in September

CHURCH OF SCOTLAND **B**

178 PEEBLES OLD PARISH CHURCH

NT 246 406

High Street, Peebles

1887 by William Young of London in Gothic style containing features from earlier church. Fine crown spire dominates the High Street. An inviting flight of steps leads up to the entrance. The chancel was reconstructed by J D Cairns 1937. Entrance screen of 1965, woodwork by Messrs Scott Morton, metalwork by Charles Henshaw & Son, glass by Helen Turner. Pulpit 1913 by P MacGregor Chalmers. Part of pre-Reformation font incorporated in table in crossing, by Mitchall Design 1998. Pipe organ by August Gern 1887, rebuilt by Henry Willis 1937. Stained glass by Cottier of London and McCartney of Wiston. Sunday Service 10am, Holy Communion 10am Easter Sunday and on last Sunday of month January, April and October

Open 10am-4pm, mid April to mid October

CHURCH OF SCOTLAND WC **B**

179 ST JOSEPH'S CHURCH, PEEBLES

NT 248 407

Rosetta Road, Peebles

The present building was opened in 1858. The couthy interior was reordered in 1971. The church includes various stained glass windows and statues. The most significant is the recently restored 14 Stations of the Cross by the Alinari Brothers of Florence. Sunday Service 9.15am. Saturday Vigil 6pm; Holy Days 9.30am. Vigil on previous evening, 7pm

Open daily 9am-6pm

ROMAN CATHOLIC **B**

ST JOSEPH'S CHURCH, PEEBLES

180 ST PETER'S EPISCOPAL, PEEBLES

NT 253 405

Eastgate, Peebles

Built 1836-37 in finely hewn ashlar with an open timber roof. The floor is paved with mosaic tiles as is the reredos, beautifully executed with devices in gold and colour. Choir seats and altar of oak. Piscina on the south side with stone shelf and foliated basin. Fine stained glass. The organ, Harrison & Harrison, is one of the smallest three-manual instruments ever built and has been praised for its compactness and excellence of tone. Services: Sunday: Holy Communion 8.30am, Eucharist 11am; Thursday: Holy Communion 10am

Open 9am-5pm or daylight hours

SCOTTISH EPISCOPAL

181 ROXBURGH PARISH CHURCH

NT 700 307

Built in 1752, repaired in 1828, with additions of 1865. Fine painted heraldic panels. Stained glass 1947 by W Wilson. The exterior has a pair of cubical sundials. In the graveyard the (roofless) burial-vault of the Kers of Chatto. Fine modern continuo pipe organ, Lammermuir Pipe Organs 1990. Signposted two and a half miles west of Kelso on A699. Services second and fourth Sundays 11.30am

Open by arrangement, telephone Mrs Palmer, North Cliff Cottages, Roxburgh 01573 450263

CHURCH OF SCOTLAND B

ROXBURGH PARISH CHURCH

182 SOUTHDEAN PARISH CHURCH

NT 631 092

Southdean, by Hawick

Built in 1876 to a design by George Grant of Glasgow on a site near to the ruins of two previous churches of twelfth and 17th centuries. Twelfth-century font. Super-altar set into the communion table, one of only two known in Scotland. Good stained glass. Memorial to James Thomson (1700–48), author of 'Rule Britannia' and 'The Seasons', whose father was parish minister. Prior to the Battle of Otterburn 1388, the Earl of Douglas and his army met at the twelfth-century church, whence the survivors returned to bury their dead. United with Hobkirk. Special Services only

Open daily all year

CHURCH OF SCOTLAND WC

183 STOBO KIRK

NT 183 377

Stobo, by Peebles

One of the oldest churches in the Borders, and of historical importance. Much of the present building dates from twelfth century. It stands on the site of a sixth-century church reputedly founded by St Kentigern (St Mungo). The twelfth-century building comprised nave, sanctuary and tower, the latter rebuilt from first floor level, probably 16th century. Major restoration in 1863 John Lessels. North aisle chapel restored in 1929 James Grieve. A new stone floor laid and a meeting room formed at first floor level of the tower in 1991. Linked with Broughton, Tweedsmuir and Skirling and united with Drumelzier. Stands 100 yards from B712, off A72, four miles west of Peebles or off A701, one and a half miles south of Broughton. Sunday Service 11.30am

CHURCH OF SCOTLAND **B**

184 TRAQUAIR HOUSE CHAPEL

NT 331 355

Traquair House, near Innerleithen

The chapel, formerly the billiard room above the brewhouse, replaced the 'secret chapel' in the main house used in penal times. Related memorabilia on view in house which also contains a priest's hole and secret stairway. Chapel has carved oak panels said to have come from the chapel of Mary of Guise in Leith, and to be of Flemish origin. Service: Mass, 7pm last Wednesday April-October

Open April to end-October 12.30pm-5.30pm, except July and August 10.30am-5.30pm. Access to Chapel is included in admission to grounds

ROMAN CATHOLIC **A**

185 TWEEDSMUIR KIRK

NT 101 245

Tweedsmuir, by Broughton

The present building was erected in 1874 by John Lessels, to replace a much earlier church of 1643. Bell of 1773 still in use. Two high circular windows in the north and south transepts and some interesting stained glass. Oak for the panelling in the porch is from a tree planted at Abbotsford by Sir Walter Scott. First and Second World War memorials. The churchyard dates back to the first church and contains table-stone graves of the 18th century and several other stones of interest, including a Covenanter's grave and one, near the gate, to the many men who died in the construction of the Talla reservoir. Linked with Broughton, Skirling and Stobo with Drumelzier. Village six miles south west of Broughton on A701. Sunday Service 10am

Open daily all year

CHURCH OF SCOTLAND **B**

186 ST MUNGO'S CHURCH, WEST LINTON

NT 148 519

Main Street, West Linton

A 'Gladstone Church' built in 1851 when it served as both church and school. Unusually, the church runs from north to south instead of east to west. Fine stained glass by C E Kempe. Services every Sunday 11am, second Sunday Choral Evensong 5.30pm

Open by arrangement, telephone the Rector 01968 672862

SCOTTISH EPISCOPAL

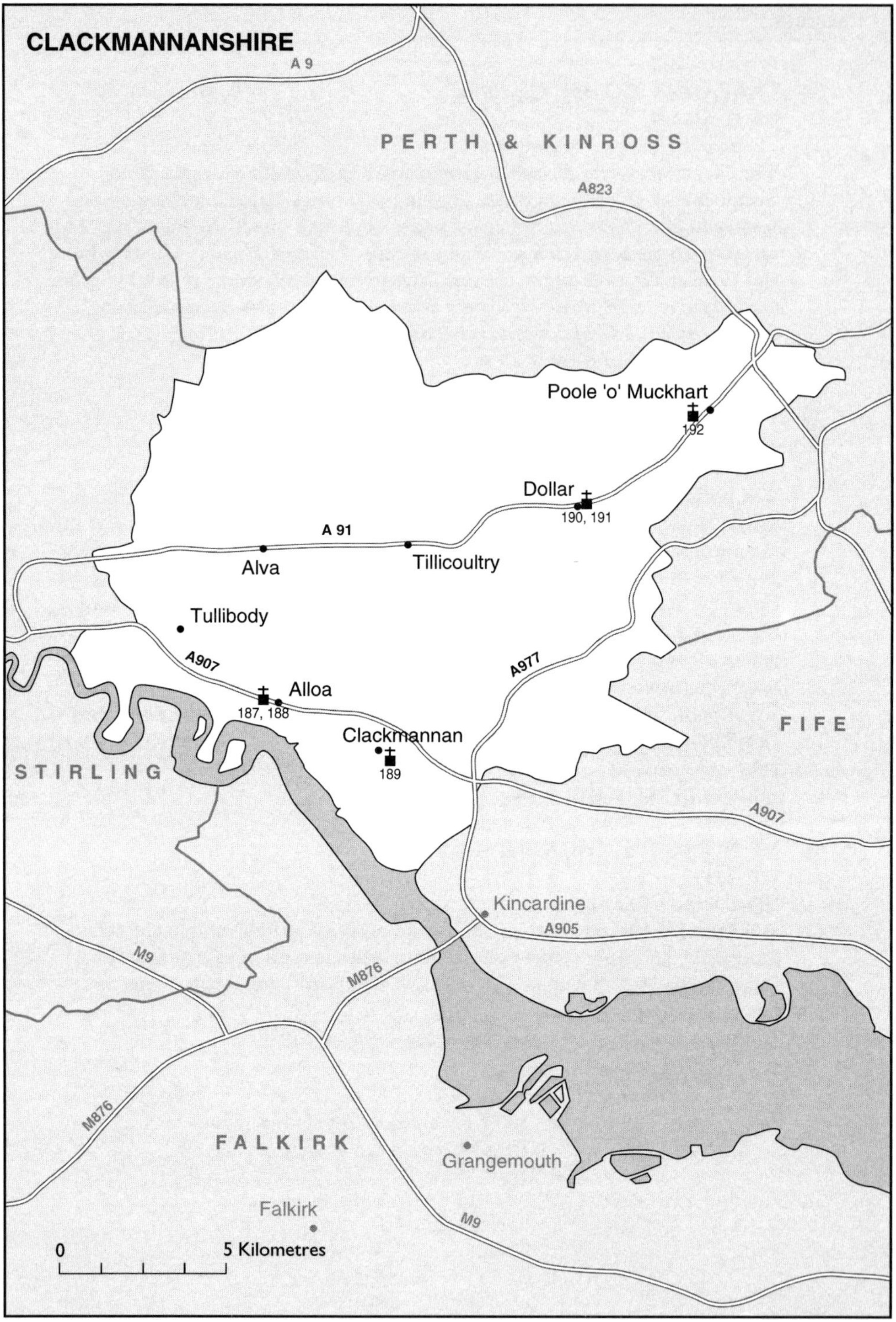
CLACKMANNANSHIRE
A 9
PERTH & KINROSS
A823
Poole 'o' Muckhart
192
Dollar
190, 191
A 91
Alva
Tillicoultry
Tullibody
A907
Alloa
187, 188
A977
Clackmannan
189
FIFE
STIRLING
A907
Kincardine
A905
M9
M876
M876
FALKIRK
Grangemouth
Falkirk
M9
0
5 Kilometres

CLACKMANNANSHIRE

187 ALLOA PARISH CHURCH (ST MUNGO'S)

NS 886 929

Bedford Place, Alloa

Delicate and picturesque Gothic Revival church by James Gillespie Graham 1819. Usual symmetry in plan, but greater felicity than normal in lacy Perpendicular. The 207 ft spire with flying buttresses is visible from most parts of the town. Interior is by Leslie Grahame MacDougall in Lorimer-derived Gothic. Sunday Service 11.15am

Open by arrangement, telephone 01259 721553. Close to Alloa Tower

CHURCH OF SCOTLAND WC **B**

188 ST JOHN'S CHURCH, ALLOA

NS 886 923

Broad Street, Alloa

Sir R Rowand Anderson designed St John's which was opened in 1869 and enlarged in 1873. Described by Thomas Bradshaw then as the 'most elegant place of worship in the County'. Early Geometric Gothic with a notable broach spire. The rich interior includes glass by Kempe, and a reredos with a mosaic of the Last Supper by the Italian Salviatti. The chancel was refurbished in 1913, its roof bearing 106 carved bosses. These, together with the woodwork of the choirstalls 1902, organ screen and war memorial are all by Lorimer. The tower contains a ring of eight bells, six hung in 1871 and a further two in 1925. Sunday Service Family Eucharist 11am

Open usually Wednesday to Friday 9.30am-12.30pm.
Other times, telephone 01259 212836

SCOTTISH EPISCOPAL WC **B**

189 CLACKMANNAN PARISH CHURCH

NS 910 918

High Street, Clackmannan

There has been a church at Clackmannan since St Serf visited from Culross in the eighth century. The present church was built in 1815 by James Gillespie Graham to replace a 13th-century church. Perpendicular Gothic with buttressed tower at the west end. Stained glass by Herbert Hendrie, Gordon Webster, Sadie Pritchard and Douglas Hamilton. Modern Makin Tocatta digital computerised organ. Graveyard has stones dating from the 17th century with several Bruce family memorials. Views over Carse of Forth. Sunday Services 11am

Open June to September 2-4pm.
Other times, telephone 01259 214238

CHURCH OF SCOTLAND WC **B**

CLACKMANNAN PARISH CHURCH

190 DOLLAR PARISH CHURCH

NS 964 980

east end of Dollar, north side of A91, Bridge Street

Built 1842/3 to replace 18th century church (ruin to north), designed by architect Tite of London. Chancel added 1926, porch added 1963. Three stained glass windows by Adam Robson and Jennifer Campbell, Union window 1979 by Douglas Hogg. Rushworth and Dreaper organ, 1926. Reredos tapestry based on Ardchattan Cross designed by Adam Robson, 1963. Sunday Service 11.15am

Open by arrangement with Rev John Purves, telephone 01259 743432

CHURCH OF SCOTLAND ♿ WC 🦻 📖 **B**

191 ST JAMES THE GREAT, DOLLAR

NS 958 980

Harviestoun Road, Dollar

A small country church with a prayerful atmosphere, set in a well-kept garden. Consecrated in 1882, the building designed by Thomas Frame & Son, Alloa. The font is a memorial to Archbishop Archibald Campbell Tait of Canterbury (1868-83). Sunday Services 8.30am and 10.30am, Thursday 9.45am

Open daily all year

SCOTTISH EPISCOPAL 🦻 ♿ **C**

192 MUCKHART PARISH CHURCH

NO 000 010

north side of A91 at west end of Pool of Muckhart

Eighteenth century. Stained glass windows removed to Fossoway Church, Crook of Devon. Various plaques. Large gravestone on east wall of the church for the Christie family, Cowden. Nearby stone to Matsui, Japanese gardener to Miss Ella Christie. Sunday Service 9.45am

Open at all times

CHURCH OF SCOTLAND WC **B**

MUCKHART PARISH CHURCH

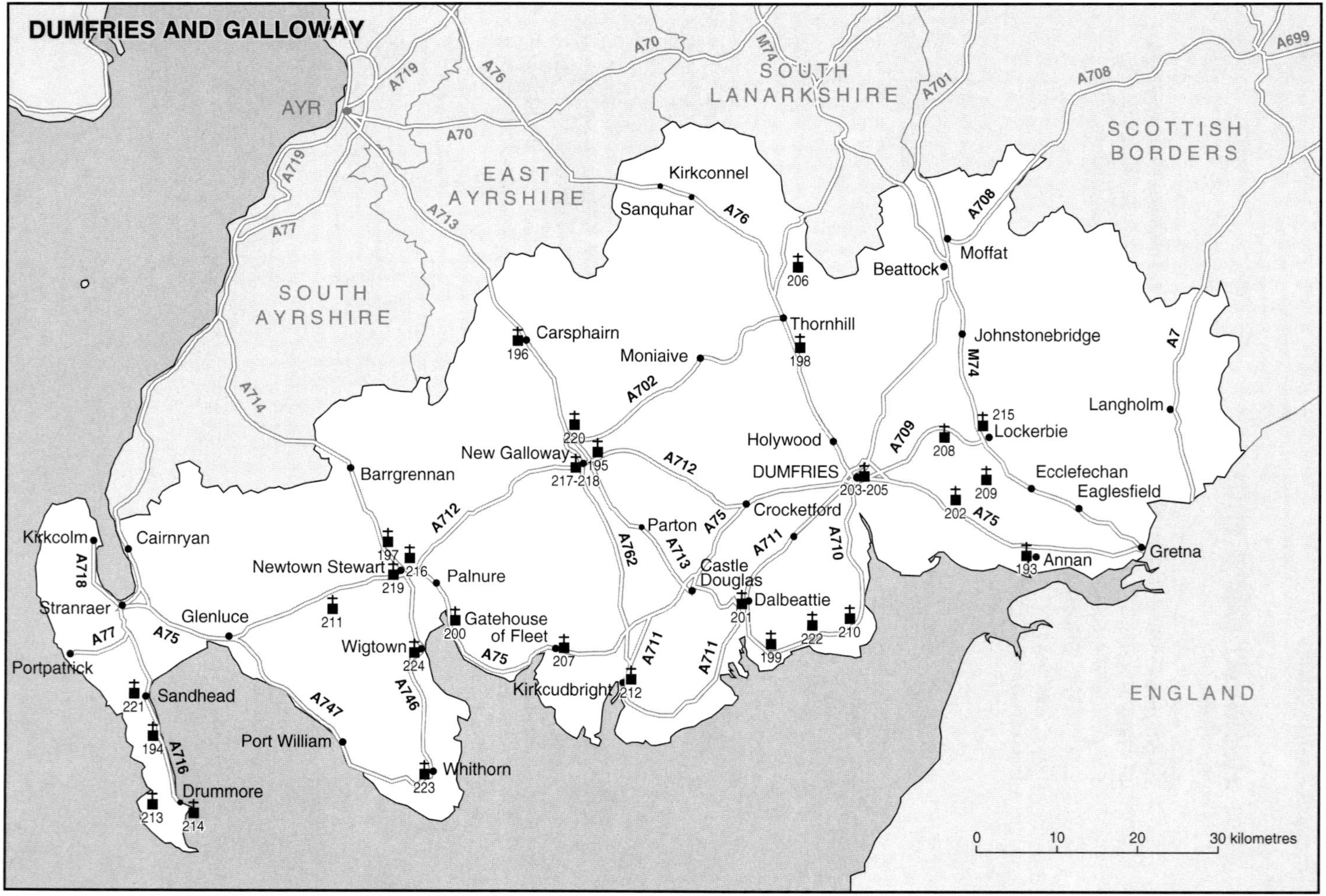
DUMFRIES AND GALLOWAY
AYR
SOUTH LANARKSHIRE
SCOTTISH BORDERS
EAST AYRSHIRE
SOUTH AYRSHIRE
ENGLAND
Kirkconnel
Sanquhar
Moffat
Beattock
Thornhill
Johnstonebridge
Carsphairn
Moniaive
Langholm
Lockerbie
Holywood
New Galloway
DUMFRIES
Ecclefechan
Eaglesfield
Barrgrennan
Crocketford
Parton
Cairnryan
Kirkcolm
Gretna
Annan
Newtown Stewart
Palnure
Castle Douglas
Dalbeattie
Stranraer
Glenluce
Gatehouse of Fleet
Wigtown
Portpatrick
Sandhead
Kirkcudbright
Port William
Whithorn
Drummore
A70
A76
A719
A77
A713
A714
M74
A701
A708
A699
A7
A702
A709
A712
A762
A713
A75
A711
A710
A718
A747
A746
A716
193
194
195
196
197
198
199
200
201
202
203-205
206
207
208
209
210
211
212
213
214
215
216
217-218
219
220
221
222
223
224
0
10
20
30 kilometres

DUMFRIES & GALLOWAY

Local Representative: The Rev J W Scott, The Manse of Durisdeer, Thornhill (*telephone* 01848 500231)

193 ST COLUMBA'S CHURCH, ANNAN

NY 199 665

Scott's Street, Annan

Built as a Congregational Church in 1794 on the site of a Secession Meeting House and re-opened as Catholic Church in 1839. Extended at both ends in 1904 by Charles Walker of Newcastle as the gift of the parish priest the Rev Lord Archibald Douglas. Stations of the Cross by Brendan Ellis 1984. Painted panels in sanctuary, Joe Burns 1997. The parish priest also serves St Francis' Church, Drove Road, Langholm (1960) and St Ninian's Church, Victory Avenue, Gretna (1925, 1918) Services: Saturday Vigil Mass 6pm; Sunday Mass 11am

Open daily 9am to 6pm. When closed key from adjacent presbytery or at 32 Scott's Street.

ROMAN CATHOLIC WC **B**

194 ARDWELL

NX 100 457

1km west of Ardwell village

Surrounded by trees, and shrubs and fronted with grass and flowerbeds, Gothic cruciform church by P MacGregor Chalmers, 1901. Tower with spire has spired octangonal corner pinnacles. Notable inside are the inscriptions in the masonry. Pulpit, reredos, screen and communion table in oak, elaborately carved. Stained glass window of the calming of the storm. Sunday Service every two weeks (normally) 10am

Open by arrangement with Mrs H McCreadie, Laundry Cottage, Ardwell Mains

CHURCH OF SCOTLAND WC **B**

195 BALMACLELLAN CHURCH

NX 651 791

Balmaclellan, Castle Douglas

A harled, 'T plan' kirk, the body was built in 1753, with the north aisle added in 1833 by William McCandlish. The stained glass west window is dated 1928 and is by Gordon Webster. The graveyard has an early 18th-century table-stone commemorating the Covenanting martyr Robert Grierson. Plaque in churchyard commemorating Sir Walter Scott's 'Old Mortality', who came from Balmaclellan. Sunday Service on first Sunday of every month at noon

Open by arrangement, telephone the Minister 01644 430380

CHURCH OF SCOTLAND

BALMACLELLAN CHURCH

196 CARSPHAIRN PARISH CHURCH

NX 563 932

Carsphairn, Castle Douglas

Built in 1815 to replace church of 1636 destroyed by fire. Central communion table. Memorials including John Semple, Covenanting minister and John Loudon MacAdam, roads pioneer. Covenanter's grave. A713 Ayr to Castle Douglas. Linked with Balmaclellan, Kells and Dalry. Sunday Service 10.30am

Open by arrangement, telephone Mr Hunter Blair 01644 460207, or Mrs Campbell 01644 460208

Carsphairn Pastoral & Horticultural Show, 1st Saturday in June

CHURCH OF SCOTLAND WC **B**

CARSPHAIRN PARISH CHURCH

197 ALL SAINTS CHURCH, CHALLOCH

NX 385 675

Challoch, by Newton Stewart

Built as private chapel of Edward James Stopford-Blair of Penninghame House and consecrated 1872. Designed by W G Habershon & Pite of London and an excellent example of a small Victorian church. Ten stained glass windows, 17 memorial plaques, pine altar and wrought iron and brass rood screen. Fine Harston two-tracker organ 1881, restored 1993 and the only example of Harston's work still in use. Located two miles north of Newton Stewart on road to Girvan, A714. Sunday Services 9am Holy Eucharist, 10.30am Sung Eucharist,1st in month 10.30am Choral Matins. Daily 8am Morning Prayer, 5.30pm Evening Prayer.

Feast days 7pm Holy Eucharist

Open daily, or telephone 01671 402101

SCOTTISH EPISCOPAL WC **A**

198 CLOSEBURN PARISH CHURCH

NX 904 923

Closeburn, by Thornhill

Built by James Barbour in 1878 alongside former (1741) church. In Gothic style with a three-stage tower. Spacious interior with an elaborate hammerbeam roof supported on foliaged corbels. Pipe organ by Henry Willis & Sons 1887. Window in the north transept by the St Enoch Glass Studios 1948. Font originally from Dalgarnock. In the graveyard is the smart mausoleum built by Thomas Kirkpatrick of Closeburn in 1742. Sunday Service 10.30am

Open by arrangement. Keys from either Mrs Lorimer, Lakehead Farm Cottages, or Mr Menzies, Closeburn Village

CHURCH OF SCOTLAND

WC **B**

CLOSEBURN PARISH CHURCH

COLVEND PARISH CHURCH

199 COLVEND PARISH CHURCH

NX 862 541

Rockcliffe, by Dalbeattie

A chaste Early Christian church by P MacGregor Chalmers 1911 of granite with red sandstone dressings, set on a rise overlooking the Solway Firth. Its bell tower is topped by a steep pyramid roof. A pretty interior with nave, aisle and transept and a timbered roof. Plain plastered walls are a foil for the sandstone columns which support round-headed arches springing from cushion capitals to form arcades into the aisle and transept. In the chancel, the deep colour of the stained glass window, the Ascension by Stephen Adam & Co 1918 forms a lovely backdrop to the High Presbyterian arrangement of furnishings. Other windows by Adam & Co and by Margaret Chilton and Marjorie Kemp 1926. A710 from Dalbeattie, turn right onto unclassified road signposted Rockcliffe. A quarter of a mile on the right. Linked with Southwick and Kirkbean. Sunday Service 11.30am

Open daily 10am-6pm

CHURCH OF SCOTLAND WC

200 KIRKMABRECK PARISH CHURCH, CREETOWN

NX 493 565

Large and tall with a tower above the front gable, built in 1834 by John Henderson. Panelling 1645 with Muir family coat of arms. In spring time churchyard and graveyard carpeted with crocuses. On A75, six miles from Newton Stewart, signposted in village. Sunday Service 11.30am

Open by arrangement, telephone Mr J Cutland, 5 Chain Road, Creetown 01671 820228

CHURCH OF SCOTLAND WC

KIRKMABRECK PARISH CHURCH, CREETOWN

201 ST PETER'S CHURCH, DALBEATTIE

NX 831 613

Craignair Street, Dalbeattie

Hall church 1814 of pinky granite with red sandstone dressings. Grey granite tower was added c.1850. Sunday Mass 9am and 11am

Open daily 9am-5pm

ROMAN CATHOLIC ♿ **B**

202 DALTON KIRK

NY 114 740

Dalton, by Lockerbie

Close by the roofless shell of the 1704 parish church stands J M Dick Peddie's 1895 sturdy Romanesque church. Unusually colourful kingpost-truss roof over the nave and scissors roof in the chancel. Three-light stained glass window of the Ascension by A Ballantine and Gardiner, 1896. The graveyard contains a late Georgian burial enclosure and the suave classical monument to the Carruthers of Whitecroft. B725, signposted off A75 Annan–Dumfries. Sunday Services 9.45am, 11.15am or 6.30pm by rotation with Hightae and St Mungo

Open by arrangement, telephone the Rev W L Kirk, Hightae Manse, Lockerbie 01387 811499

CHURCH OF SCOTLAND WC **B**

DALTON KIRK

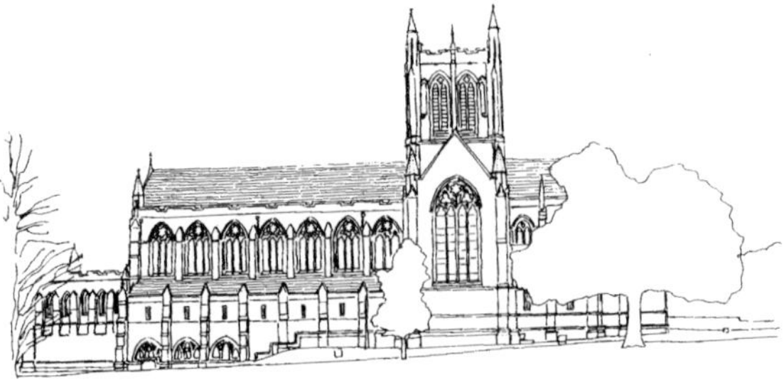

CRICHTON MEMORIAL CHURCH, DUMFRIES

203 CRICHTON MEMORIAL CHURCH, DUMFRIES

NY 983 742

Bankend Road, The Crichton, Dumfries

Completed 1897 by architect Sydney Mitchell. Richly detailed cathedral-style church with 123ft square tower. Exterior of red sandstone from Locharbriggs. Oak roof by Alexander Tweedie of Annan and stone carving by William Vickers of Glasgow. Floor is of bold design and laid out in Irish and Sicilian marble. Impressive stained glass by Oscar Paterson of Glasgow 1896. Pulpit and choir stalls 1897, organ 1902 with richly carved screen and brass angel lectern 1910. Services: Sunday 10am Church of Scotland; Thursday 11am Scottish Episcopal Eucharist. Available for weddings, concerts and other special events

Open by arrangement, telephone Crichton Development Company 01387 247544

NON-DENOMINATIONAL WC **A**

204 GREYFRIARS CHURCH, DUMFRIES

NX 971 763

Church Crescent, Dumfries

A richly ornamented Gothic edifice by John Starforth 1868 with plenty of crisply carved detail, all in red sandstone snecked rubble. The steeple dominates both the building and the townscape. The interior is a huge, almost square space, richly decorated. Clustered shafts with leafy capitals support collar-braced and kingpost-truss roofs over the nave and transepts. Stained glass by James Ballantine & Son, Powell Bros, Camm Bros and L C Levetts. Pipe organ 1921 by Ingram. Sunday Services 11am and 9.30am during summer, fortnightly Evening Services

Details of opening on notice board

CHURCH OF SCOTLAND WC **A**

GREYFRIARS CHURCH, DUMFRIES

ST GEORGE'S, DUMFRIES

205 ST GEORGE'S, DUMFRIES

NX 971 764

George Street, Dumfries

Built as a Free Church in 1844 by William McGowan, and remodelled in 1893 by James Halliday who added the Italianate front of red sandstone. Almost square interior with north and south aisles marked off by superimposed Corinthian columns. Compartmented and coved main ceiling. Sunday Service 11am, additionally July and August 9.30am (Family Service)

Open by arrangement, telephone Dr Balfour 01387 253696

CHURCH OF SCOTLAND ♿ WC **B**

206 DURISDEER PARISH CHURCH

NS 894 038

Unspoilt, peaceful, Georgian country parish church, rebuilt in 1716, topped by a belfry tower. X-plan, one arm of the cross is taller and more sophisticated, built for the Duke of Queensberry and remaining from the earlier church. Inside is the most amazing monument over the Queensberry burial vault, a baroque baldacchino carved in 1695 by John van Nost to the design of James Smith who was also architect of the later church. 'There are few buildings in which baroque magnificence and presbyterian decency are so happily combined' (George Hay, *Architecture of Scottish Post-Reformation Churches*). Martyr's Grave 1685. One mile east of A702 (signed). Sunday Service 11.45am

Open during daylight hours. Drumlanrig Castle nearby

CHURCH OF SCOTLAND ♿ (afternoon teas, Sundays July, August, September) WC **A**

DURISDEER PARISH CHURCH

207 ST MARY'S CHURCH, GATEHOUSE OF FLEET

NX 597 562

Dromore Road

Episcopalians in the area worshipped in the private chapel of Cally house until the present building of 1840 was purchased from the United Presbyterian Church and dedicated to St Mary in 1909. It is probably unique among Scottish Episcopal Churches in having a stained glass window commemorating John Knox! Sunday Service 9.45am Holy Communion, Wednesday 9.30 Holy Communion

Open daily during summer, and by arrangement, telephone H Leslie 0557 814721

SCOTTISH EPISCOPAL ♿ 👂 **B**

ST MARY'S CHURCH, GATEHOUSE OF FLEET

208 HIGHTAE KIRK

NY 090 793

Built as a Relief meeting house in 1796 and remodelled for the Reformed Presbyterians in 1865, when the windows were enlarged and the gableted west bellcote and small porch were added. On the B7020, Two and a half miles south of Lochmaben. Sunday Services 9.45am, 11.15am or 6.30pm by rotation with Dalton and St Mungo

Open by arrangement, telephone Mr William Cartledge, Knowehead Cottage, Hightae 01387 810782

CHURCH OF SCOTLAND ♿ 🛈 WC (adjoining manse)

209 ST MUNGO PARISH CHURCH, KETTLEHOLM

NY 143 771

Built under the patronage of the Rt Hon Robert Jardine MP of Castlemilk. Late Scots Gothic by David Bryce 1877 with a pinnacled-buttressed porch decorated with grotesque carved heads. Inside, a magnificently elaborate open roof. Organ 1905 by Abbot & Smith. Stained glass by James Ballantine & Son 1876. First World War memorial by F M Taubman. On the B723, three miles south of Lockerbie. Sunday Services 9.45am, 11.15am or 6.30pm by rotation with Dalton and Hightae

Open by arrangement, telephone Mr A Leslie, Lindores, Peatford, Lockerbie 01576 202827

CHURCH OF SCOTLAND ♿ 🛈 WC **B**

210 KIRKBEAN PARISH CHURCH

NX 980 592

Harled T-plan kirk said to have been designed by William Craik, sometime Laird of Arbigland. The tower on the west wall is of two lower stages 1776 with a Diocletian window in its second stage, and two upper stages, added in 1836 by Walter Newall, the first with a clock and the top a big octagonal belfry cupola of polished ashlar under a lantern. A Venetian window in the east gable of the tail of the church. Inside, plain furnishings of 1883. A memorial font, presented by the US Navy, in memory of John Paul Jones, a gardener's son from Arbigland, who founded the US Navy; designed and sculpted by George Henry Paulin 1946. In the village, turn left at the road junction to Carsethorn. Adjacent to the school on left. Linked with Colvend and Southwick. Sunday Service 10am

Open by arrangement, telephone Mr George Fazakerley 01387880662

CHURCH OF SCOTLAND **B**

KIRKBEAN PARISH CHURCH

211 KIRKCOWAN PARISH CHURCH

NX 327 610

Main Street, Kirkcowan

At the west end of the village, built in 1834 to replace a former church, of which only an ivy-clad east gable remains in its kirkyard (east end of village). The present church is a harled T-plan building with external stairs at the east and west gables leading to two galleries. A tower at the north side. Inside, three galleries in all, supported by marbled cast iron columns. Tall pulpit of 1834 and a late 19th-century chamber organ by J & A Mirrlees, brought here in 1966. Linked with Wigtown. Sunday Service 10am

Open by arrangement, telephone Mr J Adair 01671 830214

CHURCH OF SCOTLAND WC **A**

212 GREYFRIARS (ST FRANCIS OF ASSISI), KIRKCUDBRIGHT

NX 682 511

Mote Brae, Kirkcudbright

The sanctuary of Greyfriars Church is the last remaining fragment of a Franciscan friary. Dating from either the 13th or 15th centuries, it has undergone many changes in both design and use over the centuries. The MacClellan Monument, erected in 1597, is one of the most interesting features of the church. On the left of the High Altar is an ancient piscina. There are also three fine modern stained glass windows including work by Gordon Webster. The cross and candlesticks are the work of Mabel Brunton, a distinguished member of the artists' colony which flourished in the town in the 1920s. Other interesting furnishings are the 17-century dower chest and the medieval holy water stoup. Sunday Services: Holy Communion 11.30am all year, and 8.15am end May to August; Friday Holy Communion 10am

Open Easter week, July to August, and by arrangement, telephone the Rector 01557 330146

SCOTTISH EPISCOPAL **A**

213 KIRKMAIDEN OLD KIRK

NX 139 324

Kirkmaiden, Drummore

Built 1638 to replace St Catherine's at Mull of Galloway in the most southerly parish in Scotland. T-shaped church with vaults of the McDougall family of Logan underneath balcony. 'Treacle' Bible on display. Bell from Clanyard Castle, a gift from the Earl of Dalhousie 1532. Floodlit most of 2000. Service 11.30am last Sunday May-September

Open daily Easter-October or by arrangement with Mrs Symonds, telephone 01776 840601

CHURCH OF SCOTLAND WC

214 ST MEDAN'S, DRUMMORE

NX 135 367

Stair Street, Drummore

Built 1903 in red Dumfries sandstone with an attractive roof of red and yellow pine. Hymnus IV electronic organ. Morrison memorial window behind choir, 1951. John McGuffog memorial window above pulpit, designed and made by Arthur C Speirs DA of Greenock, 1996. Sunday Services 11.30am except last Sunday in month in May when service is in Kirkmaiden Old Church

Open by arrangement contact Mrs Beck, telephone 01776 840210

CHURCH OF SCOTLAND WC **B**

215 HOLY TRINITY, LOCKERBIE

NY 136 815

Arthurs Place, Lockerbie

Built as Trinity Church in 1874 for the United Presbyterian Church, became Church of Scotland 1929 and acquired in 1973 by the Catholic Church and renamed Holy Trinity. Designed by Ford Mackenzie, built in Corncockle sandstone in Gothic style with a large rose window and steeple. The organ, Ingram of Edinburgh, is a prominent feature. Plaque in vestibule commemorates 1,000 years of Christianity in the Ukraine. Copy of Lockerbie Book of Remembrance. Services: Saturday Vigil 7pm, Sunday Mass 11.15am, other days as announced

Open daily 9am-5pm

ROMAN CATHOLIC **B**

216 MONIGAFF PARISH CHURCH, MINNIGAFF

NX 410 666

Minnigaff, Newton Stewart

Church completed in 1836 to a design by William Burn. Stained glass by William Wailes of Newcastle 1868 and Ballantine, Edinburgh 1910. Font from Earl of Galloway's private chapel. Organ built in 1873, Bryceson Brothers, London. Ruins of pre-Reformation church on medieval foundations. East gable twelfth or early 13th-century. Motte and ditch. Eighth-century stone slab of Irish missionary influence. Grave stones including B-listed Heron monument. Yew tree 900 years old. Sunday Service 10am, first Sunday of month Holy Communion 9.25am

Open July and August, Monday and Friday 2-4.30pm. Or by arrangement, telephone Mrs Shankland 01671 402164. Historical display June to September

CHURCH OF SCOTLAND WC (free) **B**

217 KELLS PARISH CHURCH, NEW GALLOWAY

NX 632 784

Kirk Road, New Galloway

Built in 1822 to a design by William McCandlish. A granite T-plan church with three-stage square tower at the centre of south wall. Interior mainly reconstructed in 1911 following original layout. Galleries on three sides with pulpit on long south wall. Notable churchyard with three 'Adam and Eve' stones of 1706-7, and a delightful upright for Captain Gordon's gamekeeper, John Murray. Linked with Carsphairn, Balmaclellan and Dalry. Sunday Service 10.30am, not first Sunday

Open by arrangement 01644 430380

CHURCH OF SCOTLAND **B**

KELLS PARISH CHURCH, NEW GALLOWAY

218 ST MARGARET'S NEW GALLOWAY

NX 636 778

on edge of New Galloway on Ken Bridge road

Built 1904, chancel added 1908. The walls of the church are harled and the roofs are red tiled. The wooden panelling and furnishings are a mixture of Oregon pine and oak and the windows are variously by Kempe, Clayton & Bell and James Powell & Sons. Services 10.30am every Sunday and Wednesday.

Key at Rectory next door, The Rev John Redpath 01644 420235

SCOTTISH EPISCOPAL

ST MARGARET'S NEW GALLOWAY

219 PENNINGHAME ST JOHN'S PARISH CHURCH, NEWTON STEWART

NX 410 654

Church Street, Newton Stewart

Church completed in 1840 to a design by William Burn. Groome's *Gazetteer* describes it as 'a handsome Gothic edifice'. Organ built by J F Harston of Newark in 1878, and is believed to be the largest and most intact of all organs built by him. Renovated by Hill, Norman and Beard in 1962. Spire 151 ft. All glass replaced 1996. Church Street is parallel to town's main street. Sunday Services 10.30am, 6.30pm (except July and August)

Open Tuesday 12.30–2pm for lunchtime prayer meeting.
Or by arrangement, telephone Mr M C Dunlop 01671 402543

CHURCH OF SCOTLAND WC **A**

220 DALRY PARISH CHURCH, ST JOHN'S TOWN OF DALRY

NX 618 813

Main Street, St John's Town of Dalry

Completed in 1831 to a design by William McCandlish to replace a ruined building of 1771, it is probably the third church to occupy the site. Early records are scarce but a church, a dilapidated one at that, existed in 1427. Traditional T-shaped interior, plainly furnished. Pulpit with carved wooden canopy. Galleries on three sides. Stands near the Water of Ken with wide views of the Rhinns of Kells. Avenue of lime trees. Interesting old kirkyard with Covenanters' stone and Gordon Aisle, burial place of the Gordons of Lochinvar. Robert Burns fashioned his poem 'Tam o' Shanter' on a local tale. On A713 Castle Douglas to Ayr. Linked with Balmaclellan and Kells and Carsphairn. Sunday Service 12 noon

Open by arrangement, telephone Mr L A Young 01644 430472

CHURCH OF SCOTLAND WC **B**

221 SANDHEAD

NX 097 500

Main Street, Sandhead

Substantial timber construction with steeply pitched tiled roof and cedar-board clad walls by architects Goudie & Hill, 1962. The unusual structure uses laminated timber portal frames with obscured glass between the frames in both side walls. Flat-roofed porch with masonry bell-tower. Internally, much varnished wood. Inverted-pyramid shaped pulpit. Services Sundays 10am

Open by arrangement Mrs C McKay, 25 Main Street or Mr Cowan, Dorlin, Main Street

CHURCH OF SCOTLAND WC (Wednesdays and Sundays, 2-4pm in summer)

SOUTHWICK PARISH CHURCH

222 SOUTHWICK PARISH CHURCH

NX 906 569

Caulkerbush, by Dumfries

Standing by woodland just outside the policies of Southwick House, a stone church of local grey granite with dressings of red sandstone. By Kinnear & Peddie 1891 a mixture of Early Christian and Norman. Its crossing tower was derived from the 14th-century tower of St Monans Parish Church. A wagon roof over the nave; the chancel arch enriched with chevron decoration. On either side of the chancel arch, a neo-Norman font by Cox & Buckley 1898 and a neo-Jacobean pulpit. Wrought iron Arts and Crafts light fittings, once for oil lamps. Late 19th-century stained glass. Organ replaced in May 1999 with Ahlborn SL100. A710 from Dumfries, turn right immediately over Southwick Bridge onto B793 Dalbeattie. Linked with Colvend and Kirkbean. Sunday Service 10am

Open daily 10am–6pm

CHURCH OF SCOTLAND WC

223 ST NINIAN'S PRIORY CHURCH, WHITHORN

NX 444 403

Bruce Street, Whithorn

Built 1822 with later 19th-century tower. Simple rectangular hall church. Carved oak pulpit. Stained glass east windows gifted by the daughter of Gemmell Hutcheson RSA in memory of her father. Located on the site of Whithorn 'dig' in the former precincts of Whithorn Priory. First Scottish Christian community founded here by St Ninian, pre-dates Iona. From A75 turn south at Newton Stewart on A714 then A746. Sunday Services 10.30am and 7pm

Open Easter to end of October, 10am–5pm

CHURCH OF SCOTLAND A

ST NINIAN'S PRIORY CHURCH, WHITHORN

224 WIGTOWN PARISH CHURCH

NX 436 555

Bank Street, Wigtown

The parish church on an ancient ecclesiastical site, largely rebuilt in 1730, was by the middle of the next century thought to be 'an old mean-looking edifice'. A new church, by the London architect Henry Roberts, was built nearby in 1851, still using the Georgian T-plan with a French pavilion roof on the tower. Built of granite, it encloses a broad nave and east transept. P MacGregor Chalmers added a communion table and font, an organ chamber, and rearranged the seating in 1914. In the transept are three carved stones, one a Celtic cross shaft decorated on both faces with interlaced rings, similar to those of the same period at Whithorn. Stained glass in the east transept window by James Ballantine & Son 1867. Linked with Kirkcowan. Sunday Service 11.30am and 6.30pm (in church hall)

Open Easter to September, Monday to Friday 2-4pm

CHURCH OF SCOTLAND WC **B**

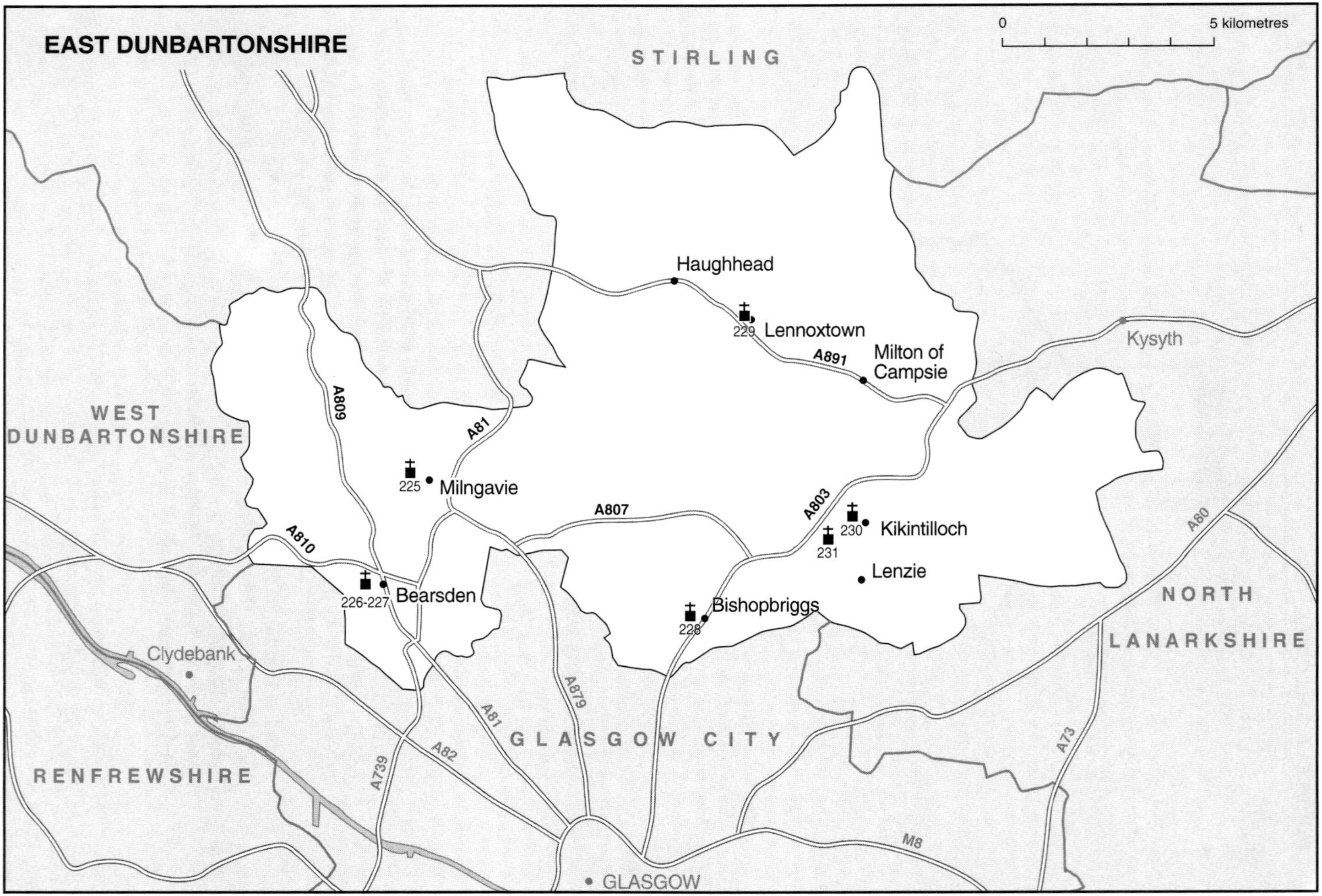
EAST DUNBARTONSHIRE
0
5 kilometres
STIRLING
WEST DUNBARTONSHIRE
NORTH LANARKSHIRE
GLASGOW CITY
RENFREWSHIRE
Haughhead
Lennoxtown
229
Milton of Campsie
Kysyth
A891
A809
A81
A807
A803
A810
A879
A82
A739
A80
A73
M8
225
Milngavie
226-227
Bearsden
228
Bishopbriggs
230
Kikintilloch
231
Lenzie
Clydebank
GLASGOW

EAST DUNBARTONSHIRE

Local Representative: Mrs Marion Smith, 30 Roman Court, Roman Road, Bearsden (*telephone* 0141 942 1236)

225 BALDERNOCK PARISH CHURCH

NS 577 751

near Milngavie

The religious history of the site goes back to the 13th century. The present church was built in 1795 on the site of an earlier church. The bell tower contains a curious panel which may have come from the nearby Roman wall. The octagonal gatehouse and stone stile feature in Moffat's play 'Bunty Pulls the Strings'. Interesting gravestones, including Archibald Bulloch from whom President Theodore Roosevelt and Eleanor Roosevelt descended. The church stands at the end of a lovely one mile walk from Milngavie. Sunday Service 11am

Open Sunday 2-4pm, June to August

CHURCH OF SCOTLAND **B**

226 BLESSED JOHN DUNS SCOTUS CHAPEL, BEARSDEN

NS 535 720

2 Chesters Road, Bearsden, Glasgow

The Chapel of Scotus College was designed by J F Stephen and dedicated in 1997. The main internal features are its barrel-vaulted ceiling and glass walls. The 14 stained glass panels representing the Stations of the Cross are by Shona McInnes and are full of rich symbolism. A number of other items were specially commissioned for the Chapel including processional cross, presidential Chair, candlesticks and a Christ-figure. A pamphlet is available giving excellent details

Open during term time 7am-9pm. Also telephone 0141 942 8384

ROMAN CATHOLIC

227 NEW KILPATRICK PARISH CHURCH, BEARSDEN

NS 543 723

Manse Road, Bearsden

Building began in 1807 on the site of an earlier church 1649 and within the original settlement established by Paisley Abbey in 1232. Very fine collection of stained glass including windows by Stephen Adam, Alfred and Gordon Webster, Norman M Macdougall, C E Stewart, James Ballantine and Eilidh Keith. By rail to Bearsden, by Kelvin Bus 118 to Bearsden Cross.

Services Sunday 10.30am and 7pm, Wednesday 12 noon

Open June to August, Wednesday 12.30-4pm, Sunday 2pm-5pm

Other times by arrangement, telephone M L Smith 0141 942 1236.

Close to Roman Bath House east of Bearsden Cross

CHURCH OF SCOTLAND **B**

228 ST JAMES THE LESS, BISHOPBRIGGS

NS 612 712

Hilton Road, Bishopbriggs

Built 1980 when the congregation moved from Springburn, this church by Glasgow architects Weddell and Thomson, preserves the most striking features of the 1881 Springburn building and contains many items from other Glasgow churches: stained glass by Edward Burne-Jones and Stephen Adam and part of the old High Altar of Iona Abbey. Pipe organ by J W Walker & Sons, 1964. Sunday Services: 9am Eucharist, 10.30am Sung Eucharist, Thursday 10.10am Morning Prayer, 10.30am Eucharist

Open Sundays and Thursdays 10am-12noon or by arrangement with the Rector telephone 0141 772 4514

SCOTTISH EPISCOPAL

229 CAMPSIE PARISH CHURCH, LENNOXTOWN

NS 629 777

Main Street, Lennoxtown

Modern church with interesting wood carving and stained glass. Craft centre and old church with fascinating graveyard at Campsie Glen, two miles. Bus 175 Campsie Glen via Kirkintilloch. Sunday Service 11am

Open by arrangement, telephone Mrs M Tindall 01360 310 911

CHURCH OF SCOTLAND A

ST DAVID'S MEMORIAL
PARK CHURCH, KIRKINTILLOCH

230 ST DAVID'S MEMORIAL PARK CHURCH, KIRKINTILLOCH

NS 654 737

Alexandra Street, Kirkintilloch

The present church by P MacGregor Chalmers 1926, adjacent to site of the original building (1843) was dedicated as a gift of Mrs Paton Thomson in memory of her parents. Two-manual pipe organ, a significant Anneessens 1899 rebuilt and enlarged. Off A803. Sunday Services 11am and (most Sundays) 6.30pm

Open every Wednesday 11am–2pm for meditation and prayer

CHURCH OF SCOTLAND

231 ST CYPRIAN'S CHURCH, LENZIE

NS 653 727

Beech Road, Lenzie

Built in 1873 by Alexander Ross of Inverness in Gothic style with a three-stage tower at the east end and a gabled porch at the west end. The use of contrasting materials gives a colourful interior. Painting of the Last Supper on the reredos. Memorial choir screen made in local iron foundry. Half mile north from Lenzie Cross. Sunday Services 8.30am, 11am and 6.30pm (not July and August)

Open by arrangement, telephone the Rector 0141 776 4149

SCOTTISH EPISCOPALIAN **B**

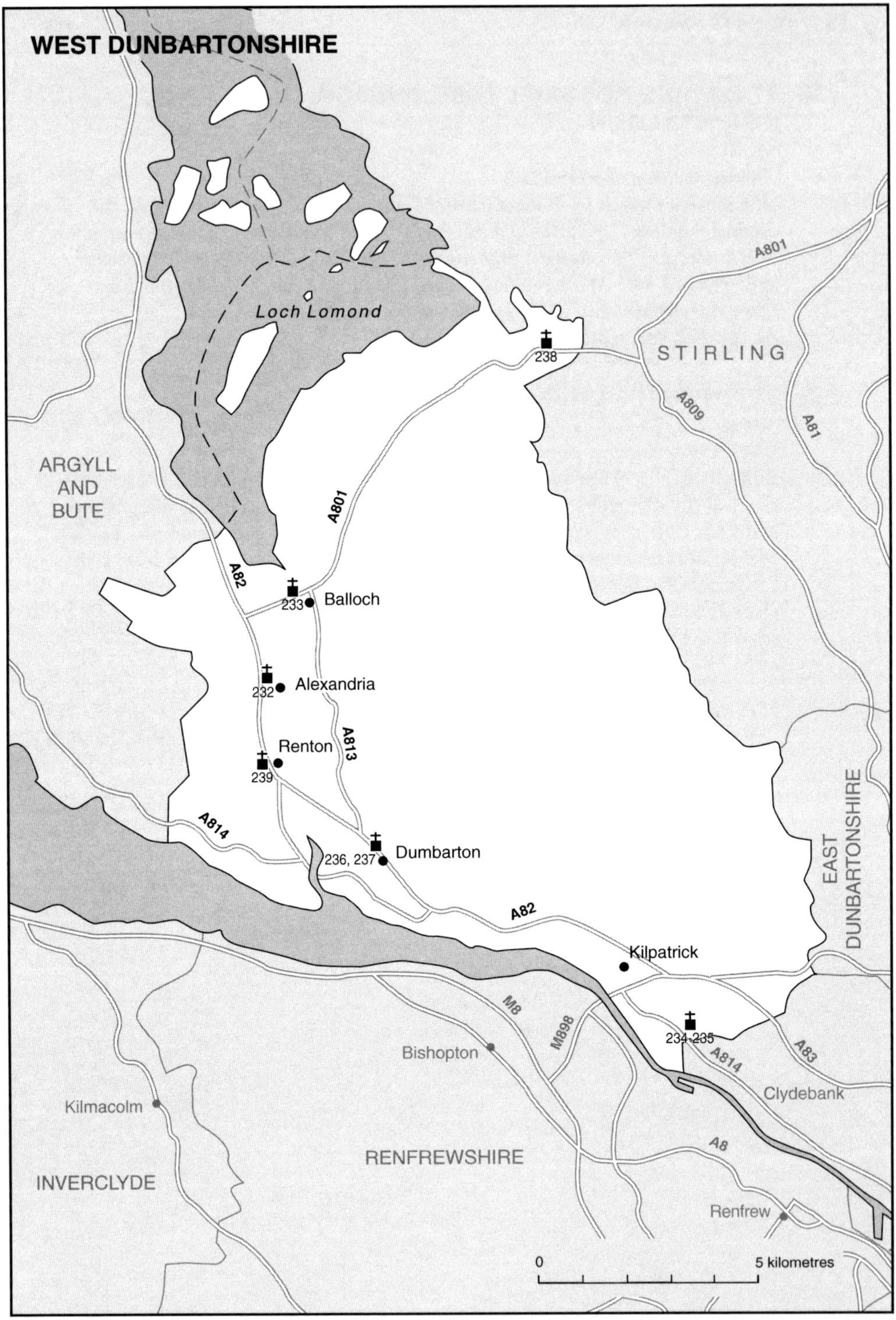
WEST DUNBARTONSHIRE
Loch Lomond
STIRLING
A801
238
A809
A81
ARGYLL
AND
BUTE
A801
A82
233
Balloch
232
Alexandria
A813
Renton
239
A814
236, 237
Dumbarton
EAST
DUNBARTONSHIRE
A82
Kilpatrick
M8
M898
234-235
A814
A83
Bishopton
Clydebank
Kilmacolm
A8
RENFREWSHIRE
INVERCLYDE
Renfrew
0
5 kilometres

WEST DUNBARTONSHIRE

232 ST MUNGO'S CHURCH, ALEXANDRIA

NS 389 796

Main Street, Alexandria

Dedicated 1894, J M Crawford, architect, in pointed Gothic style. Early 20th-century addition of side aisle. Simple interior with simple altar furniture. Open timber roof with curved brace supported on stone corbels. Three-light stained glass window in memory of Agnes J Burham of New York featuring Christ in Majesty, St Michael the Archangel, St Agnes and St Agatha. Sunday Services Eucharist 9am, Sung Eucharist 11am; Wednesday Eucharist 10am

Open by arrangement, telephone the Priest-in-charge, St Mungo's Rectory 01389 752633

SCOTTISH EPISCOPALIAN **B**

233 ALEXANDRIA PARISH CHURCH, BALLOCH

NS 389 798

Lomond Road, Balloch

Building refurbished and upgraded in 1995-6. Digital organ by Allen. A number of items produced by the congregational Sewing Group include the Heritage Tapestry 30 by 27 inches, finely embroidered pulpit falls and communion table cords, four hand sewn banners (two on local themes) crafted in 1998 and 1999 for the Millennium. Several noteworthy items of stained glass by Gordon Webster. Contemporary Noah's Ark mural in main hall. In the grounds, a War Memorial commemorating members of the congregation killed in action 1914-18 and 1939-45. Off A82. Five to ten minutes walk from Balloch railway station. Sunday Service 11am and Jazz Praise services at 7pm usually on last Sunday of February and following alternate months

Open by arrangement lunches/afternoon teas for groups by arrangement, Miss E McCreadie 01389 752370

CHURCH OF SCOTLAND

ALEXANDRIA PARISH CHURCH, BALLOCH

234 KILBOWIE ST ANDREW'S PARISH CHURCH, CLYDEBANK

NS 497 702

Kilbowie Road, Clydebank

For the congregation founded as St John's on the Hill 1897 the present church was built in 1904 on land gifted by William Black of Auchentoshen. In simple Perpendicular style, a low cruciform church of red sandstone. The battlemented belfry added 1933. Recent refurbishment. Memorial side chapel with tapestry and stained glass window by Eilidh Keith 1997 dedicated to the victims of the Clydebank blitz. The bell, 1933, is one of few remaining in this former industrial community of Scotland. M8 Junction 19, A82 to A8014 turn off. Five minutes walk from railway station. Sunday Service 11am, except July and August

Open 18 March 2000 10am-4pm, 7-9pm (Blitz Memorial Day). Other times by arrangement, and Doors Open Day, telephone Rev R Grahame 0141 951 2455

CHURCH OF SCOTLAND

235 ST JOSEPH'S CHURCH, CLYDEBANK

NS 510 733

Faifley Road, Clydebank

Replacing a Coia church which was burned down, the building is one of the newest in the country, being opened in 1997. The award-winning design by Jacobsen & French utilises tall windows to provide light while natural wood is featured extensively. Sunday Services 9 and 11.30am, 6pm; Saturday Vigil 6pm;. Daily Mass 9.30am

Open Wednesday 9-11am, Saturday 5-7pm, Sunday 9-12.30 and 5-7pm

ROMAN CATHOLIC

ST JOSEPH'S CHURCH, CLYDEBANK

236 RIVERSIDE PARISH CHURCH, DUMBARTON

NS 398 752

High Street, Dumbarton

Built in 1811 to a design by John Brash on the site of earlier 13/14th-century and 17th-century churches. The steeple and pedimented gable command the westward curve of the High Street. Urns perch on the belfry and adorn the gatepiers. The interior was refurbished 1886. Stained glass includes the Queen Margaret window by the Abbey Studio of Glasgow and Ascension window by C E Stewart. Eleventh/twelfth-century Crusader stone now housed in gallery. Sunday Service 11.15am

Open weekdays 9.30am-12.30pm

CHURCH OF SCOTLAND **A**

237 ST AUGUSTINE'S CHURCH, DUMBARTON

NS 397 752

High Street, Dumbarton

Built in 1873, the architect Sir R Rowand Anderson designed the building in the Gothic Revival Style. Stained glass at baptismal font by Stephen Adam with others to a design by Carl Alnquist. The organ was designed and built for the church by Smith and Brock. Sunday Services 9 and 11am

Open Saturday mornings, and by arrangement, telephone Church Office 01389 734514

SCOTTISH EPISCOPAL A

ST AUGUSTINE'S CHURCH, DUMBARTON

238 THE CHURCH OF KILMARONOCK

NS 452 875

by Drymen

The present church building dates from 1813 and has a stout classical dignity. Parish long-established when documented records began; the screen at the entrance to the nave lists incumbents since 1325. Memorial wall plaques. Ancient stones in graveyard. North side of A811, three miles west of Drymen. Sunday Service 11am, May to September

Open by arrangement, telephone the Rev Andrew Mitchell 01360 660295.

Occasional events by the Friends of Kilmaronock

CHURCH OF SCOTLAND B

THE CHURCH OF KILMARONOCK

239 RENTON TRINITY PARISH CHURCH

NS 390 780

Renton

Building originally constructed as Renton Old Parish Church 1892, architects H & D Bradlay. United with Renton Union Church and Renton Millburn Church 1969. Building has since been refurbished and upgraded. Five stained glass windows by Oscar Paterson, Glasgow 1912–1922. Sunday Services 11am and at 6.30pm 2nd Sunday of March, June, September, December

Open Thursdays 10.30am–1.30pm.

Or by arrangement, telephone Rev Cameron Langlands 011389 752017

CHURCH OF SCOTLAND A

DUNDEE CITY

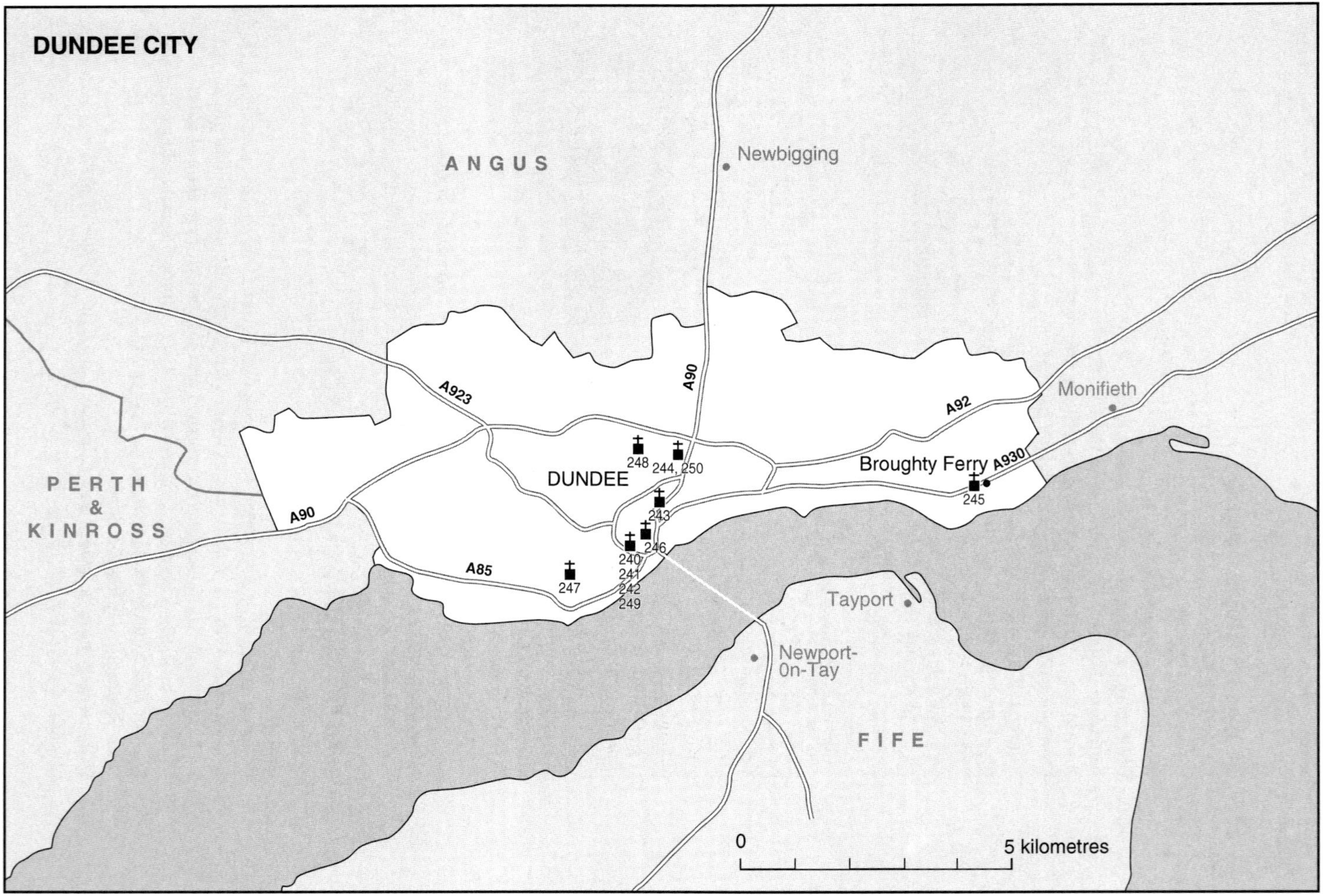
ANGUS
Newbigging
PERTH
&
KINROSS
A923
A90
A90
A92
Monifieth
DUNDEE
Broughty Ferry
A930
248
244, 250
243
246
240
241
242
249
247
245
A85
Tayport
Newport-
0n-Tay
FIFE
0
5 kilometres

DUNDEE

240 DUNDEE PARISH CHURCH (ST MARY'S)

NO 401 301

Nethergate, Dundee

Founded in 1190 by Earl of Huntingdon. Rebuilt 1844 by William Burn. Beautiful 19th and 20th century stained glass windows. 1914–18 war memorial. Impressive organ installed in 1865. Reading desk with interesting history. North of Discovery Point and railway station. Sunday Service 11am, Holy Communion last Sunday of month

Open May to September, Monday, Tuesday, Thursday, Friday 10am–12 noon

CHURCH OF SCOTLAND WC B

241 MEADOWSIDE ST PAUL'S CHURCH

NO 401 300

114–116 Nethergate, Dundee

Built in 1852, replacing the Mariners' Church, to a design by Charles Wilson. It 'boasts a fine spire terminating the elevation of Nethergate before it is disrupted by the ring road'. Hammer beam roof. Organ by Walker & Co 1902 overhauled by Rushworth & Dreaper 1971. Stained glass, some by Jones & Willis, and by Alexander Russell. A hall complex, M J Rodgers 1988. A feature of the garden is an artistic stone wall by David Wilson. Sunday Service 11am

Open Wednesday 12 noon–1.30pm for prayer and meditation

CHURCH OF SCOTLAND (Cornerstone Coffee House adjoining) WC B

242 ST ANDREW'S CATHEDRAL

NO 400 299

150 Nethergate, Dundee

Designed by George Mathewson in 1835, impressive arcaded interior. Outstanding 19th and 20th-century stained glass by Mayer of Munich. Sunday Mass 10.30am, 7pm. Weekday Mass 10am

Open Monday to Saturday 9am–3pm

ROMAN CATHOLIC

GLASSITE KIRK NOW PART OF THE CHURCH HALLS OF THE ST ANDREW'S PARISH CHURCH

ST ANDREW'S PARISH CHURCH

243 ST ANDREW'S PARISH CHURCH

NO 404 307

King Street, Dundee

Trades Kirk with interesting history, dating from 1774, Samuel Bell with plans by James Craig, Edinburgh. Beautiful stained glass. Includes Glassite kirk 1777 now part of church hall complex. Handsome spire with peal of fine musical bells. Lovely gardens. Teas on Saturdays. Next to Wellgate Shopping Centre. Sunday Service 11am all year; also 9.30am June, July and August

Open Tuesday, Thursday, Saturday 10am-12 noon all year. Also Doors Open Day

CHURCH OF SCOTLAND (Saturdays) WC **A**

244 ST JOHN THE BAPTIST CHURCH

NO 411 314

116 Albert Street, Dundee

The present building was consecrated in 1886. Designed with a French style roof by the Rev Edward Sugden 1885. The sanctuary and chancel are panelled in late Gothic style, the details suggested by the woodwork in King's College Chapel, Aberdeen. Open wood roof and pillars give this interior a Scandinavian feel. Reredos by William Hole. The font cover is a splendid carved wooden spire

Open Thursday 9-11am. Other times by arrangement, telephone Rev James Forbes 01382 461640

SCOTTISH EPISCOPAL WC **B**

245 ST MARY'S CHURCH, BROUGHTY FERRY

NO 461 310

Queen Street, Broughty Ferry

Designed by Sir George Gilbert Scott 1858 and added to 1870. Sir Robert Lorimer extended the chancel 1911. The pulpit, screen, choir stalls and reredos are all by Lorimer. Garden of Remembrance. On the main road from Carnoustie and Monifieth to Dundee. Frequent bus service. Sunday Services 8.30am, 11am, 6.30pm. Weekdays Matins 7am, Evensong 6pm

Open daily all year

SCOTTISH EPISCOPAL **A**

246 ST PAUL'S CATHEDRAL

NO 404 303

Castlehill, 1 High Street, Dundee

Designed by Sir George Gilbert Scott, the Cathedral stands on the site of Dundee's ancient Castle. Gothic in style, but Gothic with a difference. Tall, graceful columns give an impression of lightness and airiness. East end of High Street at junction with Commercial Street. Walking distance from rail and bus stations. Sunday Services 8am, 9.40am, 11am, 6.30pm

Open Monday to Saturday 11am-5pm

SCOTTISH EPISCOPAL WC **A**

247 ST PETER'S FREE CHURCH

NO 390 298

St Peter Street, Dundee

1836, by Hean Brothers. Remarkably douce for a revivalist kirk: yet this was the seat of the Rev Robert McCheyne (1813-43) a major player in the Evangelical revival, who made these sober rafters ring. An elegant, classical church with a gallery carried on cast-iron columns. Original pulpit. The plain simplicity of the building is ennobled by the tower and stone spire against its east gable. The church has served different denominations since its opening, Free, United Free, and Church of Scotland. It became a Free Church again in 1987. From city centre, west for one mile along High Street, Nethergate and Perth Road. Turn right into St Peter Street. Sunday Services 11am and 6.30pm. Wednesday Prayer Meeting 7.30pm

Open by arrangement, telephone Rev D Robertson 01382 861401

FREE CHURCH OF SCOTLAND WC **B**

248 ST SALVADOR'S CHURCH

NO 403 313

Church Street, Dundee

Glorious painted interior with stencilled wall decoration and open roof, built in 1868 in early Arts and Crafts Gothic by G F Bodley. Carnegie Street end of Church Street, off Hilltown. Buses 20 and 22. Daily Services: Tuesday 9.30am, Wednesday 10am, Thursday 12.30pm, Friday/Saturday 8am. Evensong daily 5.30pm except Sunday 5pm. Sunday Services 9am, 11am, 5pm

Open most mornings. Also Doors Open Day, September

SCOTTISH EPISCOPAL **B**

249 THE STEEPLE CHURCH

NO 402 301

Nethergate, Dundee

Church building dates from 1788, Samuel Bell. Entry through 15th-century St Mary's Tower. A landmark, known as Old Steeple. City centre. Sunday Services 11am and 6.30pm (7pm July and August)

Open July to August, Tuesday 10am-1pm, Saturday 12 noon-3pm.
Also Doors Open Day and other summer activities.
Mary Slessor Exhibition, July to August (details in Church)

CHURCH OF SCOTLAND **B**

THE STEEPLE CHURCH

250 STOBSWELL PARISH CHURCH

NO 411 315

Albert Street, Dundee

On a prominent site, by Charles Edward and Thomas S Robertson 1874. The buildings have recently undergone extensive refurbishment. L-shaped church. Fine stained glass windows by William Wilson. From city centre buses 15, 17, 32, 33, 35 and 36. Sunday Service 11am (10.30am, July and August)

Open Dundee Doors Open Day, September

CHURCH OF SCOTLAND ♿ 👂 WC (for disabled) **B**

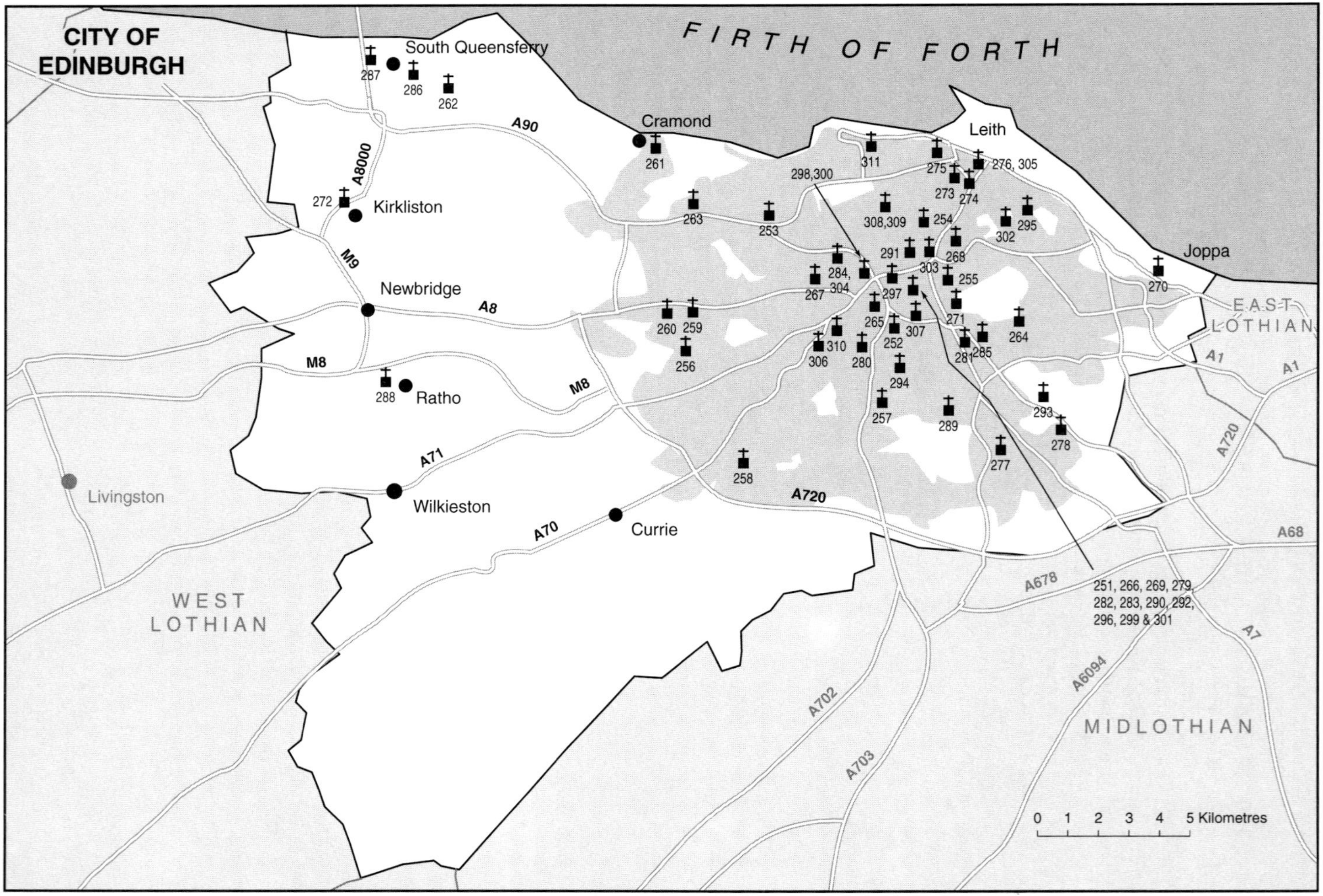
CITY OF EDINBURGH
FIRTH OF FORTH
South Queensferry
Kirkliston
Newbridge
Ratho
Wilkieston
Currie
Cramond
Leith
Joppa
Livingston
WEST LOTHIAN
EAST LOTHIAN
MIDLOTHIAN
A90
A8000
M9
A8
M8
A71
A70
A720
A678
A68
A1
A7
A6094
A702
A703
287
286
262
272
288
261
263
253
260
259
256
258
298,300
311
275
276, 305
273
274
308,309
254
302
295
291
268
303
284, 304
267
297
255
270
271
265
307
264
310
252
281
285
306
280
294
257
289
293
278
277
251, 266, 269, 279, 282, 283, 290, 292, 296, 299 & 301
0 1 2 3 4 5 Kilometres

EDINBURGH

251 AUGUSTINE UNITED CHURCH

NT 257 734

41 George IV Bridge, Edinburgh

Built 1857-61 by J J M & W H Hay with Romanesque, Renaissance and Classical elements for the congregation of the second Scottish Congregational Church in Edinburgh. The projecting centre of the gable front is carried up as the 'bride's-cake' tower which is topped by a spire of three diminishing octagonal stages. Composite hammerbeam and kingpost roof. The Bradford computer organ 1994 uses the pipes and case of the former Ingram organ 1929. Major alterations to interior, to plans by Stewart Tod and Partners 1995. Two stained glass windows by Robert Burns, formerly in the gallery, now at ground floor level. Now, with the merger of several congregations, a member of the United Reformed Church. Sunday Service 11am, Holy Communion first and third Sundays

Normally open Monday to Friday 12noon-2pm, April to September

UNITED REFORMED WC WC **B**

252 BARCLAY CHURCH

NT 249 726

Bruntsfield Place, Tollcross, Edinburgh

1864 in powerful Ruskinian Gothic, this is Frederick T Pilkington's greatest achievement. Spire 230 ft is well known landmark. Spectacular theatrical space within with double gallery. Painted ceiling. Hundred metres south of King's Theatre. Sunday Services 11am and 6.30pm

Open July to August, Tuesday and Thursday 2-5pm.

Other times and details of special events, telephone J Baker 0131 229 0899

CHURCH OF SCOTLAND WC **A**

253 BLACKHALL UNITED FREE CHURCH

NT 216 750

1 House o' Hill Road, Edinburgh

Modern church completed in 1968. A90 at the junction between Telford Road and Queensferry Road. LRT buses 32, 52 and 41a, SMT 43.

Sunday Services 11am

UNITED FREE CHURCH OF SCOTLAND WC

254 BROUGHTON ST MARY'S PARISH CHURCH

NT 256 748

12 Bellevue Crescent, Edinburgh

A burgh church, built to serve Edinburgh's spreading New Town. Designed in 1824 by Thomas Brown as centrepiece of Bellevue Crescent. Neo-classical style, graceful interior with fluted Corinthian columns supporting gallery. Original pulpit. Nathaniel Bryson's stained glass 'Annunciation' is of particular note. Robert Stevenson, lighthouse builder and grandfather of Robert Louis Stevenson, elder 1828-43. Ten to fifteen minutes walk from east end of Princes Street. City buses 8, 9, 19, 39 to Bellevue Crescent.
Sunday Service 10.30am

BROUGHTON ST MARY'S PARISH CHURCH

Open May to September, Wednesday 10am-12 noon, and Monday to Saturday during Edinburgh Festival: 14-19 August 2000, 10-4pm, 13-18 August 2001, 10-4pm and on Edinburgh Doors Open Day in September each year

CHURCH OF SCOTLAND A

255 CANONGATE KIRK

NT 265 738

Canongate, Royal Mile, Edinburgh

This interesting and recently restored 17th-century church was opened in 1691, its plan by James Smith being unique among 17th-century Scottish churches. Restored in 1991, Stewart Tod Partnership. The churchyard contains the remains of many famous Scots, including economist Adam Smith. 'Open Kirk' information sheets in several languages. New Frobenius organ Opus 1000, first in Scotland, now installed. On the Royal Mile opposite Huntly House Museum. LRT bus 1 from Castle. Sunday Services Family Service 10am, Parish Worship 11.15am

CANONGATE KIRK

Open mid June to mid September, Monday to Saturday, 10.30am-4.30pm.
Churchyard open all year

CHURCH OF SCOTLAND A

256 CARRICK KNOWE PARISH CHURCH

NT 203 721

Saughton Road North, Edinburgh

Built in 1953, and described as of Norman design with a strong Scottish character. The last post war church to be built of stone – the external walls of Blaxter dressed stone, and Darney rubble, both from Northumberland Quarries. Furnishings in Scottish Border oak, commissioned by the Church of Scotland as part of their exhibit for the Empire Exhibition in Glasgow of 1938 – beautiful examples of ecclesiastical craftsmanship. Baptismal bowl gifted by Her Majesty Queen Elizabeth The Queen Mother. Tapestry, Dovecot Studios, Edinburgh. Opposite Union Park. Buses 1 and 6. Sunday Service 11am

Open every morning except Wednesday 9.30am-12 noon

CHURCH OF SCOTLAND **A**

257 CLUNY PARISH CHURCH

NT 246 707

Cluny Drive, Edinburgh

Built as St Matthew's 1890 by Hippolyte Blanc, inspired by late 13th-century Gothic. United with South Morningside 1974 which is now the Church Centre. Chancel with Italian marble floor added 1900. Thirteen stained glass windows on side aisles of nave and St Andrew Window in North Transept. East Window: 'Four Apostles', Sir Edward Burne-Jones 1900; West Window: four scenes from the ministry of Jesus, Percy Bacon & Co 1905. Last 'Father Willis' organ installed 1901. Sunday Services summer 9.30am and 11am; autumn, winter, spring 11am and 6.30pm

Open Edinburgh Festival, Tuesdays 17, 24 and 31 August, Wednesdays 18, 25 August and 1 September, Thursdays 19, 26 August, and 2 September, with organ recitals at 12.30pm; or by arrangement, telephone 0131 447 6745 (Church Office, Tuesday to Friday, 9am-12noon)

CHURCH OF SCOTLAND

COLINTON PARISH CHURCH (ST CUTHBERT'S)

258 COLINTON PARISH CHURCH (ST CUTHBERT'S)

NT 216 692

Dell Road, Edinburgh, at foot of Colinton village, beside Water of Leith

The church of 1650 was rebuilt in 1771 and enlarged by David Bryce in 1837. Sydney Mitchell transformed the building in a neo-Byzantine style between 1907 and 1908. The angel decorated, barrel-vaulted nave is supported on sandstone columns. Mitchell adorned the semi-circular apse with murals and fine woodwork including the pulpit, communion table and rood-screen. Both the latter and the marble font are beautifully inscribed. To the south of the church, Page and Park have built new rooms which, through their contemporary design, embrace the wonderful woodland setting. The Offertory House of 1807 heralds this most interesting of buildings with its ancient graveyard set within a bend of the Water of Leith. Sunday Services 9.30 and 11am

Open Monday to Thursday 9am-4pm, Friday 9am-12.30pm. Swing Cafe – open for morning coffee and light lunches, Monday to Friday 10am-2pm. Contact the Church Office, telephone 0131 441 2232

CHURCH OF SCOTLAND **B**

259 CORSTORPHINE OLD PARISH CHURCH

NT 201 728

Kirk Loan, Corstorphine, Edinburgh

Interesting 15th-century church with tower, pre-Reformation relics, Scottish heraldic panels and fine medieval tombs, including those of the founders Sir Adam Forrester, Lord Provost of Edinburgh (died 1405) and Sir John Forrester, Lord Chamberlain of Scotland in the reign of James I. Fine Victorian stained glass. Interesting gravestones in churchyard. Sunday Services 10am and 11.30am

Open Wednesdays 10.30am-12 noon, except December and January. Coincides with opening of Dower House (Corstorphine Trust). Special events during Edinburgh Festival, August

CHURCH OF SCOTLAND (partial) **A**

CORSTORPHINE OLD PARISH CHURCH

260 CORSTORPHINE UNITED FREE CHURCH

NT 199 727

Glebe Road, Corstorphine, Edinburgh

Intimate, secluded, friendly little church. Various ante-rooms and large hall. Good grassed area for barbecues. Off St John's Road opposite Harp Hotel. Sunday Service 10am (this may be altered in 2000)

Open by appointment, telephone the Session Clerk 0131 339 6832

UNITED FREE CHURCH OF SCOTLAND

261 CRAMOND KIRK

NT 190 768

Cramond Glebe Road, Edinburgh

A cruciform kirk of 1656 with 15th-century tower. Interior altered 1701, 1811, large reconstruction 1911 by Donald McArthy and James Mather. Pitch pine hammerbeam roof, oak furnishings, white marble font. Burgerhuys bell 1619. Jock Howieson mosaic. Plan of kirkyard available. Roman settlement remains. Off Whitehouse Road. City buses 40 and 41. Sunday Services 9.30 and 11am, July and August 10am

Open daily during Edinburgh Festival 2-5pm. Cramond Village exhibition at the Maltings

CHURCH OF SCOTLAND WC B

262 DALMENY PARISH CHURCH (ST CUTHBERT'S)

NT 144 775

Main Street, Dalmeny, near South Queensferry

The most complete example of Romanesque architecture in Scotland. Dates from c.1130. Superb medieval south doorway, arch stones elaborately carved with animals, figures and grotesque heads. Historic graveyard. Off A90, follow signs for Dalmeny and South Queensferry. Sunday Service 11.30am

Open April to September, Sunday 2-4.30pm. Other times key from the Post Office or Manse, or 5 Main Street. Parties please telephone in advance Mr W Ross 0131 331 1479

CHURCH OF SCOTLAND WC A

DALMENY PARISH CHURCH (ST CUTHBERT'S)

263 DAVIDSON'S MAINS PARISH CHURCH

NT 207 752

1 Quality Street off Queensferry Road

Originally Cramond Free Church. A small T-plan kirk with flat Gothic windows by David Cousin 1843. The timber bellcote with a prickly slated hat was added to the centre gable in 1866. Interior enlarged to the north in 1970. Major refurbishment to the chancel area in 1999. To the east the little school and house by Robert R Raeburn 1846 were extended with a hall by Auldjo Jamieson & Arnott 1933 maintaining the domestic scale by means of a dormered roof. Fully refurbished in 1995. Essentially a village church. Sunday Services: July to August 10am and 6.30pm, September to June 11am and 6.30pm

Open Tuesday to Thursday 10am-2pm. At other times telephone the Beadle, Mr John Brown 0131 336 2065

CHURCH OF SCOTLAND WC

DAVIDSON'S MAINS PARISH CHURCH

264 DUDDINGSTON KIRK

NT 284 726

Old Church Lane, Duddingston Village, Edinburgh

Attractive twelfth-century church, situated beside Duddingston Loch bird sanctuary, south of Arthur's Seat. Dr Neil's garden lies adjacent in the church glebe land. During the ministry of the Rev John Thomson 1804–1840 (himself a noted landscape painter), the English painter Turner, and the Scottish writer Sir Walter Scott, both visited the manse. City bus 42/46 to Duddingston Road. Sunday Services 10am and 11.30am

Open June to September, Saturday 11am-5pm, Sunday 2-5pm

CHURCH OF SCOTLAND **A**

265 EDINBURGH METHODIST MISSION

NT 248 730

Central Hall, West Tollcross, Edinburgh

1901 by Dunn & Findlay, Edinburgh. Several alterations have been made to suit the changing needs of the congregation. Main hall has a curved and ribbed ceiling on arches rising from Ionic columns. Leaded windows of clear 'cathedral' glass embellished in the style of Glasgow Art Nouveau. Lower landings are decorated with mosaic tiles. A well-known venue for concerts, conferences and meetings. Half mile south of Princes Street west end, via Lothian Road. LRT buses 10, 11, 15-18, 23, 24, 27, 45, 47. Sunday Services 11am

Open Monday to Friday 9am-10pm, Saturday 9am-12.30pm.

Venue for the National Association of Youth Orchestras during Edinburgh Festival, daily performances

METHODIST (lift access via Dunbar Street) WC **B**

266 EDINBURGH SEVENTH-DAY ADVENTIST CHURCH

NT 258 732

3 Bristo Place, Edinburgh

A red sandstone building, by Sydney Mitchell & Wilson 1900, this church is unusual in having its sanctuary on the first floor. The rather handsome staircase is flanked by a tiled wall. The sanctuary interior is well lit by four large windows looking onto the street. Pulpit and furnishings in pine; two galleries, one of which houses a pipe organ by Gray & Davison. Services Saturday 10am (Bible Study) and 11.15am (Worship Service)

Open by arrangement, telephone Pastor David West 0131 667 3881.

Edinburgh Fringe Festival Venue, August

SEVENTH-DAY ADVENTIST

EDINBURGH SEVENTH-DAY ADVENTIST CHURCH

267 CHURCH OF THE GOOD SHEPHERD

NT 228 734

Murrayfield Avenue, Edinburgh

Designed by Sir Robert Lorimer and dedicated in 1899, the building contains some fine examples of stained glass, including a modern window depicting The Good Shepherd. There is a fine Willis organ which was rebuilt in 1967. Sunday Services: 8.30am Holy Communion, 10am Sung Communion, 4th Sundays Matins; Wednesday 11am Holy Communion

Open Edinburgh and Scottish Churches Doors Open Days.

Or by arrangement, telephone James Young 0131337 7615

SCOTTISH EPISCOPAL WC **B**

268 GREENSIDE PARISH CHURCH

NT 263 745

Royal Terrace, Edinburgh

T-plan design by Gillespie Graham 1839 with tower added in 1851, set amidst Playfair's great terraces. Connections with Robert Louis Stevenson who knew it as 'the church on the hill'. Off London Road. Sunday Services 11am and 6.30pm (no evening service July and August)

Open by arrangement, telephone the Session Clerk 0131 669 5324

CHURCH OF SCOTLAND WC **B**

GREENSIDE PARISH CHURCH

GREYFRIARS TOLBOOTH & HIGHLAND KIRK

269 GREYFRIARS TOLBOOTH & HIGHLAND KIRK

NT 256 734

Greyfriars Place, Edinburgh

The first post-Reformation church built in Edinburgh 1620 altered 1722, 1858, 1938 and 1990. The National Covenant signed here in 1638. Fine 19th-century coloured glass by Ballantine, and Peter Collins organ 1990. Historic kirkyard, former Franciscan Friary garden, has fine examples of 17th-century monuments, the Martyrs' Monument, Covenanters' Prison and memorial to Greyfriars Bobby. South end of George IV Bridge. City buses 2, 12, 23, 24, 27, 28, 29, 40, 42, 45, 47. Sunday Services: 11am and 12.30pm (Gaelic), 1st Sunday of month 9.15am Holy Communion, 2nd Sunday of month 6pm Evening Service; Thursdays all year 1.10-1.30pm, Lunchtime Service with organ music

Open April to October, Monday to Friday 10.30am-4.30pm, Saturday 10.30am-2.30pm, November to March Thursday 1.30-3.30pm. Churchyard open all year Monday to Friday 8am-6pm, Saturday and Sunday 10am-4pm.

Special events: year round programme of concerts and lectures (programme available). Tours for groups, telephone Visitors Officer 0131 226 5429

CHURCH OF SCOTLAND (by arrangement) **A**

270 ST PHILIP'S, JOPPA

NT 313 736

Abercorn Terrace, Joppa, Edinburgh

A really striking edifice in the Early Decorated style by J Honeyman 1877. Broach spire 170 ft over a lofty belfry. Aisled nave with entry in the south gable. Inside, a remarkably complete interior. Clustered piers with leafy capitals support the nave arcade, foliated corbels on the clerestorey support the wood-lined tunnel-roof. Fine stained glass windows to aisles. Sunday Service 11am

Open by arrangement, telephone Mr Mitchell 0131 669 3641

CHURCH OF SCOTLAND **B**

271 KIRK O' FIELD PARISH CHURCH

NT 264 732

146 Pleasance, Edinburgh

Built as Charteris Memorial Church in 1912. Late Scots Gothic by James B Dunn. Lorimerian vine enrichment on the vestibule ceiling. Wagon-roofed nave with west gallery. Memorial to the Rev A H Charteris 1908. Mission Hall 1891 dedicated to St Ninian. City buses 2, 2a, 21. Sunday Service 11am

Open the first Saturday in September, 10am-1pm

CHURCH OF SCOTLAND

272 KIRKLISTON PARISH CHURCH

NT 125 744

The Square, Kirkliston

Mainly twelfth-century church. Has two Norman archways, the largest of which was blocked up in the 19th century. Two beautiful modern stained glass windows. In the 19th century a small watchtower was built in the graveyard where the earliest identifiable stone is dated 1529. Sunday Service 11am

Open by arrangement, telephone Mrs Keating 0131 333 3298, or Mrs Brechin 0131 333 3252

CHURCH OF SCOTLAND **A**

KIRKLISTON PARISH CHURCH

273 EBENEZER UNITED FREE CHURCH, LEITH

NT 266 764

31 Bangor Road, Leith

The Ebenezer congregation was founded in 1891. The original church building in Great Junction Street was demolished in 1979 to make way for new housing. The present building, by Sir Frank Mears & Partners, was opened in 1984. Bangor Road runs south from Great Junction Street in Leith. Sunday Services 11am and 6.30pm

Open 1st Saturday of each month, 10am-12 noon

UNITED FREE CHURCH OF SCOTLAND

274 LEITH METHODIST CHURCH

NT 268 761

1 Junction Place, Leith

Built 1932 by Maclennan & Cunningham as 600-seater Central Hall in artificial stone and harl on site of former Secession Church. In Methodist use from 1868. Horizontally subdivided in 1987 with flexible worship area upstairs and community centre downstairs. Off Great Junction Street, behind McKenzie-Millar. Sunday Service 11am

Open weekdays, except Wednesday 10am-2pm, Saturday 10am-12 noon

METHODIST A

275 NORTH LEITH PARISH CHURCH

NT 263 765

Madeira Street, Leith

Georgian building designed by William Burn 1816. Renovated 1950 Ian G Lindsay & Partners, and 1993 Stewart Tod & Partners. Impressive two-storey 'country house' front. Light interior with galleries supported by Ionic columns. Stained glass James Ballantine. Three-manual pipe organ, built by Wadsworth of Manchester 1880. Small graveyard and garden. Off Ferry Road, close to Leith Library. Sunday Services 11am all year, 6.30pm (excluding July and August)

Open Wednesday 9.15am-11.15am.
Or by arrangement, telephone the Church Office 0131 553 7378

CHURCH OF SCOTLAND WC A

NORTH LEITH PARISH CHURCH

276 SOUTH LEITH PARISH CHURCH

NT 271 761

Kirkgate or Constitution Street, Leith

A church was erected in 1483 as a chapel attached to the collegiate Church of Restalrig. The present building dates from 1847, built to a design by Thomas Hamilton. Tower and porch incorporate coats of arms of four successive Scottish monarchs. Fine hammerbeam roof. Italian marble pulpit. Stained glass and emblems of the Trade Guilds. Set in ancient graveyard with interesting monuments. At the foot of Leith Walk. Sunday Services 11am, also 6.30pm October to May, and 9.30am June to July

Open June to August, third Sunday 2-4pm. Also Mondays to Fridays 11am-2pm during August

CHURCH OF SCOTLAND WC A

277 LIBERTON KIRK

NT 275 700

Kirkgate, Liberton, Edinburgh

Sitting in a commanding position overlooking the city, a church was founded here in 1143 by David I, although there is evidence of an earlier church dating from AD 800. The present building was erected in 1815 to replace a former church destroyed by fire. Designed by James Gillespie Graham, it is a rectangular semi-Gothic building with corbelled parapet tower and thin pinnacles. A memorial stained glass window depicting Cornelius, by Ballantine 1905. Three striking contemporary pulpit falls by D Morrison. The kirkyard contains many stones of special interest, including a table-top tomb to a local farmer, its ends carved in relief with agricultural scenes. Sunday services 9.30am and 11am (10.30am, July and August)

Open Monday to Friday 9am–5pm by arrangement, telephone Mrs W Munro 0131 664 3795

CHURCH OF SCOTLAND WC **A**

278 LIBERTON NORTHFIELD PARISH CHURCH

NT 280 699

280 Gilmerton Road, Edinburgh

Built 1869 as a Free Church to designs by J W Smith. North-east tower and broach spire added by Peddie & Kinnear 1873. Interior with raked floor and an ornate arch-braced timber roof springing from short ashlar colonnettes with a variety of leafy capitals. Transepts entered by triple arches expressed on the exterior by triple gables. Virtually unaltered organ by E F Walcker 1903. Sunday Services 11am and 6pm

Open by arrangement, telephone Mr Macleod 0131 467 1898.
Flower Festival weekend, late September

CHURCH OF SCOTLAND WC **B**

279 MAGDALEN CHAPEL

NT 256 734

41 Cowgate, Edinburgh

The chapel was built in 1541 by Michael McQuhane and his wife Janet Rhynd. Its main features are the medieval stained glass roundels. The panelling records gifts from members of the Incorporation of Hammermen who were patrons of the chapel until 1862. The chapel is now owned by the Scottish Reformation Society and serves as its headquarters

Open Monday to Friday 9.30am–4pm. Other times by arrangement.
Parties welcome, telephone Rev A S Horne 0131 220 1450

INTER-DENOMINATIONAL **A**

280 CHRIST CHURCH, MORNINGSIDE

NT 245 719

Holy Corner, Bruntsfield, Edinburgh

French Gothic by Hippolyte Blanc, a member of the congregation, 1876. Gables and flying buttresses face on to the road; the main entrance is beneath the tower. Original murals in chancel and nave roof. Extensive stained glass by Ballantine. Sunday Services: Holy Communion 8am, Eucharist 10am, Evensong (winter) 6.30pm, Compline (summer) 9pm, Monday-Friday: Morning Prayer and Eucharist 8am, Thursday Holy Communion 11am

Open 11am-3pm Wednesday and Friday

SCOTTISH EPISCOPAL WC B

281 ST COLUMBA'S CHURCH, NEWINGTON

NT 265 721

9 Upper Gray Street, Edinburgh

A free treatment of the classic Renaissance style by R M Cameron, 1888. West façade has a large semicircular window and pedimented gable finished with a plain Latin cross. Oblong interior with open timber roof and semicircular end forming a chancel and apse. The chancel arch is a later addition. Notable features include a collection of statues in the window niches. Extensive natural lighting from roof lights and west window. Two-manual pipe organ by Matthew Copley, 1997. Masses: Monday-Friday 9.30am, Saturday 11am, Sunday 11am and 6.30pm

Open after Masses or by arrangement with the Parish Priest, telephone 0131 667 1605

ROMAN CATHOLIC WC WC (toilet adapted in church hall) B

282 NICOLSON SQUARE METHODIST CHURCH

NT 261 732

Nicolson Square, Edinburgh

By Thomas Brown 1815 set diagonally across the corner of the square behind a forecourt. Classical two-storey front based on Adam's design for the west block of the University. Inside, fluted cast-iron columns support the U-plan gallery. Furnishings date from the late 19th century. Organ by Forster & Andrews of Hull. Interesting modern chapel in basement created in 1989 by Nira Ponniah. Small public garden at rear. Sunday Services 11am and 6.30pm

Open Monday to Friday 9.30am-3.30pm. Fringe performances during Edinburgh Festival, and concerts at other times

METHODIST (cafe in basement) WC A

NICOLSON SQUARE METHODIST CHURCH

283 OLD ST PAUL'S

NT 260 737

Jeffrey Street, Edinburgh

The hidden gem of the Old Town. Dating from 1884, Hay & Henderson. Entrances in Carrubber's Close and Jeffrey Street give little clue to the splendour within. Historic Episcopal church with Jacobite past has magnificent furnishings. A living church with daily worship and a prayerful atmosphere. Off Royal Mile. Sunday Services 8am, 10.30am, 5pm Holy Eucharist, 6.30pm Evensong. Daily Worship 12.20pm

Open daily, 9am–6pm

SCOTTISH EPISCOPAL WC **B**

284 PALMERSTON PLACE CHURCH

NT 241 734

Palmerston Place, Edinburgh

Inspiration for Peddie & Kinnear's design of 1875 came from the 17th-century St Sulpice in Paris. A notable feature is the central ceiling motif of a dove within a sunburst. Wells Kennedy organ, 1991, incorporates the oak case of the earlier 1902 organ. Meeting place for the Presbytery of Edinburgh and the Synod of the Scottish Episcopal Church. Sunday Services 11am, 6.30pm (except July and August)

Open by arrangement, telephone 0131 220 1690

CHURCH OF SCOTLAND WC **B**

285 PRIESTFIELD PARISH CHURCH

NT 271 721

Dalkeith Road, Edinburgh

Built in 1877, Sutherland & Walker, in the Italian Lombardic style. Beautiful stained glass windows designed by three young artists in 1921. Other features of note are the handsome pulpit and organ gallery and a most unusual baptismal font. On Dalkeith Road, A68. City buses 2, 14, 21, 33, 2a, c3, c11, 85, 86. Sunday Service 11am

To visit during building reconstruction in 2000, contact Minister 0131 667 5644

CHURCH OF SCOTLAND WC A

286 QUEENSFERRY PARISH CHURCH, SOUTH QUEENSFERRY

NT 130 782

The Loan, South Queensferry, Edinburgh

Well-used and well-loved Burgh Church, built in 1894 and extended in 1993. Tastefully lit and decorated. Of special interest is the display of Banners. Centre of village. Sunday Services 10am and 11.30am

Open all year, Monday to Friday 10-11.30am. Access to historic graveyard (1635-early 1900s) can be arranged in advance, telephone 0131 331 1100

CHURCH OF SCOTLAND

A

QUEENSFERRY PARISH CHURCH, SOUTH QUEENSFERRY

287 PRIORY CHURCH OF ST MARY OF MT CARMEL, SOUTH QUEENSFERRY

NT 129 784

Hopetoun Road, South Queensferry, Edinburgh

Orginally a Carmelite Friary founded in 1330, the church fell into disrepair during the 16th century. It was restored for the use of the Episcopal church in 1890, the work being begun by John Kinross. Later work was carried out in the 1960s by Ian Lindsay. Font cover designed by Lorimer. Fourteenth-century aumbry. Mass dial on outside south wall. Sunday Services 9.30 and 11am; Thursday 10am

Open by arrangement, telephone the Church Office 0131 331 5540. Also open during Ferry Fair Week in August

SCOTTISH EPISCOPAL WC A

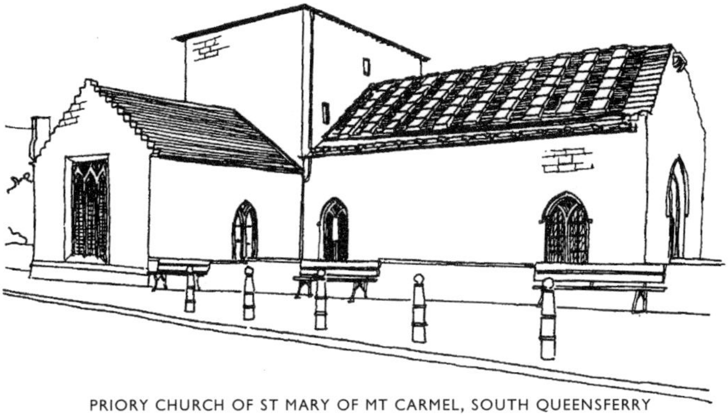

PRIORY CHURCH OF ST MARY OF MT CARMEL, SOUTH QUEENSFERRY

288 RATHO PARISH CHURCH

NT 138 710

Baird Road, Ratho, Edinburgh

An interesting medieval cruciform church, with later aisles. The east aisle dated 1683, the south 1830. To the west of the south aisle is a twelfth-century doorway, partially visible, with scalloped capitals and decorated hoodmould. Twentieth-century refurbishment revealed a Celtic cross stone which might suggest early worship on this site. In the south porch a 13th-century tomb slab belonging to one of the Knights Templar who owned Ratho in the Middle Ages. In the graveyard are several interesting headstones and a panelled coffin formed of a single stone. Sunday Service 11am

Open by arrangement, telephone Mrs Watson 0131 333 1732

CHURCH OF SCOTLAND WC A

289 REID MEMORIAL CHURCH

NT 261 710

West Savile Terrace, Edinburgh

Church, hall and church officer's house by Leslie G Thomson 1933 form an architectural oasis. A lofty, cruciform church with meticulous neo-Perpendicular detail. Stained glass windows by James Ballantine, pipe organ Rushworth & Dreaper, painting on reredos of Last Supper by William R Lawson. Cloister court to rear with carved panel of Christ at the well of Samaria by Alexander Carrick. On local bus routes 24, 38, 38a, 40 and 41.

Sunday Services 10.30am and 1st Sunday of month 6.30pm

Open 16, 18, 23, 25 and 30 August, 1 September, 11am–5pm.

Or by arrangement, telephone Mr Philip 0131 662 1494

CHURCH OF SCOTLAND WC A

290 SACRED HEART CHURCH

NT 252 730

28 Lauriston Place, Edinburgh

Stone fronted building designed by Father Richard Vaughan SJ 1860, altered by Archibald Macpherson 1884. Holyrood Madonna of carved wood, probably late 16th century. Stations of the Cross by Peter Rauth 1874. Conservators presently working on these works of art in stages. Buses to Tollcross. Masses: Saturday Vigil 6.30pm; Sunday 7.45, 10 and 11.15am, and 8pm

Open every day

ROMAN CATHOLIC **B**

291 ST ANDREW'S AND ST GEORGE'S PARISH CHURCH

NT 255 741

George Street, Edinburgh

This beautiful elliptical church with its delicate spire and Adam style plaster ceiling has been described as the architectural gem of the New Town. Built in 1784, designed by Major Andrew Frazer. Two fine 20th-century stained glass windows, one by Douglas Strachan. Light lunches in undercroft. At the east end of George Street and one block north of Princes Street. Sunday Services 9am, 9.45am, 11am. Weekday Prayers 1pm (Communion Service Tuesday)

Open all year, Monday to Friday 10am-3pm. Undercroft open 12-2pm, telephone 0131 225 3847/fax 0131 225 5921. Special Edinburgh Festival programme of events. Week-long Christian Aid book sale in May

CHURCH OF SCOTLAND **A**

292 ST ANDREW'S ORTHODOX CHAPEL

NT 257 728

23a George Square, Edinburgh

Built in 1779 as a one-storey and basement villa across the centre lane on the west side of George Square. Large Venetian window faces onto George Square. Orthodox furnishings and icons. Services: Saturday 6.30pm, Sunday and Feasts 9.00 Matins and 10.30am Liturgy

Open by arrangement, telephone Archimandrite John Maitland-Moir 0131 667 0372

ORTHODOX **A**

293 ST BARNABAS EPISCOPAL CHURCH

NT 290 693

4 Moredun Park View, Edinburgh

Small modern church in housing scheme 1950. Altered in 1969. St Barnabas tapestry. Moredun Scheme is between A7 and A772 on south side of city. Sunday Service 10.30am Eucharist, Tuesday 6.30pm Prayer Group

Open Wednesday mornings

SCOTTISH EPISCOPAL **A**

ST BENNET'S

294 ST BENNET'S

NT 248 717

42 Greenhill Gardens, Church Hill, Edinburgh

The chapel attached to the home of the Archbishops of St Andrews and Edinburgh. A charming Byzantine church built by R Weir Schultz 1907, under the will of the third Marquess of Bute, to take the outstanding Italianate classical interior designed by William Frame in 1889 for the chapel at House of Falkland. Porch by Reginald Fairlie 1934. There are examples of stained glass windows by Gabriel Loire of Chartres dating from the 1970s; other windows were installed in 1999 commemorating the 1600th anniversary of St Ninian and the 1400th anniversary of St Columba, as well as a millennium window. The chapel contains memorabilia of the Archbishops since the restoration of the hierarchy. Buses 11, 15, 16, 17 and 23 to Church Hill. Service times as announced

Open weekdays 9am–5pm

ROMAN CATHOLIC ♿ WC **A**

295 ST CHRISTOPHER'S

NT 292 748

Craigentinny Road, Edinburgh

Built by James McLachlan in 1934–8, the foundation stone was laid by John Buchan, author of *The Thirty Nine Steps*. The exterior is of variegated red brick with round arched windows and tiled roof. The interior is a darker plum-coloured brick with a low wagon roof and segmental arches. The organ came from St Catherine's Grange church and was rebuilt with all speaking pipes in 1975. There are two stained glass windows by Sax Shaw and one by George Reid. Sunday Service 10.30am. Communion on last Sunday in January, March and June to October

Open Saturday 10am–12 noon Tuesdays and Saturdays, and by arrangement, telephone Mr R Mutch 0131 669 6735

CHURCH OF SCOTLAND WC

ST CHRISTOPHER'S

296 ST COLUMBA'S BY THE CASTLE

NT 254 735

Johnston Terrace, Edinburgh

By John Henderson 1847 a single-nave building of six bays under a pitch-slated roof with a battlemented tower. Four-bay aisleless nave and one-bay chancel; the sixth bay forms the entrance and vestibule to the west end. Triple arcading at the west wall, originally supporting a gallery, now subsumed into a suite of rooms served by a new staircase. Stone altar, font and pulpit. Gifted oak panelling on lower east wall c1914. The blocked east window has been filled with a mural 'Christ Enthroned' by John Busby 1962. Pipe organ, James Conacher & Sons 1880, rebuilt in 1965 by N P Mander and relocated in 1998 by Lightoller. Church hall, originally a school, below the church. Redevelopment and refurbishment, Simpson & Brown 1998. Sunday Service Eucharist 10am and at other times as announced

Open by arrangement, telephone the Rector 0131 228 6470

SCOTTISH EPISCOPAL **B**

297 ST CUTHBERT'S PARISH CHURCH

NT 248 736

Lothian Road, Edinburgh

The present church, the seventh on the site, is over 100 years old, 1894 by Hippolyte Blanc, retaining the 1790 spire. Altered in 1990 Stewart Tod. Tradition has it that St Cuthbert had a cell church here. If so, Christian worship has taken place here for 1300 years. Furnishings include scroll-topped and Renaissance style stalls, marble communion table, murals and stained glass window by Tiffany. One of the finest romantic organs in Scotland, rebuilt 1997. Display of life of St Cuthbert in vestibule. Interesting graveyard, with many famous names, is an oasis in the centre of the city. Buses to Princes Street and Lothian Road. Sunday Services 9.30am, 11am, 6.30pm (Service of Healing)

Open mid May to mid September, Monday to Friday 10am-4pm, Saturday 10am-12 noon

CHURCH OF SCOTLAND WC **A**

298 ST GEORGE'S WEST CHURCH

NT 245 736

Shandwick Place, Edinburgh

Designed by David Bryce 1869 with campanile by Sir R Rowand Anderson 1881. Special features are the rose window and the pulpit. Woodwork excellent, mainly original. The organ by Thomas Lewis 1897. The first organist was Alfred Hollins, famous blind organist and composer (1897-1942). City Centre West End. Sunday Services 11am and 7pm; Prayers Monday to Friday 1pm

Busy Church Centre and cafe open Monday to Friday 10am-3.30pm, Saturday 10.30am-12.30pm, all year

CHURCH OF SCOTLAND WC **B**

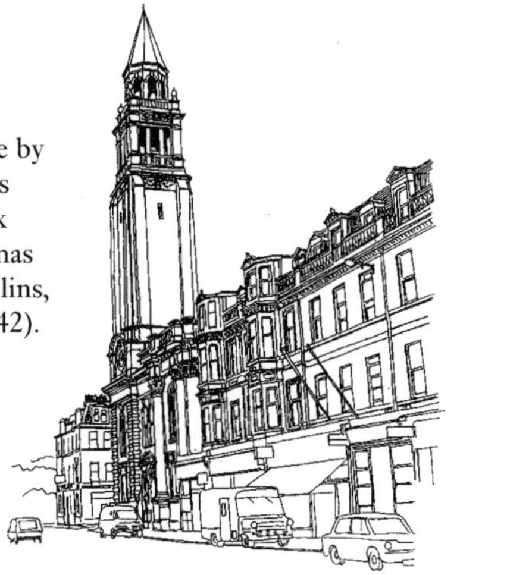

ST GEORGE'S WEST CHURCH

299 ST GILES' CATHEDRAL

NT 257 736

High Street, Edinburgh

St Giles was founded in the 1100s and mostly rebuilt during the 15th and 16th centuries. It was the church of John Knox during the Reformation and played an important part in the history of that time. The church contains fine examples of late medieval architecture and a wide range of traditional and modern stained glass and memorials. The magnificent Rieger organ was installed in 1992. The Thistle Chapel, designed by Robert Lorimer for the Order of the Thistle, was added in 1911. Sunday Services 8, 10, 11.30am and 6, 8pm

Open Easter to mid September, Monday to Friday 9am-7pm, Saturday 9am-5pm, Sunday 1pm-5pm. Mid September to Easter, Monday to Saturday 9am-5pm, Sunday 1pm-5pm

CHURCH OF SCOTLAND WC **A**

300 ST JOHN THE EVANGELIST

NT 247 736

Princes Street, Edinburgh

Designed by William Burn 1817. Recently cleaned and restored. Notably good stained glass. Sir Walter Scott's mother, Anne Rutherford and Sir Henry Raeburn RA are buried in Dormitory Garden. Undercroft includes a cafe restaurant, Christian bookshop (multi-denominational), One World Shop, and Peace and Justice Centre. At the foot of Lothian Road and opposite the Caledonian Hotel. Sunday Services 8am Holy Communion, 9.45am Sung Eucharist, 11.15am Choral Matins, 6pm Choral Evensong, 8pm Eucharist with music from Taizé. Further details on answering machine (0131 229 7565). Weekday Service 1pm, Communion Service Wednesday 11am

Open daily in working hours

SCOTTISH EPISCOPAL (Cornerstone Cafe) WC **A**

ST JOHN THE EVANGELIST

301 ST MARGARET'S CHAPEL

NT 253 735

Edinburgh Castle, Edinburgh

The oldest surviving structure in the castle built by King David I (1124–53). Interior divided into two by a fine arch decorated with chevron ornament. Semi-circular east chancel. Copy of the Gospel Book owned by St Margaret to whom the chapel was dedicated by her son, David I. Stained glass windows depicting St Andrew, St Ninian, St Columba and St Margaret by Douglas Strachan c.1930. Magnificent views from castle ramparts. Other attractions within the castle (Historic Scotland) include 'Honours of the Kingdom' exhibition, now with the Stone of Destiny

Open summer 9.30am–6pm, winter 9.30am–5pm (last ticket sold 45 minutes before closing)

NON-DENOMINATIONAL WC **A**

302 ST MARGARET'S PARISH CHURCH

NT 284 745

27 Restalrig Road South, Edinburgh

Rebuilt by William Burn 1836 on the foundations of the previous 15th-century church. The flowing window tracery follows the original design, stained glass by William Wilson 1966. Attached to the south-west corner is the hexagonal St Triduana's Chapel, once the lower storey of a two-tier chapel built for James III about 1477. The vault springs from a central pier, its six shafts topped by capitals with crinkly foliage. Notable 17th and 18th-century monuments in the graveyard. Sunday Service 10.30am

Open Monday to Friday 11am–1pm or by arrangement, Mr Skakle 0131 661 2510, or the church office 0131 554 7400.

See web page at: www.st-margarets.freeserve.co.uk

CHURCH OF SCOTLAND WC **A**

ST MARGARET'S PARISH CHURCH

303 ST MARY'S CATHEDRAL

NT 259 743

Broughton Street, Edinburgh

There has been a church on the site since 1814. However, all that remains of the original, designed by James Gillespie Graham, is the neo-Gothic façade. Following a fire in 1892 it was decided to enlarge the church. This led to the addition of the present sanctuary and side aisles. In 1932 it was decided to heighten the roof by 20 feet. The interior contains the superb baldacchino designed in 1928 by Reginald Fairlie. It stands over the High Altar whose tabernacle was designed by Betty Koster and cast by George Mancini.

Sunday Services: 7.30am, 9.30am and 11.30am; Saturday 10am, 12.45pm and 6pm Vigil; Monday to Friday 7.30am and 10am, 12.45pm. 7.30pm Mass on Sunday

Open daily 7am-6pm (later on Saturday/Sunday)

ROMAN CATHOLIC A

ST MARY'S CATHEDRAL, EDINBURGH

304 ST MARY'S EPISCOPAL CATHEDRAL

NT 242 735

Palmerston Place, Edinburgh

Built in 1879 to the award-winning design of Sir Gilbert Scott, this neo-Gothic building reflects the spirit of that age: it is massive, its three spines lend distinction the Edinburgh skyline and it rejoices in a wealth of ornate and symbolic detail, the evidence of a flourishing craftsmanship. Of particular note are the pelican lectern, Lorimer's rood and the J Oldrid Scott's reredos of the high altar, featuring the Scottish saints Columba and Margaret. In the grounds stand the 17-century Old Coates House (now the Theological Institute of the Scottish Episcopal Church) and the Song School, famous for its recently restored murals, painted by Phoebe Anna Traquair 1888-92 on the theme of 'Benedicite omnia opera'. The Cathedral maintains an internationally renowned choir, which sings on Sundays and for Evensong on weekdays. During holiday periods the Cathedral welcomes visiting choirs. The Cathedral is open daily; the Song School may be viewed by appointment. Services; for full details contact the Cathedral answering machine on 0131 225 6293

Open daily 7.30am-6pm (5pm Saturday).

SCOTTISH EPISCOPAL WC A

305 ST MARY, STAR OF THE SEA, LEITH

NT 272 762

106 Constitution Street, Edinburgh

E W Pugin and Joseph A Hansom's church 1854 had no chancel, no north aisle and was orientated to the west. The north aisle was added in 1900 and the chancel in 1912 when the church was turned round and the present west entrance made. Inside the church has simple pointed arcades and a high braced collar roof. Access from Constitution Street or New Kirkgate.

Services: Monday to Friday 9am and 12.15pm; Saturday 10am and Vigil Mass 6pm; Sunday 10am and 11.30am

Open Monday to Friday 9am-11am, Saturday 9am-11.30am, Sunday 9am-12.30pm

ROMAN CATHOLIC ♿ 👂 WC **B**

306 ST MICHAEL'S CHURCH

NT 234 722

1 Slateford Road, Edinburgh

One of architect John Honeyman's most notable buildings, completed 1883. Square 41m tower and longest aisle in the city. Sanctuary illuminated by clerestoried nave beneath dark-timbered roof. Unusual reredos bearing Ten Commandments, Beatitudes and the Creed. Pulpit and lectern decorated with biblical fruits by Gertrude Hope. Organ by Brindley and Foster 1895. Stained glass, including work by Douglas Strachan (1895-1925). The building was extensively restored in 1998 and provides for a variety of worship, cultural and outreach activities. Bus routes 4, 28, 34 and 44. Sunday Services 11am, June to August 10am and 11am. Occasional Evening Services

Open Edinburgh Doors Open Day, and by arrangement, telephone 0131 337 5646

CHURCH OF SCOTLAND

♿ 👂 WC

ST MICHAEL'S CHURCH

307 ST MICHAEL'S AND ALL SAINTS' CHURCH

NT 251 729

Brougham Street, Edinburgh

A shrine of the Anglo-Catholic movement in Scotland. The church was mostly built in 1867 but the west end not completed until 1876 and the Lady Chapel added in 1897, all to designs by Sir R Rowand Anderson. Austere Gothic externally but the interior is a magnificently spacious setting for a sumptuous display of furnishings, including an elaborate Spanish pulpit of c.1600, carved and painted altarpieces by William Burges (1867) and Hamilton More-Nisbet (1901), and a huge high altar reredos, again carved and painted, by C E Kempe (1889). Extensive collection of stained glass with windows by Wailes, Clayton & Bell, Kempe, and Sir Ninian Comper. Sunday Services 8am Low Mass, 11am High Mass, 6.30pm Choral Evensong and Benediction; Tuesday 8am Low Mass; Wednesday 12.30pm Low Mass; Thursday 6pm Low Mass; Friday 10.30am Low Mass; Saturday 12.30pm Low Mass

Open all year Wednesday 12 noon-2.30pm, Friday 10am-2pm, Saturdays during Edinburgh Festival, and by arrangement, telephone the Rector 0131 229 6368

SCOTTISH EPISCOPAL (Saturdays during Edinburgh Festival) **A**

308 ST STEPHEN'S CENTRE

NT 250 746

St Vincent Street, Edinburgh

Built 1828 as St Stephen's Church, this is the ecclesiastical masterpiece of W H Playfair. Severe Greek detail but Baroque in spirit, with a large tower dominating the vista from Queen Street downhill through the Northern New Town. Interior recast in 1956 when a floor was inserted at the level of the former gallery whose cast iron Egyptian columns were retained. No Services

Open Monday-Friday 9am-9pm,
telephone Development Officer, David Nicholson 0131 556 2661

CHURCH OF SCOTLAND

309 STOCKBRIDGE PARISH CHURCH

NT 247 748

Saxe Coburg Street, Edinburgh

Classical church by James Milne 1823 with an Ionic pilastered and pedimented front and a small domed steeple. The interior contains the original U-plan gallery. In 1888 Hardy & Wight added the apse which was decorated in 1987 with war memorial murals by the German artist Reinhardt Behrens depicting the Lothian coastline 'at the going down of the sun and in the morning ....' Historic two-manual organ by August Gern installed 1995.

Sunday Service 11am, Wednesday Service 1pm

Telephone the Administrator, Graham Donaldson 0131 332 0122

CHURCH OF SCOTLAND **A/B**

STOCKBRIDGE PARISH CHURCH

310 VIEWFORTH ST DAVID AND ST OSWALD

NT 244 725

104 Gilmore Place, Edinburgh

Originally a Free Church. Built by Pilkington and Bell 1871 to an orthodox four-square plan with restrained detail. The massive upward growth contrasts with the fragile shafted geometric window in the central gable. Octagonal belfry, truncated in 1976. Powerful interior, rebuilt after a fire in 1898, with very thin cast-iron columns supporting huge transverse beams over the side galleries. Organ reconstructed 1976 from two instruments by Blackett & Howden 1899 and Forster & Andrews 1904. Sunday Service 10.30am. Shared by Associated Presbyterian congregation. Sunday Services 12 noon, Wednesday 7pm

Telephone the Church Administrator 0131 229 1917

CHURCH OF SCOTLAND WC **B**

WARDIE PARISH CHURCH

311 WARDIE PARISH CHURCH

NT 246 768

Primrose Bank Road, Trinity

A jolly Gothic church with Francophile detail, by John McLachlan 1892. Distinctive silhouette with central lantern and conical pinnacles. Inside, a clear-span tunnel roof. A complete and perfect set of Gothic oak furnishings by Scott Morton & Co 1935 including the organ case (organ by Rushworth & Dreaper). Sunday Service 11am, 10.30am, July and August

Open Tuesday, Thursday and Friday 9am-12 noon.

Telephone the Church Office 0131 551 3847

CHURCH OF SCOTLAND ♿ 👂 WC

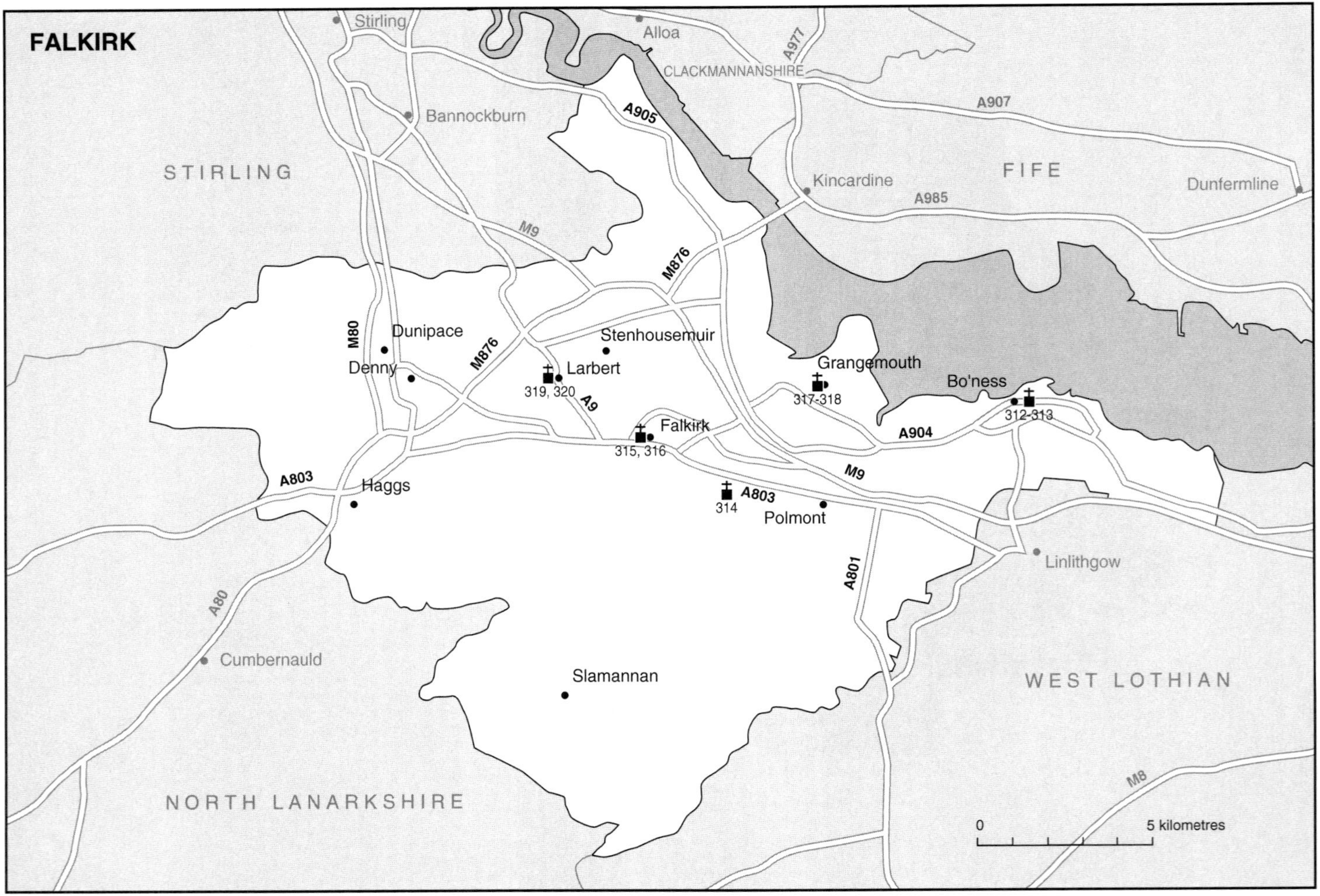
FALKIRK
Stirling
Alloa
A977
CLACKMANNANSHIRE
A907
Bannockburn
A905
STIRLING
Kincardine
FIFE
Dunfermline
A985
M9
M876
M80
Dunipace
Stenhousemuir
M876
Grangemouth
Denny
Larbert
319, 320
A9
317-318
Bo'ness
312-313
Falkirk
315, 316
A904
M9
A803
Haggs
314
A803
Polmont
A801
Linlithgow
A80
Cumbernauld
Slamannan
WEST LOTHIAN
NORTH LANARKSHIRE
M8
0
5 kilometres

FALKIRK

Local Representative: Mr Alan Naylor, Candiehill, Candie, Avonbridge, Falkirk (*telephone* 01324 861583)

312 ST CATHERINE'S CHURCH, BO'NESS

NS 999 812

Cadzow Crescent, Bo'ness

The congregation was formed in 1888 and moved to the present building in 1921. The hall was added in 1928. The sanctuary windows depict the children of the Bible. Organ by Miller of Dundee. Off Dean Road, adjacent to Douglas Park. Services: Sunday 11.30am Sung Eucharist; Wednesday 10.15 Said Eucharist

Open by arrangement, telephone the Rector 01324 482438

SCOTTISH EPISCOPAL ♿ WC

313 CARRIDEN PARISH CHURCH, BO'NESS

NT 019 812

Carriden Brae, Carriden, Bo'ness

The first church of Carriden was consecrated in 1243 by Bishop David de Bernam, although it is believed that the parish goes back to the time of St Ninian, c. AD 396. The present church is the third. Designed by P MacGregor Chalmers, 1909, in simple Romanesque style with a west tower and stone spire. The bell was cast in Rotterdam, Peter Oostens 1674. Inside a wooden sailing ship 'The Ranger' hangs from the barrel shaped pitch pine roof. Six-bay nave. Baptistry chapel with a wall painting thought to be of the Scottish School. Sounding board on north wall, 1655. A fine stone arcaded baptismal font, two-manual pipe organ moved from the John Knox Church, Gorbals after the blitz of 1941. Sunday Service 11.15am

Open Tuesday 9am-12 noon

CHURCH OF SCOTLAND ♿ 👂 WC **B**

314 BRIGHTONS PARISH CHURCH

NS 928 778

Main Street, Brightons

Built in 1847. Local quarry owner Alexander Lawrie gifted the stone to build the church to a design by Brown & Carrick of Glasgow. T-plan church with small steeple with bell. Side galleries added in 1893. Chancel area modernised 1935. Windows 1993 by Ruth Golliwaws of New Orleans, USA. B805, four miles south of Falkirk; or B810, half mile from Polmont Station. Sunday Services 11am and 1st Sunday, September to May, 6pm

Open for prayer, September to June, Thursday 10am-12 noon

CHURCH OF SCOTLAND ♿ 👂 WC

315 FALKIRK FREE CHURCH

Beaumont Drive, Newcarron, Falkirk

The present congregation began in 1991 and moved into its new building in 1998. The building reflects modern architecture but maintains a spiritual and practical ambience. An interdenominational conference in two parts is planned for 2000: 'The Church in the Third Millennium' and 'The Church - Her Ultimate Experience.' Sunday Services 11am and 6.30pm, Prayers: Wednesday and Saturday 7.30pm, Saturday 7pm

Open by arrangement, telephone The Rev R MacLeod 01324 631008

FREE CHURCH OF SCOTLAND

316 FALKIRK OLD AND ST MODAN'S PARISH CHURCH

NS 887 800

Manse Place, off High Street, Falkirk

Dating from 1811, although twelfth-century pillars remain in the vestibule. There has been a Christian church on this site for 1200; local legend links the earliest foundation with the Celtic St Modan in the sixth century. The square tower dates from the 16th century, and the gable marks of the earlier nave and chancel are visible. Above the tower an 18th-century bell tower with 13 bells. Two late 19th-century stained glass windows; pipe organ of same period. Twelfth-century sanctuary cross. Major refurbishment in the 1960s. Sunday Services: winter 11.15am and 6.30pm, summer 9.30 and 11.15am

Open Monday to Friday 12 noon-2pm. Lunches served

CHURCH OF SCOTLAND **B**

317 ST MARY'S CHURCH, GRANGEMOUTH

NS 932 818

Ronaldshay Crescent, Grangemouth

The present church was built in 1938 to replace a 'tin kirk' of 1901; the architect was Maxton Craig of Edinburgh. A small hall was added in 1978. The west window, 1962, depicts the industries of Grangemouth. Altar cross, candlesticks and vases by Edward Spencer, the Artificers' Guild, his last work. Adjacent to Zetland Park in the centre of the town. Services: Sunday 8.30am Said Eucharist, 10am Sung Eucharist; Tuesday 10am Said Eucharist

Open 1st Saturday of month, 12 noon-2pm.

Or by arrangement, telephone the Rector 01324 482438

SCOTTISH EPISCOPAL

318 GRANGEMOUTH: ZETLAND CHURCH

NS 931 818

Ronaldshay Crescent, Grangemouth

Building by Wilson & Tait completed 1911. Cruciform in plan with a south aisle and north and south transepts. Four arches support a timber barrel roof and there is a small gallery at the end of the nave. Second World War memorial stained glass window by Douglas Hamilton, Glasgow, with four lights depicting Peace, Victory, Willingness to Lay Down Life and The Glory of the King of Heaven. Willis organ of 1890 installed 1983 and Memorial Chapel furnished in the south transept 1990 used for private prayer and small services. Grounds have won Falkirk Council's Church Gardens award for past six years. Sunday Services 11.15am, and 6.15pm last Sunday of month October to November, January to March

Open Wednesday mornings, 9.30-11.30am, March to October

CHURCH OF SCOTLAND ♿ WC B

319 LARBERT OLD CHURCH

NS 856 822

Denny Road, Larbert

LARBERT OLD CHURCH

Near site of earlier chapel – twelfth-century dependency of Eccles Kirkton of St Ninian's and Cambuskenneth Abbey. The present church was built in 1820, architect David Hamilton replacing a pre-Reformation church which was located within the adjacent churchyard. The chancel was added in 1911. The fine oak panelling dates from 1887. There are good memorial windows including Gordon Webster and Stephen Adam. The apsidal triptych of the Transfiguration is believed to be the only example of Frank Howard's work (1805-66) in Scotland and was executed by Edmundson of Manchester. There are some interesting memorial plaques. The graveyard includes the burial place of James Bruce, Abyssinian explorer, and Master Robert Bruce, the post-Reformation divine, as well as the early partners of the Carron Company. The bell tower has a carillon of chimes dating from 1985. Sunday Services 11.30am and 6.30pm

Open Saturdays in August 2000 2pm-5pm

CHURCH OF SCOTLAND ♿

320 OUR LADY OF LOURDES AND ST BERNADETTE, LARBERT

NS 865 829

323 Main Street, Larbert

The present building designed by Reginald Fairlie, dating from 1930s, was intended to be a hall but used for worship until a permanent church could be built. When this plan was abandoned in the 1950s the building was adapted to become exclusively the place of worship. Entrance porch by Sam Sweeney added 1995. Marian Grotto in grounds 1983 to mark the Golden Jubilee, recently embellished and decorated by local talent from within the church community. Sunday Services 11.30am and 6.30pm Mass

Open 9am-dusk, or apply to Presbytery adjacent to Church

ROMAN CATHOLIC ♿

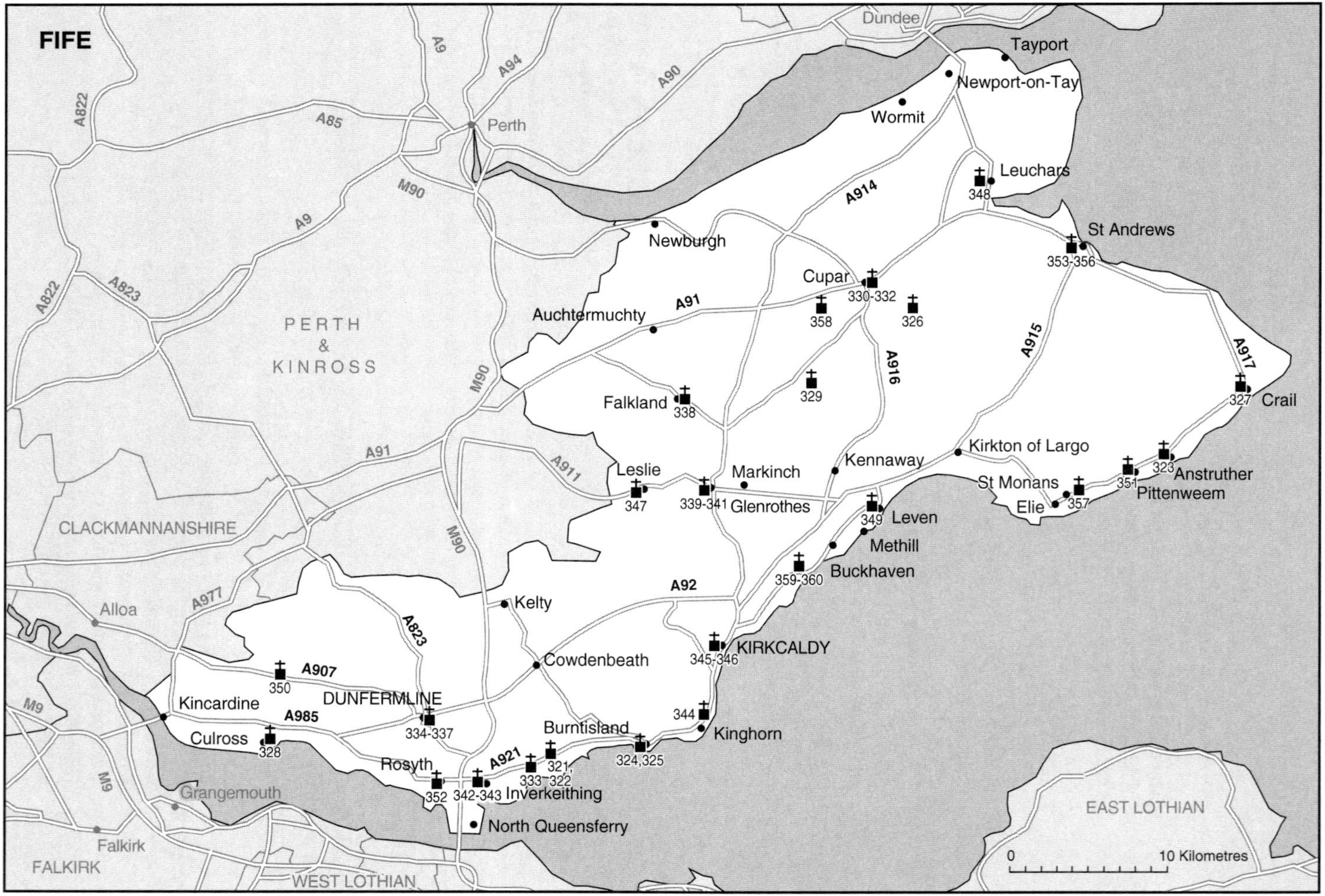
FIFE
Dundee
Tayport
Newport-on-Tay
Wormit
Perth
A9
A94
A90
A822
A85
M90
Leuchars
348
A914
St Andrews
Newburgh
353-356
Cupar
330-332
A823
A91
358
326
Auchtermuchty
PERTH
&
KINROSS
A916
A915
A917
329
Falkland
338
327
Crail
A91
Kirkton of Largo
Kennaway
A911
Leslie
Markinch
323
Anstruther
351
St Monans
Pittenweem
347
339-341
Glenrothes
357
Elie
349
Leven
CLACKMANNANSHIRE
Methill
M90
359-360
Buckhaven
A92
Alloa
Kelty
A977
A823
KIRKCALDY
345-346
Cowdenbeath
350
A907
DUNFERMLINE
M9
Kincardine
A985
344
334-337
Burntisland
Kinghorn
Culross
324,325
328
Rosyth
A921
321,
333-322
M9
Grangemouth
352
342-343
Inverkeithing
EAST LOTHIAN
North Queensferry
Falkirk
0
10 Kilometres
FALKIRK
WEST LOTHIAN

FIFE

Local Representative: The Rev Malcolm Trew, 155 Park Road West, Rosyth
e-mail: malcolm.trew@virgin.net

321 ST COLUMBA'S CHURCH, ABERDOUR

NT 186 851

Inverkeithing Road, Aberdour

Built in 1843 for the Earl of Moray as a private chapel for his employees in Aberdour. It was transferred to the Scottish Episcopal Church in 1918. A cruciform plan, tall and light with lancet windows. The west window blocked off by the addition of a balcony, which has recently been enclosed. A921 from Dalgety Bay, in the village on the right. Linked with St Peter's, Inverkeithing and St Serf's, Burntisland. Sunday Service 11am

Open by arrangement, telephone Mrs Clifford 01383 860521, or Mrs Greenwood 01383 860408

SCOTTISH EPISCOPAL WC

322 ST FILLAN'S, ABERDOUR

NT 193 855

Hawkcraig Road, Aberdour

One of the finest examples of Norman architecture in Scotland, this 'miniature Cathedral' sits in its own graveyard overlooking Aberdour harbour. The early church, standing in 1123, consisted of the nave and chancel, lit by deep splayed windows which still exist. The church was enlarged in the 15th century by the addition of a side aisle, and in the 17th by the small transeptual aisle, now used by the choir. The church fell into disrepair in the 18th century and was restored in 1925. 'Even to enter St Fillan's is to worship.' Sunday Service September-May 10.30am, June-August 10am

Open every day

CHURCH OF SCOTLAND

BURNTISLAND PARISH CHURCH

323 ANSTRUTHER PARISH CHURCH

NO 567 037

Burial Brae (off Crail Road), Anstruther

James Melville (brother of Andrew, the leading Covenanter) inspired the purchase of land in 1590 for a new church, but he was exiled by James VI and the church was not built until 1634. Described in 1837 as 'one of the most elegant country churches anywhere to be seen'. Tahitian Princess buried outside the south wall. Many interesting features. Anstruther is the birthplace of Thomas Chalmers. A917 Crail, 400 yards east of St Andrews cross road. Bus services, Fife Scottish 95 and 57, Minibus M1 and M611, Stagecoach x23. Sunday Service 11am, Healing Service second Sunday of month 2pm

Open April to September, Tuesday 2-3pm, Thursday 11am-12 noon.

All year coffee morning, Tuesday 10am-12 noon in Hew Scott Hall (converted 13th-century West Anstruther Church)

CHURCH OF SCOTLAND **B**

324 BURNTISLAND PARISH CHURCH

NT 234 857

East Leven Street, Burntisland

Built in 1592 to an unusual square plan. The first post-Reformation church built in Scotland, still in use. The General Assembly of the Church of Scotland met in Burntisland in 1601 in the presence of James VI when a new translation of the Bible was approved. Information available on the churchyard. Extensive refurbishment completed in 1999. Sunday Services 11am and 6.30pm

Open June to August, 2-4pm. Other times key from tourist office, or Curator, telephone 01592 873275

CHURCH OF SCOTLAND WC **A**

325 ST SERF'S CHURCH, BURNTISLAND

NT 230 864

Ferguson Place x Cromwell Road, Burntisland

Built in 1905 to a design by Truro Cathedral architect J L Pearson, the stone is from the local Grange quarry. The chancel is divided from the nave by a fine Gothic arch. The east end of the chancel is semi-octagonal behind a tri-form arch springing from slender columns, surmounted by a Gothic arch. Linked with St Peter's, Inverkeithing and St Columba's, Aberdour. Sunday Service 9.30am; Tuesday 11am

Open by arrangement, telephone Mrs M McQuarrie 01592 873117

SCOTTISH EPISCOPAL WC **B**

326 CERES CHURCH

NO 399 117

Kirk Brae, Ceres

Built 1806 to a design by Alexander Leslie, with a battlemented tower, its spire added in 1852, the building has the original box pews and long communion tables running the full length of the church. Crenellated tower with obelisk corner pinnacles. The 17th-century stone-slated Lindsay vault in the kirkyard was possibly attached to the medieval church. Linked with Springfield Church. Sunday Service 11.00am

Open on Doors Open Day, September, and by arrangement, telephone the Minister 01334 828233

CHURCH OF SCOTLAND **B**

CERES CHURCH

327 CRAIL PARISH CHURCH

NO 613 080

Marketgate, Crail

Built in 1243 with alterations 1526, 1796. Restored 1963 Judith Campbell. Pictish cross slab, 17th-century carving. Pipe organ 1936, Harrison & Harrison. Graveyard. Hourly bus service Dundee–Leven. Sunday Services 11.15am, also June to late August 9.30am

Open 14 June to 28 August, Monday to Saturday 2-4pm

CHURCH OF SCOTLAND **A**

328 CULROSS ABBEY

NS 989 863

Kirk Street, Culross

Built on the site of a Celtic Christian Culdee church. Abbey founded in 1217 by Malcolm, seventh Earl of Fife; dedicated to St Mary and St Serf. Much of the original building remains, although a great deal of it is in ruins. The monks' choir forms the present parish church, in continuous use since 1633. Modernised in 1824 and restored in 1905 by Sir R Rowand Anderson. Many features of interest. Situated in 16th-century small town of Culross. Seven and a half miles west of Dunfermline. Sunday Service 11.30am

Open daily, summer 10am-dusk, winter 10am-4pm

CHURCH OF SCOTLAND **A**

CULTS KIRK

329 CULTS KIRK

NO 347 099

Kirkton of Cults, south side of A914, ½ mile from Pitlessie, 4 miles SW of Cupar

A place of worship since the 12th century, the present kirk built 1793. Bell inscribed *John Meikle, Edinburg, fecit for the Kirk of Cults, 1699.* Lepers window, Laird's Pew, Memorials, one by Chantry of Sir David Wilkie RA, our most famous son of the manse, one by Samuel Joseph of his father and mother. Wilkie Hall, Pitlessie village, collection of etchings and engravings by Wilkie, viewing by appointment 01337 830491. Flower Festival in Kirk 24-25 June 2000. Sunday Service 11.30am until July 2000, then 10am

Open 8am-8pm

CHURCH OF SCOTLAND B

330 CUPAR OLD AND ST MICHAEL OF TARVIT PARISH CHURCH

NO 380 146

Kirkgate, Cupar

The tower dates from 1415; its spire and belfry (containing two bells 1485 and 1689) were added in 1620 and the four-face clock in 1910. The church itself was rebuilt in 1785. Inside are war memorials on the east and south walls and the guidon of the Fife and Forfar Yeomanry. A recess in the west wall contains the 15th-century recumbent figure of a knight ('Muckle Fernie'). Adjacent graveyard contains hand of David Hackston, a Covenanter from Rathillet. Sunday Services 11am, and 6.30pm September to April

Open Saturdays 10am-12pm, June-August,
or by appointment 01334 653036

CHURCH OF SCOTLAND WC A

CUPAR OLD AND ST MICHAEL OF TARVIT PARISH CHURCH

331 ST JAMES THE GREAT CHURCH, CUPAR

NO 376 146

St Catherine Street, Cupar

Built in 1866 to a design by Sir R Rowand Anderson. Fine choir screen, reredos and panelling, Lorimer 1920. Town centre, A91 Stirling to St Andrews. By rail from Edinburgh and Dundee. By coach from Kirkcaldy, Dundee, St Andrews and Stirling. Services Sunday 8am and 11am; Wednesday 10am

Open weekdays, 10am-3pm

SCOTTISH EPISCOPAL WC **B**

332 ST JOHN'S PARISH CHURCH, CUPAR

NO 373 147

Bonnygate, Cupar

The 150 ft spire with belfry dominates the view of Cupar from the many approaches. Built 1878, Campbell Douglas & Sellars, Glasgow when first Cupar Free Church became too small. Galleried interior. Set on a raised area in stepped gardens. Sunday Service 11am. Mid-week half hour service every Wednesday 9.30am

Open all year, Wednesday 9.30am-11.30am. Other times by arrangement 01334 655851

CHURCH OF SCOTLAND WC **B**

333 DALGETY PARISH CHURCH, DALGETY BAY

NT 155 836

Regents Way, Dalgety Bay

A hall church designed by Marcus Johnston, built in 1981. Worship area and suite of halls which are used by congregation and local community groups. War memorial in grounds. Sunday Services 9.30am and 11.30am, all year; also second Sunday 6.30pm, October to March

Open by arrangement, telephone Mr W Wood, 13 Doune Park, Dalgety Bay 0138 822 529

CHURCH OF SCOTLAND

334 DUNFERMLINE ABBEY

NT 090 873

St Margaret Street, Dunfermline

Founded in 1072. Consists today of the nave of medieval monastic church (1150) and the modern parish church (1821) erected over foundations of original Choir. Burial place of King Robert the Bruce and numerous other Scottish royals including Malcolm III (Canmore) and his queen St Margaret of Scotland. Exquisitely carved pulpit by William Paterson, Edinburgh 1890. Fine pipe organ of 1882, rebuilt Walker in 1986. Signposted from outskirts of city. Sunday Services 9.30am and 11am

Open April to October, Monday to Saturday 10am-4.30pm, and Sunday 2-4.30pm. Abbey shop also open as above. Groups by arrangement, telephone Mr F Tait 01383 872242

CHURCH OF SCOTLAND

A

DUNFERMLINE ABBEY

335 ST LEONARD'S, DUNFERMLINE

NT 096 869

Brucefield Avenue

The most striking feature of the church, P McGregor Chalmers, 1904, is a round Celtic tower. Inside, the semi-circular apse has a dramatic painting of the Risen Christ surrounded by Gospel characters, designed by the architect and painted by Mr A Samuel, 1927. Heraldic gallery dedicated to the Scottish Wars of Independence led by Wallace and Bruce. Sunday Service: June-August 10am, September-May 9.30am and 11am

Open Tuesday and Thursday mornings (church office)

CHURCH OF SCOTLAND **B**

ST LEONARD'S, DUNFERMLINE

336 ST MARGARET'S MEMORIAL CHURCH, DUNFERMLINE

NY 096 876

Holyrood Place, Dunfermline

A commanding building forming part of the ancient gateway to the town at the East Port. Built in 1896 to a design by Sir R Rowand Anderson in twelfth-century Transitional style. Stained glass circular window by John Blyth, stone reredos by Hew Lorimer, wood carving by Steven Foster and historical prints by Jurek Pütter. Three new stained glass windows by Douglas Hogg.

Services: Saturday 6.30pm; Sunday 9am and 11am; Weekdays 10am

Open by arrangement, telephone Father Barr 01383 625611

ROMAN CATHOLIC WC **B**

337 VIEWFIELD BAPTIST CHURCH, DUNFERMLINE

NT 095 875

East Port, Dunfermline

Gothic design by Peter L Henderson, 1882-84. Front façade skewed giving a vestibule narrower at one side than the other and making necessary the cylindrical addition for the east gallery staircase. Wood vaulted ceiling upheld by laminated wood arches, supported internally by six cast-iron pillars. Pipe organ.

Sunday Services 11am and 6.30pm

Church Office open 9.30am-2.30pm every weekday

BAPTIST WC (open 10am-2pm Monday-Friday, in adjacent Viewfield Centre)

338 FALKLAND PARISH CHURCH

NO 252 074

The Square, Falkland

On the site of an earlier building, the present church was completed in 1850 to a design by David Bryce and gifted to the people of Falkland by Onesiphorus Tyndall Bruce, of the family of Bruce of Earlshall. The style is Victorian Gothic. Centre pews convert to long communion tables. Stained glass 1897. A912 Perth–Kirkcaldy. Bus service 36 from Perth. Sunday Service 2000 – 10am, 2001 – 11.30am

FALKLAND PARISH CHURCH

Open 13 June to 6 September 2000, Tuesday and Wednesday 2pm-4pm. 12 June to 5 September 2001, Tuesday and Wednesday 2pm-4pm

CHURCH OF SCOTLAND B

339 ST COLUMBA'S PARISH CHURCH, GLENROTHES

NO 270 009

Rothes Road, Glenrothes

Built in 1960 and designed in conjunction with the theologians at St Mary's College of St Andrews University with the emphasis on how the Scottish Reformation could be best expressed in a church building. The sanctuary features seating around three sides, with the Lord's table in the centre. Mural of Alberto Morocco measuring 59' by 9' of scene from the last days of Christ. Iron bell tower is a landmark in the centre of the town. Sunday Service 11am September-May, 10am June-August

Open 10am-12.30pm Tuesday, Thursday and Friday

CHURCH OF SCOTLAND

340 ST LUKE THE EVANGELIST, GLENROTHES

NO 273 008

Ninian Quadrant, Glenrothes

By J Cassells 1960 the church is in a Perpendicular style, set alongside a playpark in the earliest and most central part of the new town of Glenrothes. Furnished with the warmth of pine, its interior is light and airy with an unusual layout, and houses several items of interest. Sunday Services 9.15 and 10.45am

Open Monday and Thursday 10am-1pm, Tuesday 9am-10.30am, Sunday 9am-12.30pm

SCOTTISH EPISCOPAL A

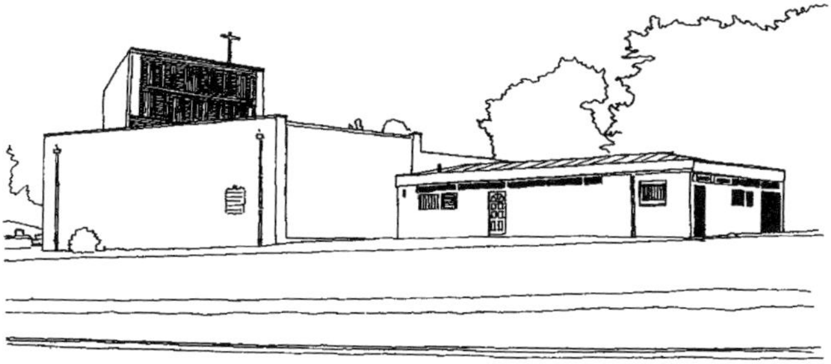

ST PAUL'S CHURCH, GLENROTHES

341 ST PAUL'S CHURCH, GLENROTHES

NO 281 005

Warout Road, Glenrothes

Completed 1957 from design by Isi Metzstein and Andy McMillan of Gillespie, Kidd & Coia. Described by *The Scotsman* as 'the most significant piece of architecture north of the English Channel' and in *The Twentieth Century Church* as 'a homage to architecture's liberating function'. Interior contains the 'Catalonian' altar crucifix 1957 and 'The Madonna' or 'Lady Piece' by Benno Schotz 1960. Carved Stations of the Cross and figure of St Paul by Harry Bain 1983. Follow Woodside Road from town centre, corner of Woodside Road/ Warout Road. Sunday Services 9am and 11.30am

Open first Saturday of the month, 11am-6pm

ROMAN CATHOLIC B

342 ST PETER'S PARISH CHURCH, INVERKEITHING

NT 131 830

Church Street, Inverkeithing

A Norman foundation, church dedicated to St Peter 1244. The present building is a nave and aisles church by Gillespie Graham 1827 attached to a 14th-century tower. Refurbished 1900, P MacGregor Chalmers. Fourteenth-century stone font, one of the finest in Scotland, thought to have been gifted by King Robert III for the baptism of his son the Duke of Rothesay. Sunday Service 11.15am

Open July-August, Friday 2-4pm, Saturday 10am-12noon, 2pm-4pm

CHURCH OF SCOTLAND

ST PETER'S PARISH CHURCH, INVERKEITHING

343 PETER'S EPISCOPAL CHURCH, INVERKEITHING

NT 128 827

Hope Street, Inverkeithing

The church was built to serve the Scottish Episcopal community in Jamestown, at one time outside the Royal Burgh of Inverkeithing. The nave was built in 1903 to a design by Henry F Kerr and the chancel added in 1910. The interior was altered in 1980 to form a worship area and hall. Set in well-kept gardens on the southern approach to the town from the Forth Road Bridge. Linked with St Columba's, Aberdour and St Serf's, Burntisland.

Sunday Service Holy Communion 11am

Open by arrangement, telephone Mrs D Macdonald 01383 414194

SCOTTISH EPISCOPAL WC

344 KINGHORN PARISH CHURCH

NT 272 869

St James Place, Kinghorn

The Kirk by the Sea for over 750 years has an unrivalled view across the beach to the Firth of Forth and Edinburgh. It has an historic bell tower and a 'Sailors' Aisle' built in 1609 celebrating the naval connection and a model of the first Unicorn. Sunday Services: 9.30am and 11am (except first Sunday of month: 10.30am in church hall)

Open every Tuesday 6pm–8 pm

CHURCH OF SCOTLAND

KINGHORN PARISH CHURCH

345 KIRKCALDY OLD PARISH CHURCH

NT 280 917

Kirk Wynd, Kirkcaldy

Consecrated in 1244 by the Bishop of St Andrews, the ancient tower offers excellent views of Kirkcaldy. The body of the church is by James Elliot 1808. Good stained glass windows, some by Morris & Co from Burne-Jones designs of 1886. Historic graveyard.

Sunday Service 11am

Open during August, Friday and Saturday 10am–4pm

CHURCH OF SCOTLAND WC **B**

KIRKCALDY OLD PARISH CHURCH

346 ST BRYCEDALE, KIRKCALDY

NT 279 917

St Brycedale Avenue, Kirkcaldy

Built as a Free Church 1877-81 by James Matthews of Aberdeen. A 60-metre tower and spire and associated pyramid-roofed twin towers lift the church out of the ordinary. In 1988, a transformed church at first-floor level was created above a multi-purpose ground-floor. Organ by Brindley & Foster 1893. Stained glass includes windows by Adam & Small 1881, Douglas Strachan 1923, and Edward Burne-Jones (executed by William Morris & Co) 1889. On junction of Kirk Wynd and St Brycedale Avenue. Services each Sunday 11am, and fourth Sunday 7pm

Open Monday to Thursday 9am-10pm, Friday 9am-3pm. Coffee Bar open Monday to Thursday 10am-9pm, Friday 10am-3pm, Saturday 10am-1pm

CHURCH OF SCOTLAND **B**

347 ST MARY, MOTHER OF GOD, LESLIE

NO 251 018

High Street, Leslie

Originally Leslie Free Church by R Thornton Shiells 1879. In 1900 it was renamed the Logan United Free Church after the Minister at that time. Closed as a Free Church in 1956 and opened as Roman Catholic in 1959. Tower 120 ft and spire. Stained glass by John Blyth, painting of the Crucifixion by Geoffrey Houghton-Brown. Sunday Service: 9.30am

Open 1st Saturday of each month 11am-6pm

ROMAN CATHOLIC **B**

ST MARY, MOTHER OF GOD, LESLIE

348 ST ATHERNASE CHURCH, LEUCHARS

NO 455 214

Main Street, Leuchars

Twelfth-century Norman church in a historic conservation setting. The belfry was added c.1700, and nave restored in 1858. Chancel and apse of outstanding architectural interest. Sunday Service 11am

Open March to October daily 9.30am-6pm. Teas, Tuesdays 10am-4pm. Tours for groups, telephone Church Officer, 18 Schoolhill, Leuchars 01334 838884

CHURCH OF SCOTLAND **A**

ST ATHERNASE CHURCH, LEUCHARS

349 SCOONIE KIRK, LEVEN

NO 383 017

Durie Street, Leven

Scoonie Kirk is the original Parish Church of Leven with its roots going back over 16 centuries. The church moved to its present site in 1775. In 1904 the building was extended following a design by the eminent church architect P MacGregor Chalmers which incorporated some of the earlier building. The unique pipe organ was built by the French organ builder August Gern 1884 and was restored 1992. The building also has some very striking stained glass windows. Sunday Services 9.30am (all age worship), 11.00am (traditional worship)

SCOONIE KIRK, LEVEN

Open Easter to Sept, Tuesdays 11am-1pm

CHURCH OF SCOTLAND **B**

350 CHURCH OF THE HOLY NAME, OAKLEY

NT 025 885

Station Road, Oakley

Built by the Smith-Sligo family of Inzievar House to a design by Charles Gray. Consecrated October 1965. Outstanding features include stained glass windows by Gabriel Loire of Chartres. Carved Stations of the Cross also by Gabriel Loire. Services: Vigil Mass Saturday 6.30pm; Sunday Mass 10.15am

Open by arrangement, telephone the Parish Priest at Priest's House (adjacent via grass path to right of church)

ROMAN CATHOLIC

CHURCH OF THE HOLY NAME, OAKLEY

PITTENWEEM PARISH CHURCH

351 PITTENWEEM PARISH CHURCH

NO 549 026

Kirkgate, Pittenweem

This ancient monument has developed over a long time. The earliest work is around 1200. The Church was extended in 1532 with an entrance from Cove Wynd and the addition of the Tolbooth Tower with Bailies Loft. The interior was refurbished in 1883 in Victorian style with new entrance, galleries and stairs. The bell dates from 1662 while the clock in the tower is a fine example by John Smith. Stained glass by William Wilson and John Blyth of the 1950s and 1960s. Sunday Service 11.30am

Open weekdays 8am-6pm. Keys from the Post Office (C & A Campbell's) in Market Place

CHURCH OF SCOTLAND WC **A**

352 ROSYTH METHODIST CHURCH

NT 114 842

Queensferry Road x Woodside Avenue, Rosyth

Founded in 1916, the present building was opened in 1970. A sanctuary of A-frame design with single storey hall and ancillary rooms adjoining by Alan Mercer, architect. Striking 30 ft high mural, painted in Byzantine style by Derek Seymour. Sunday Services 9.30am (Scottish Episcopal), 11am (Methodist)

Open by arrangement, telephone Mr Martin Rogers 01383 415458

METHODIST

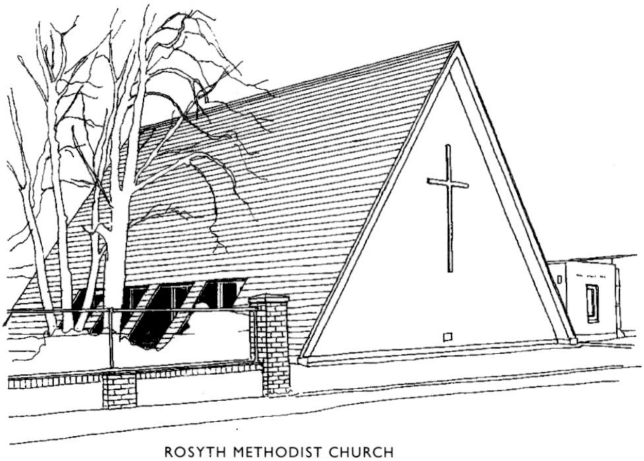

ROSYTH METHODIST CHURCH

353 ALL SAINTS', ST ANDREWS

NO 512 168

North Castle Street, St Andrews

Complex of church hall, rectory and club in Scottish vernacular with an Italian flavour. Orange pantiled roofs and lots of crowsteps. Slated chancel and bell tower by John Douglas of Chester 1906-9; the rest is by Paul Waterhouse 1919-24. Woodwork of rood, chapel altarpiece and front canopy by Nathaniel Hitch, stone Madonna and Child by Hew Lorimer 1945, marble font and wrought iron screen by Farmer & Brindley. Three windows by Herbert Hendrie, Louis Davis and Douglas Strachan. Sunday Services 8am, 10am and 6pm

Open daily 10am-4.30pm

SCOTTISH EPISCOPAL (Ladyhead book and coffee shop) WC **B**

354 PARISH CHURCH OF THE HOLY TRINITY, ST ANDREWS

NO 509 167

South Street, St Andrews

Tower and occasional pillars 1412, completely rebuilt on original ground-plan in 1909, architect McGregor Chalmers. South porch commemorates John Knox preaching here. Much fine stained glass by Strachan, Davis, Hendry, Wilson and others: clerestory windows have badges of all Scottish regiments of First World War. Elaborate memorial pulpit of Iona marble, alabaster and onyx. Decorated font of Caen stone. Memorial tomb of Archbishop Sharp. Oak barrel roof. Hunter and Memorial Aisle has much fine wood-carving. Seventeenth century sacramental silver. Harrison and Harrison organ. Twenty-seven-bell Taylor of Loughborough Carillon. Sunday Services 11am and 6pm

Open Tuesday and Saturday 10am-12noon, as advertised, or by arrangement telephone Mr Armour 01334 474494

CHURCH OF SCOTLAND WC **A**

355 HOPE PARK CHURCH, ST ANDREWS

NO 505 167

St Mary's Place, St Andrews

Completed in 1865, Peddie & Kinnear. Unusual canopy pulpit. Stained glass. Pewter communion ware, pulpit falls. A91 St Andrews, turn right at first mini roundabout. Three hundred yards on left opposite bus station. Rail service to Leuchars. Sunday Services 9.30am and 11am. Evening service as advertised in local press

Open Holy Week and Christmas week, Monday to Friday 10am-4pm, July to August, Wednesday 10am-4pm

CHURCH OF SCOTLAND WC A

356 ST ANDREW'S CHURCH, ST ANDREWS

NO 509 164

Queen's Terrace, St Andrews

1869 by Sir R Rowand Anderson. Fine 19th-century stained glass in the east and west walls. Two bays of excellent modern stained glass work. A Biblical Garden developed by BBC television's Beechgrove Garden Hit Squad is part of the popular, well-kept grounds for this vibrant and enthusiastic congregation. Sunday Services Holy Communion 8am and 10am, Choral Evensong 5.30pm (not Sundays after Christmas, Easter, nor in July and August); Monday to Friday Morning Prayer 8.30am

SCOTTISH EPISCOPAL WC B

357 ST MONANS PARISH CHURCH

NO 523 014

Braehead, St Monans

Occupying a striking position close to the sea, the church was built by Sir William Dishington 1370, with alterations by William Burn 1828 and Ian G Lindsay 1961. Fourteenth-century sedilia, piscina and aumbry. Medieval consecration crosses. Early 19th-century votive model ship of the line, heraldic bosses. External angled buttresses and 'buckle' corbels. A917 to St Monans, signposted. Sunday Service 10.30am

Open April to October during daylight hours

CHURCH OF SCOTLAND A

ST MONANS PARISH CHURCH

SPRINGFIELD CHURCH

358 SPRINGFIELD CHURCH

NO 342 119

Manse Road, Springfield, near Cupar, Fife

Built in 1861 to a plain, rectangular design. It contains notable late Victorian stained glass windows. The building was refurbished in 1970.

Linked with Ceres Church. Sunday Service 9.45am

Open by arrangement, telephone the Minister 01334 828233

CHURCH OF SCOTLAND

359 WEMYSS PARISH CHURCH

NT 340 968

Main Road, East Wemyss

Red sandstone church 1937 Peter Sinclair. United with West Wemyss and Lower Wemyss in 1976, now known as Wemyss Parish Church. Light oak furnishings, pipe organ, memorial stained glass. Surrounded by gardens with lovely views. A915 Kirkcaldy–Leven. Sunday Service 11.35am

Open by arrangement, telephone Mr Barker 01592 714874, or Miss Tod 01592 651495. Open in conjunction with Wemyss Environmental Centre Open Day. Guided parties to famous caves, some with Pictish and Viking markings, and Macduff Castle

CHURCH OF SCOTLAND

360 THE CHURCH AT WEST WEMYSS

NT 328 949

Main Street, West Wemyss

Built in 1890 Alexander Tod, simple crow-stepped cruciform church of pink sandstone. Spiral tracery in the gable's big rose window. Repurchased from the Church of Scotland in 1972 by Captain Michael Wemyss, who agreed to maintain the building externally if the church continued to be used for worship. The congregation of Wemyss Parish Church is responsible for the interior and continuing worship. Beautiful mural by William McLaren on the inner wall of the transept which now accommodates halls, vestry and kitchen. Old graveyard. Signed off A915 Kirkcaldy–Leven. Sunday Service 10am

Open by arrangement, telephone A Tod, Corner Cottage, 40 South Row, Coaltown of Wemyss 01592 651498

CHURCH OF SCOTLAND **A**

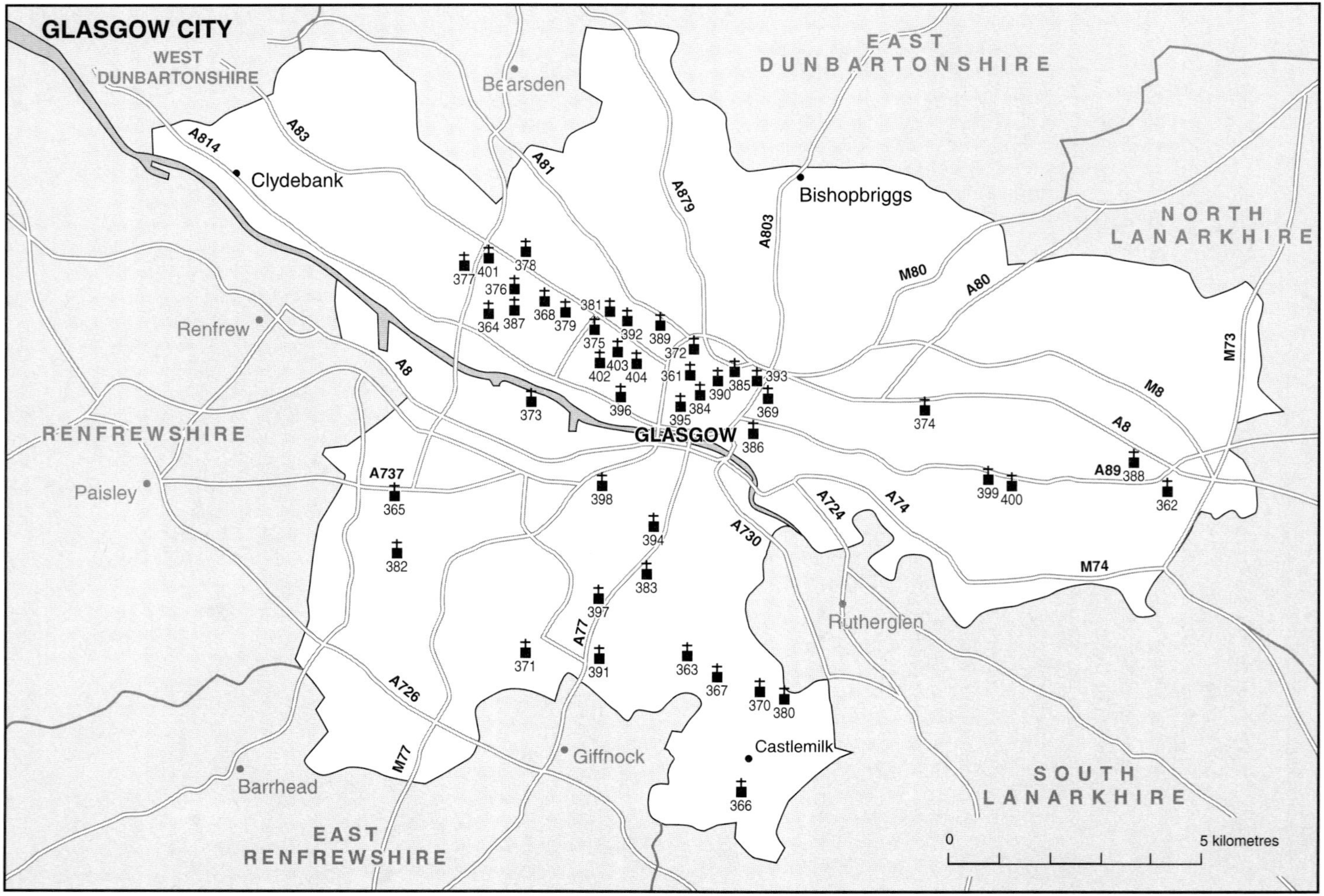
GLASGOW CITY
WEST DUNBARTONSHIRE
EAST DUNBARTONSHIRE
NORTH LANARKHIRE
RENFREWSHIRE
EAST RENFREWSHIRE
SOUTH LANARKHIRE
Clydebank
Bearsden
Bishopbriggs
Renfrew
Paisley
GLASGOW
Rutherglen
Giffnock
Barrhead
Castlemilk
A814
A83
A81
A879
A803
M80
A80
M73
M8
A8
A89
A74
A724
A730
M74
A737
A77
A726
M77
361
362
363
364
365
366
367
368
369
370
371
372
373
374
375
376
377
378
379
380
381
382
383
384
385
386
387
388
389
390
391
392
393
394
395
396
397
398
399
400
401
402
403
404
0
5 kilometres

GLASGOW

Local Representative: Mrs Jane Boyd, Manager, Renfield St Stephen's Church Centre, 260 Bath Street, Glasgow G2 4JP (*telephone:* 0141 332 4293)

ADELAIDE PLACE BAPTIST CHURCH

361 ADELAIDE PLACE BAPTIST CHURCH

NS 584 658

209 Bath Street, Glasgow (corner of Bath Street and Pitt Street)

Built 1877 T L Watson. 1995 stunning redevelopment of decaying building creating a multi-functional centre including sanctuary, guest house, cafe and nursery. Westbound M8, junction 15 along Cathedral Street and Bath Street. Eastbound M8, junction 19, left into Pitt Street. Sunday Services 11am and 7pm

Open daily 8am-8pm. Takes part in Glasgow Doors Open Day. Also wide variety of concerts and other events, telephone 0141 248 4970 for details

BAPTIST WC **B**

362 BAILLIESTON ST ANDREW'S CHURCH

NS 681 639

Church Street, Baillieston, Glasgow

Present church completed 1974 following the union of Baillieston Old and Rhinsdale Churches in 1966. Sexagonal design with slim spire, by James Houston & Sons of Kilbirnie. Allen organ installed. Sunday Services 11am and 6.30pm

Open Monday, Wednesday and Friday 9.30am-12 noon

CHURCH OF SCOTLAND

BATTLEFIELD EAST PARISH CHURCH

363 BATTLEFIELD EAST PARISH CHURCH

NS 586 613

1220 Cathcart Road

The first church on this site was by John Honeyman 1865 in Early English style. It became the hall in 1912 when the adjacent red sandstone church by John Galt was opened. Spacious interior with galleries supported on cast-iron columns and a fine timber wagon roof. Stained glass includes windows by Sadie McLennan (1971) and Susan Laidler (1980). Pipe organ by Ingram of Edinburgh. Near Mount Florida railway station. Sunday Service 11am, and occasional Evening Service 6.30pm

Open Tuesdays to Fridays 9.30am–12.30pm.

Ring bell on door of glass corridor for the Beadle

CHURCH OF SCOTLAND **B**

364 BROOMHILL CHURCH

NS 549 674

Randolph Road, Glasgow

Red sandstone church 1902, and hall 1899, designed by Stewart & Paterson. Stained glass by Guthrie & Wells, Glasgow, Abbey Studio, Edinburgh and Brian Hutchison. Pipe organ refurbished by Harrison and Harrison 1997. Located at corner of Randolph Road/Marlborough Avenue. City buses 6, 16, 44.

Sunday Services 11am and 6.30pm

Open by arrangement, telephone

Mr J Boyle 0141 339 2552

CHURCH OF SCOTLAND **B**

BROOMHILL CHURCH

365 CARDONALD PARISH CHURCH

NS 526 639

2155 Paisley Road West, Glasgow

Opened 1889 as a mission church. This is the first church designed by P MacGregor Chalmers. Early English Gothic of Ballochmyle red sandstone. Stained timber roofs open to the top. Chancel has alabaster and stone pulpit by Jackson Brown & Co and fine workmanship in its oak communion table, reading desk and elders' benches. North wall screen by Ross & Manson. Rich and varied collection of stained glass windows including three-light chancel window by J & W Guthrie, centenary window by Roland Mitton, series of six windows by Sadie McLellan, a new window by Arthur Speirs (1998). Sunday Services 11.15am, Communion Sundays 11.15am and 6.30pm

Open Tuesdays, January to May, September to December 10am-11am. Viewing by arrangement 11am-12noon, 0141 882 1051. Open daily Christmas week 10am-12noon

CHURCH OF SCOTLAND **B**

366 CARMUNNOCK PARISH CHURCH, 'THE KIRK IN THE BRAES'

NS 599 575

Kirk Road, Carmunnock

Rebuilt 1767 on pre-Reformation site and repaired in 1840. External stone staircases to three galleries. Laird's gallery. Stained glass by Norman Macleod MacDougall. Ancient graveyard has watch-house with original instructions for grave watchers 1828, and burial vault of Stirling-Stuart family, Lairds of Castlemilk. City bus 31. Sunday Service 11am

Open March to October, Saturday 1.30-3pm. Other times by arrangement, telephone 0141 644 1578. Conducted tours, Sunday 2pm on Glasgow Doors Open Day

CHURCH OF SCOTLAND (in village) **B**

CARMUNNOCK PARISH CHURCH, 'THE KIRK IN THE BRAES'

367 CATHCART OLD PARISH CHURCH

NS 587 606

119 Carmunnock Road

Original design 1923 by Clifford & Lunan, but completed 1928 by Watson, Salmon & Gray. The size is enhanced by the low porch and range of vestries. South transept contains a display of the Church's history over 800 years, the north transept was converted in 1962 to the McKellar Memorial Chapel. Tapestry of The Last Supper by Charles Marshall, stained glass by R Douglas McLundie. Organ by John R Miller, 1890, restored and converted to electro-mechanical action 1994. Services: 11am, Thursday 10.45am.

Open Monday-Friday 10am-2pm

CHURCH OF SCOTLAND **B**

368 CATHEDRAL CHURCH OF ST LUKE

NS 563 675

27 Dundonald Road, Dowanhill, Glasgow

Formerly Belhaven United Presbyterian Church by James Sellars 1877, powerfully vertical Normandy Gothic. The congregation of St Luke's relocated here in 1960. The main front is inspired by Dunblane Cathedral. Marvellous display of stained glass, Stephen Adam 1877, richly stencilled roof timbers, and original light fittings and furniture. Modern iconostasis featuring icons some of which were painted on Mount Athos in the traditional Byzantine style. Sunday Service 10.30am-1pm

Open by arrangement, telephone Mr N Pitticas 0141 339 7368

GREEK ORTHODOX **B**

CATHEDRAL CHURCH OF ST LUKE

369 CATHEDRAL CHURCH OF ST MUNGO

NS 603 656

Castle Street, Glasgow

Dedicated in 1136, the largest and most complete of Scotland's medieval cathedrals still in use. Medieval stone screen. Crypt with shrine of St Mungo. Modern tapestry. Sunday Services 11am and 6.30pm

Open daily, April to September, 9.30am-1pm, 2pm-6pm, Sunday 2-5pm; October to March, 9.30am-1pm, 2pm-4pm, Sunday 2pm-4pm.
Light lunches, etc, in adjacent St Mungo's Museum

CHURCH OF SCOTLAND (May to September) **A**

370 CROFTFOOT PARISH CHURCH

NS 603 602

318 Croftpark Avenue, Glasgow

Keppie & Henderson 1936. A neat Byzantine design in red brick with ashlar facings. Carved patterns, symbolising scriptural themes, decorate the main door portico, nave and chancel columns and chancel furnishings. The bell is the Second World War memorial. Ten minute walk from Croftfoot railway station. Sunday Services 11am and 6.30pm

Open Monday to Friday, 9am-noon, and 1.30pm-4pm, except public holidays. Tours, telephone Mr W Yule 0141 637 7613

CHURCH OF SCOTLAND

(Wednesday am) **B**

CROFTFOOT PARISH CHURCH

371 EASTWOOD PARISH CHURCH

NS 558 607

5 Mansewood Road, Glasgow

1862-63 by Charles Wilson, succeeded by David Thomson. Gothic style, cruciform with a tower and broach spire. Inside, the four arms of the timber roof meet in a cross of free-flying beams. Stained glass by various artists fills almost every window. Sunday Service 11.15am

Open by arrangement, telephone Mr Smith 0141 633 0117

CHURCH OF SCOTLAND **B**

372 GARNETHILL SYNAGOGUE

NS 502 661

129 Hill Street, Glasgow

Opened in 1879, the first purpose-built synagogue in Scotland. It was designed by John McLeod of Glasgow in Romanesque-cum-Byzantine style. A round-arched portal with highly decorated orders leads to the body of the synagogue. Ladies' gallery is carried on octagonal piers with ornate Byzantine capitals. Stained glass by J B Bennet & Sons. Refurbished in 1996. From Sauchiehall Street walk up Garnet Street to Hill Street. Services Saturday 10am, Jewish Festivals 9.30am

Open by arrangement, telephone the caretaker, Mr Gibson, 32 Minerva Street, Glasgow G3 8LD (0141 204 1236). Scottish Jewish Archives open by arrangement, telephone 0141 332 4911

JEWISH (three steps) **B**

GOVAN OLD PARISH CHURCH (ST CONSTANTINE'S)

373 GOVAN OLD PARISH CHURCH (ST CONSTANTINE'S)

NS 554 659

866 Govan Road, Glasgow

Affectionately called 'the people's cathedral'. Set well back in a churchyard of great antiquity, the present building is the last in a long series of churches on this site. Completed in 1888, the design by R Rowand Anderson proved very influential for the next 50 years. Its style is Early English in the Scottish manner, with details based on Pluscarden Priory near Elgin. A set of twelve windows by Charles E Kempe. Good stained glass by Burlison & Grylls and Clayton & Bell in the Steven Chapel and by Shrigley & Hunt in the baptistry. Archaeological excavation has provided a fresh context for the large collection of early medieval sculpture including hogback stones, cross shafts, cross slabs and the richly ornamented and recently conserved Govan Sarcophagus. Fine pipe organ by Brindley and Foster. City buses and underground to Govan Station. Sunday Service 11am; Daily service Monday to Friday 10am

Open first Wednesday in June to third Saturday in September, Wednesdays 10.30am–12.30pm, and Wednesdays, Thursdays and Saturdays 1–4pm.

Also open by arrangement, telephone 0141 445 1941

CHURCH OF SCOTLAND **A**

374 HIGH CARNTYNE PARISH CHURCH

NS 636 653

358 Carntynehall Road, Glasgow

First church extension charge of Church of Scotland. Congregation met in 'the hut' until building was completed by J Taylor Thomson 1932. Original single bell still in use. Extensive suite of halls built alongside the church in 1955. Buses 41, 42, 51, 20a. Sunday Services 11am and 6.30pm; Wednesday 9.30am

Open daily 10am–12 noon

CHURCH OF SCOTLAND (by arrangement) WC **B**

375 HILLHEAD BAPTIST CHURCH

NS 568 671

Cresswell Street, off Byres Road, Glasgow

Designed by T L Watson 1883, in Greek Revival style. The impressive harmony and richness of the original dark woodwork and pews gives an intimacy to this interior where sunlight is filtered through delicately coloured glass. Fine Lewis pipe organ. Near to Botanic Gardens. Sunday Service 11am and 6.30pm

Open Tuesday to Friday, 12.30–2pm

BAPTIST **B**

376 HYNDLAND PARISH CHURCH

NS 559 675

79 Hyndland Road, Glasgow

William Leiper 1887 in red Ballochmyle sandstone. Timber roof and columns with richly carved foliage capitals. Gleaming original terrazzo floor. Original furnishings, Henry Willis pipe organ, and fine stained glass, including windows by Douglas Strachan, Gordon Webster, William Wilson and Sax Shaw. Major refurbishment 1997 including lighting of timber roof. City buses 44, 59; also by rail and underground. Sunday Service 11am (10.30am July and August), also October to Easter 7pm

Open easily by arrangement, telephone Church Officer next door, Mr Harry MacDonald 0141 338 6705

CHURCH OF SCOTLAND

A

HYNDLAND PARISH CHURCH

377 JORDANHILL PARISH CHURCH

NS 544 682

28 Woodend Drive, Glasgow

Church 1905 and hall, west aisle and gallery 1923 by James Miller in Perpendicular style. Battlemented and pinnacled tower. Mock hammerbeam roof spans the broad interior. Further extensions to hall 1971 and sanctuary refurbishment 1980 by Wylie Shanks. Organ by Lewis 1923. Woodend Drive is off Crow Road (A739 Clyde Tunnel to Bearsden). Sunday Services 10.30 and 6.30pm (October to June), and Wednesday at 10am (September to June)

Open Monday to Friday 8.30am–12.30pm and 1.30pm–5pm

CHURCH OF SCOTLAND **B**

378 ST JOHN'S RENFIELD, KELVINDALE

NS 558 683

Beaconsfield Road, Kelvindale, Glasgow

Bold and striking church in a commanding position. Topped by an openwork flèche, the stonework has the understated detail characteristic of its time, 1931 (architect James Taylor Thomson). Light and lofty interior, complete with original fitments, and stained glass by Douglas Strachan and Gordon Webster. Turn off Great Western Road to Kelvindale. Sunday Service 11am all year, 8.30pm September to Easter, and first Sunday of month Easter to August

Open Wednesday, Thursday, Friday 9.30am–12.30pm

CHURCH OF SCOTLAND [wheelchair] [hearing] [WC] **B**

379 KELVINSIDE HILLHEAD PARISH CHURCH

NS 567 673

Saltoun Street, Observatory Road, Dowanhill, Glasgow

1876 by James Sellars, the design is said to have been much influenced by William Leiper. A tall apsed church, the west front is full of carving. The interior was recast in 1921 by P MacGregor Chalmers. Communion table of Rochette marble. Good stained glass by Burne-Jones for William Morris & Co, 1893 and Sadie McLennan 1958. Organ by H Willis & Son 1876, restored in 1930. At junction of Saltoun Street with Observatory Road. City buses and underground to Hillhead. Sunday Services 11am; also October to May 6.30pm

Open Saturday 10.30am–12.30pm all year. Other times, telephone the Minister 0141 339 2865.

Venue for many concerts

CHURCH OF SCOTLAND [wheelchair] [guide] [guidebook] [hearing] [refreshments] [WC] **A**

KELVINSIDE HILLHEAD PARISH CHURCH

380 KING'S PARK PARISH CHURCH

NS 601 608

242 Castlemilk Road, Glasgow

Red brick with stone dressings, Romanesque in style by Hutton & Taylor 1932, an innovation in church design specially evolved by the Presbytery of Glasgow. The commission was the result of an architectural competition. Notable collection of stained glass windows by Sadie McLennan, Gordon Webster, Douglas Hamilton and others. Set in a pleasant small garden. Ample parking. By rail to King's Park or Croftfoot, ten minutes walk. City buses 12, 22 to Castlemilk Road. Sunday Services 11am, 6.30pm, 10.30am only July to August

Open Monday to Friday 9.30am–12 noon, all year except public holidays. Tours, telephone Mr R Pitman 0141 649 4301

CHURCH OF SCOTLAND [wheelchair] [children] [guide] [guidebook] [hearing] [refreshments] (Tues am) **A**

KING'S PARK PARISH CHURCH

381 LANSDOWNE PARISH CHURCH

NS 576 669

416 Great Western Road, Glasgow

Built 1863 to a design by John Honeyman. Spire 218 ft, one of the slimmest in Europe, a powerful landmark on Great Western Road. Pulpit said to be highest free-standing in Scotland. Box pews. Beautiful stained glass, Alfred and Gordon Webster, and war memorial frieze by Evelyn Beale. Pipe organ 1911, Norman & Beard, said to have the finest tuba rank in Glasgow with some wonderful flutes. On corner with Park Road, opposite Kelvinbridge underground. City buses 20, 66, 51, 11 from city centre. Sunday Service 11am (creche available)

Open by arrangement. Also Glasgow Doors Open Day, telephone the Minister 0141 339 2794, or Mr J Stuart 0141 339 2678

CHURCH OF SCOTLAND **A**

382 ST JAMES'S PARISH CHURCH, POLLOK

NS 530 626

183 Meiklerig Crescent, Pollok, Glasgow

Church built 1895 as Pollokshields Titwood Church, and moved stone by stone from its original site four miles away by Thomson, McCrae & Sanders, and rededicated in 1953. Congregation worshipped in a school hall and then in a wooden hut until the building was completed. Good stained glass. 50 bus from Glasgow city centre. M8, Junction for Paisley Road West. Sunday Service 11am

Open Saturdays 10am–12 noon. Close to Pollok House, the Burrell Collection, Crookston Castle and Ross Hall

CHURCH OF SCOTLAND **B**

383 QUEEN'S PARK BAPTIST CHURCH

NS 579 266

180 Queen's Drive and Balvicar Drive, Glasgow

'QP', an evangelical-charismatic church, is a changing church and recent years have seen significant growth which parallels spiritual renewal in the fellowship, preaching, ministry, outreach and worship. Since October 1995 the church occupies two nearby sites: a Romanesque building (Camphill), McKissack & Rowan 1887; and a French Gothic building (Queen's Drive), William Leiper 1876. The interiors of both buildings have been significantly modernised and renovated to make them relevant places for Christian worship and work in the 21st century. The Camphill building was fully stone cleaned and repaired during 1998-9. Queen's Drive/Pollokshaws Road, two minutes from Queen's Park Station. Sunday Services 10.30am and 6.30pm

Open Sundays, and other times by arrangement, telephone Dr J Brooks 0141 423 3962

BAPTIST **A** (Camphill) **B** (Queen's Drive)

384 RENFIELD ST STEPHEN'S PARISH CHURCH AND CENTRE

NS 582 659

260 Bath Street, Glasgow

Designed as an Independent Chapel by London architect J T Emmett in 1852 in Decorated Gothic style. Built in beautiful polished Kenmuir sandstone with a tall clerestoried nave supported on clustered columns with finely moulded capitals and arches, each with carved musical angels. The main stained glass windows are by Norman Macdougall 1905 and represent the Apostles flanking Christ in Glory. The Gothic furnishings are post First World War. Side chapel and extensive halls were added by Munro & Partners in the 1960s. Small garden with fountain. Sunday Services 11am and 7pm

Open daily 8am-7pm. Oasis Restaurant open 8am-7pm

CHURCH OF SCOTLAND

385 ST ALOYSIUS CHURCH

NS 586 660

23 Rose Street, Glasgow

Fine late-Renaissance style church, designed in 1910 by Belgian-born architect Charles Menart, with a 150 ft campanile, domed crossing and ornate marble-lined interior. The church is in the care of the Jesuit Order, and Jesuit saints figure in the stained glass. The shrine of St John Ogilvie SJ is in the east transept, with mosaics depicting his martyrdom in Glasgow in 1615. Near Glasgow School of Art and Sauchiehall Street. Sunday Services 9am, 10.30am, 12 noon (Sung), and 9pm

Open daily 7.30am to 6.30pm and on Sunday until 10pm. Full details of services on website: www.aloyius.glasgow.ukgateway.net

ROMAN CATHOLIC **A**

ST ALOYSIUS CHURCH

386 ST ALPHONSUS CHURCH

NS 600 646

217 London Road, Glasgow

A late work by Peter Paul Pugin, 1905. Rock-faced sandstone screen façade. The tracery in the gable window formalised into a saltire cross. Inside, the nave arcades have polished granite piers. One hundred and fiftieth anniversary commemorative window 1996 by Lorraine Lamond. Church is in the middle of the 'Barras', 500 metres east of Glasgow Cross. Services: Saturday 5pm (Vigil); Sundays 10am, 11am, 12 noon, 4.45pm

Open Monday to Friday 12 noon-2pm, Saturday and Sunday 9am-6pm

ROMAN CATHOLIC WC **B**

387 ST BRIDE'S CHURCH

NS 559 676

69 Hyndland Road, Glasgow

Designed by G F Bodley, who built the chancel (1904), the nave (1907) and part of the north aisle. H O Tarbolton completed the church (1913-16) including rebuilding part of the nave, and adding two north aisles and the tower. The interior scheme is mainly Bodley's. Carved woodwork by Scott Morton & Co. Sculpture of Our Lady and Child by Eric Gill, 1915. Two-manual organ by Hill. Sunday Services Sung Eucharist 10.30am; Daily Eucharist, times vary

Open by arrangement, telephone Mr Rae 0141 332 8430 and Rev R F Jones 0141 334 1401

Occasional Choral Evensong, usually with visiting choirs and concerts as advertised

SCOTTISH EPISCOPAL WC **B**

ST BRIDE'S CHURCH

388 ST BRIDGET'S CHURCH, BAILLIESTON

NS 680 642

15 Swinton Road, Baillieston, Glasgow

Built 1893 by Pugin & Pugin in light sandstone. Notable 'Creation' rose window above sanctuary area and carved 'Christ Triumphant' below. Mosaic work 'Suffer the Children', 'Nativity', 'Glories of Mary', 'Annunciation', and stained glass windows 'Christ with Saints' and 'Sacred Heart' 1945–9 by the John Hardman Studios. 'St Bridget' and 'St Colmcille' windows by Shona McInnes (1999). Located 200 yards west of Edinburgh Road/Coatbridge Road A8/A89. Sunday Services 9am and 10.30am, 12 and 6pm; Daily Service 9.30am; Saturday 6.30pm.

Open for some hours each day. Otherwise contact Church House adjacent

ROMAN CATHOLIC

ST BRIDGET'S CHURCH, BAILLIESTON

ST COLUMBA'S CHURCH

389 ST COLUMBA'S CHURCH

NS 583 671

74 Hopehill Road, Glasgow

By Gillespie, Kidd & Coia, completed in 1941, the year of the Clydebank and Govan blitz, and the cost met by the families of the area, each of whom paid 6d per brick. Italian Romanesque style with an imposing west front. Sculpture of the Paschal Lamb over central door. Painted panels of the Stations of the Cross by Hugh Adam Crawford, from the Catholic Pavilion at the Glasgow Empire Exhibition 1938. In the sanctuary a marble reredos with a carved crucifix by Benno Schotz. North of St George's Cross, via Maryhill Road. Saturday Vigil Mass 6pm; Sunday Mass 11am and 5pm

Open at any time, by contacting the Priest in the house adjacent

ROMAN CATHOLIC **A**

390 ST GEORGE'S – TRON PARISH CHURCH

NS 590 655

165 Buchanan Street, Glasgow

Designed by William Stark and completed 1808. Originally St George's Parish Church and the eighth burgh church to be built in Glasgow in what was then the extreme west-end of the city. St George's united with Tron St Anne's in 1940. Baroque-style tower with five stages capped by a ribbed dome and obelisk. Plain, galleried interior with flat ceiling. The Christ-centred life and ministry of the Rev Tom Allan (1955-64) was instrumental in the awakening of the evangelical Christian church in Glasgow and beyond. Sunday Service 11am and 7pm; Wednesday Prayer Meeting 7.30pm, except May, June and September

Open one day each week 12 noon-2pm (to be announced).

Other times by arrangement, telephone Mr William Bradford 0141 332 0187

CHURCH OF SCOTLAND **A**

ST GEORGE'S – TRON PARISH CHURCH

391 ST MARGARET'S, NEWLANDS

NS 569 610

Kilmarnock Road, Newlands, Glasgow

The church, a 'classic of the Romanesque Revival', was designed by Dr Peter MacGregor Chalmers and built in stages between 1910 and 1935. A basilica with double apse, it is splendid in size and simple beauty. The stained glass windows include examples by Morris & Co, the St Enoch Studio and Gordon Webster. Sunday Services: 9am Said Eucharist, 10.30am Sung Eucharist, 6.30pm Evensong; Tuesdays 10am; and Thursdays 10.30am, Said Eucharist

Open 9-12noon, Monday to Friday. Other details from Church Office 0141 636 1131

SCOTTISH EPISCOPAL (Anglican) ♿ 🦻 **B**

ST MARGARET'S, NEWLANDS

392 ST MARY'S CATHEDRAL

NS 578 668

300 Great Western Road, Glasgow

Fine Gothic revival church by Sir George Gilbert Scott with outstanding contemporary murals by Gwyneth Leech and newly restored Phoebe Traquair reredos. Three-manual pipe organ. Glasgow's only full peal of bells. A82, three quarters of a mile west of St George's Cross. Two minutes walk Kelvinbridge Underground.

Sunday Services: 8am Eucharist, 10am Sung Eucharist, 12 noon Eucharist, 6.30pm Choral Evensong

Open daily, 9.30am-5pm

SCOTTISH EPISCOPAL WC WC **A**

393 ST MUNGO'S CHURCH

NS 600 659

Parson Street, Glasgow

Designed by the London architect George Goldie 1869 in French Gothic style. The church is in the care of the Passionist congregation. Five apsidal chapels include St Paul of the Cross – founder of the Passionists – St Margaret of Scotland, and Our Lady of Sorrows which has a Portuguese polychrome wood statue. Late 19th-century stained glass by Mayer of Munich. Gothic-style timber confessionals. Opposite Charles Rennie Mackintosh's Martyrs School, and five minutes walk from Glasgow Cathedral and the St Mungo Museum. Sunday Services 10am, 12 noon and 7pm

Open Monday to Friday 9.30am-1pm, 5.30-6.30pm; Saturday 9.30am-1pm, 4.30-8pm; Sunday 9.30am-1pm, 6.30-8pm

ROMAN CATHOLIC WC **B**

394 ST NINIAN'S CHURCH, POLLOKSHIELDS

NS 582 632

1 Albert Drive, Pollokshields, Glasgow

The foundation stone of St Ninian's was laid on September 16th 1872, and building commenced to a design by David Thomson. Completed in 1877, and extended west in 1887. The apse is decorated with frescoes painted by William Hole 1901, and the charming little sacristy designed by H D Wilson, a member of the congregation, in 1914. Good stained glass including windows by Heaton, Butler & Bayne. The windows in the chancel represent The Gospel Story, by Stephen Adam. Disabled access at rear of church, notification required to use this entrance. Sunday Service Holy Communion (Said) 8.30am, Sung Eucharist and Sermon 10.15am, Evening Prayer (Said) 6.30pm

Open by arrangement, telephone Mrs Y Grieve 0141 638 7254

SCOTTISH EPISCOPAL (from rear of church, notification needed) WC WC **B**

395 ST VINCENT STREET – MILTON FREE CHURCH

NS 583 656

265 St Vincent Street, Glasgow

Alexander Thomson's masterpiece, distinctive Victorian Presbyterian church, designed in the classical style, and embellished by a unique Thomsonian combination of Egyptian, Indian and Assyrian influences, 1859. Owned by Glasgow City Council. Sunday Services 11am and 6.30pm

Open by appointment. Also Doors Open Day, telephone Mr Sieczowski 0141 649 1563

FREE CHURCH OF SCOTLAND **A**

396 SANDYFORD HENDERSON CHURCH

NS 570 659

13 Kelvinhaugh Street, Glasgow

Early Gothic style, 1854-56, by London architect J T Emmett, completed by John Honeyman. Several fine stained glass windows. Local attractions include Kelvingrove Art Gallery, Kelvin Hall, Scottish Exhibition and Conference Centre and the Victorian architecture of St Vincent Crescent. Sunday Services: 11am and 6.30pm, Saturday 7.30pm prayer and Bible study

Open by arrangement, telephone Prof A Nash 0141 886 5871

CHURCH OF SCOTLAND **B**

SANDYFORD HENDERSON CHURCH

397 SHAWLANDS UNITED REFORMED CHURCH

NS 570 622

111 Moss-side Road, Shawlands, Glasgow

Formerly a Churches of Christ church, by Miller & Black 1908, in red sandstone. Open baptistry. Three hundred yards from Shawlands Cross. Sunday Service 11am

Open Thursday 10.30-11.30am

UNITED REFORMED

398 SHERBROOKE ST GILBERT'S CHURCH, POLLOKSHIELDS

NS 561 636

240 Nithsdale Road, Pollokshields, Glasgow

The original building by William Forsyth McGibbon was ravaged by fire in 1994, its centenary year. Now the church is restored by James Cuthbertson, architect. The interior features the work of Scottish craftsmen: stained glass windows, inspired by the themes of creation, the Cross and rebirth, by Stained Glass Design Partnership, Kilmaurs; three-manual pipe organ by Lammermuir Pipe Organs; pulpit, tables and font by Bill Nimmo, East Lothian. Close to Dumbreck railway station, and on 59 bus route. Sunday Service 10.30am

Open by arrangement, telephone the Church Officer 0141 427 1968

CHURCH OF SCOTLAND **B**

399 SHETTLESTON METHODIST CHURCH

NS 643 642

1104 Shettleston Road, Glasgow

Former Primitive Methodist Church of 1902 which replaced a tin tabernacle of 1889. The Church incorporates windows from the former Parkhead Methodist Church. Opposite Shettleston Police Station. Services: Sunday 11am; Tuesday 10.30am

Open by arrangement, telephone the Church Office 0141 778 5063

METHODIST

400 SHETTLESTON OLD PARISH CHURCH

NS 649 370

111 Killin Street, Shettleston, Glasgow

Church by W F McGibbon, opened in 1903. Fine collection of stained glass, including windows by Alfred Webster and Gordon Webster. Fine two-manual organ. Train to Shettleston. City buses 40, 62, 260. Sunday Service 11am

Open by arrangement, telephone the Church Officer 0141 778 2484

CHURCH OF SCOTLAND **B**

401 TEMPLE-ANNIESLAND CHURCH

NS 547 699

869 Crow Road, Glasgow

Red sandstone Gothic-style church built by Badenoch & Bruce 1905. Adjoining hall was original United Presbyterian church built in 1899 by Alexander Petrie. U-plan interior with red pine panelled gallery and pews. War memorial, from Temple Parish Church (united with Temple-Anniesland 1984 and now demolished) with unique clock designed and built 1921 by first minister, Rev J Carswell. Sunday Services 11am and 6.30pm, July to August 11am only; Thursday 11am

Open Thursdays 10am-12noon (not July)

CHURCH OF SCOTLAND **B**

402 UNIVERSITY MEMORIAL CHAPEL

NS 568 666

The Square, Glasgow University, Glasgow

1923-27 by Sir J J Burnet in Scots Gothic and in harmony with the University buildings of Sir George Gilbert Scott. The structure is reinforced concrete, faced with stone. Tall interior with sculpture by Archibald Dawson. Ten of the stained glass windows are by Douglas Strachan in a cycle depicting the whole of human life as a spiritual enterprise. Other windows by Gordon Webster and Lawrence Lee. The chapel incorporates the Lion and Unicorn Stair salvaged from the Old College. Sunday Service 11am; Monday to Friday 8.45am

Open 9am-5pm Monday to Friday, 9am-noon Saturday

Chapel Choir Service December. Tours available from visitors' centre

ECUMENICAL (all in visitors' centre) **A**

403 WELLINGTON CHURCH

NS 570 667

University Avenue, Glasgow

T L Watson's Roman Classical church with mighty Corinthian columned portico 1884. Renaissance style interior with fine plaster ceilings. Pipe organ Forster & Andrews. Refectory situated in crypt. City buses 44, 59. Underground to Hillhead or Kelvinbridge, ten minutes walk. Sunday Services 11am and 7pm

Open April to September, Monday to Saturday 12 noon-2pm. Crypt open, Monday to Friday, during University term. Also Glasgow Doors Open Day

CHURCH OF SCOTLAND (& lunch during term time) WC **A**

WELLINGTON CHURCH

404 WOODLANDS METHODIST CHURCH

NS 576 665

229 Woodlands Road, Glasgow

Built for Swedenborgians by David Barclay 1909 in use by Methodists since 1977. A wide stair leads to the church. 1876 organ from Cathedral Street Swedenborgian Church, amalgamated with pipes from Willis organ at St John's, Sauchiehall Street. Windows by Guthrie & Wells and George Benson, and war memorial window from St John's. Nearest rail station Charing Cross. Services: Sunday 11am; Tuesday 12.30pm

Open by arrangement, telephone the Church Office 0141 332 7779

METHODIST

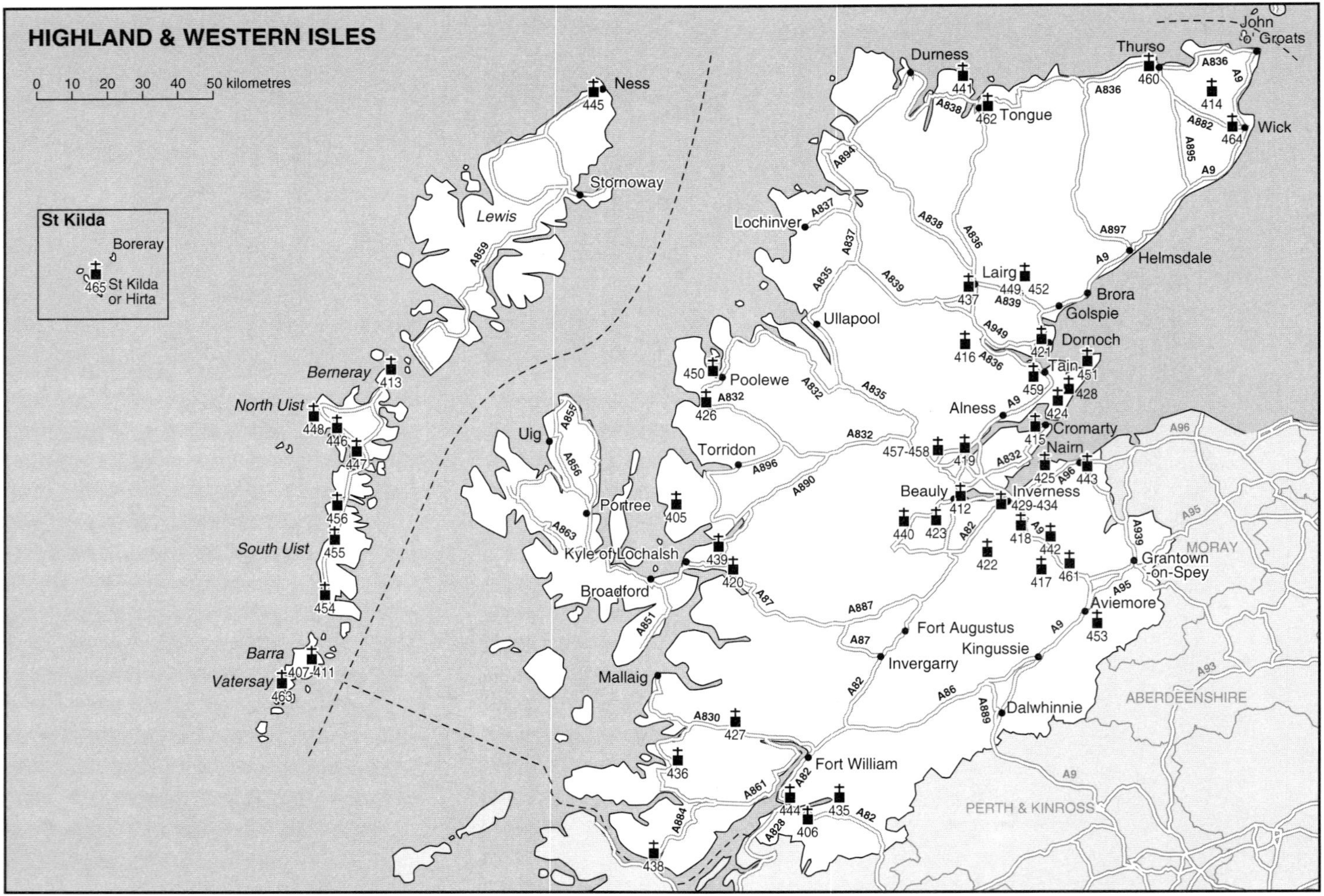
HIGHLAND & WESTERN ISLES
0 10 20 30 40 50 kilometres
St Kilda
Boreray
St Kilda or Hirta
465
Ness
445
Stornoway
Lewis
A859
Berneray
413
North Uist
448
446
447
456
South Uist
455
454
Barra
407-411
Vatersay
463
Uig
A855
A856
Portree
A863
Kyle of Lochalsh
Broadford
A851
Mallaig
405
439
420
Durness
441
A838
462
Tongue
Thurso
460
John o' Groats
A836
A9
414
A882
464
Wick
A895
A894
A837
Lochinver
A835
Ullapool
A838
A836
A897
Helmsdale
Lairg
437
449, 452
A839
Brora
Golspie
A949
416
421
Dornoch
451
Tain
459
428
424
Alness
Cromarty
415
Nairn
425
443
A96
450
Poolewe
A832
426
Torridon
A896
A890
457-458
419
Beauly
412
Inverness
429-434
440
423
A82
418
442
422
417
461
A939
Grantown -on-Spey
MORAY
A95
Aviemore
453
A87
A887
Fort Augustus
Invergarry
Kingussie
A86
A889
Dalwhinnie
ABERDEENSHIRE
A93
A830
427
Fort William
436
A861
444
435
406
A828
A884
438
PERTH & KINROSS

HIGHLAND & WESTERN ISLES (EILEAN SIAR)

Local Representatives: Ms Atisha McGregor Auld, Tollie Farm, Poolewe, Ross-shire (*telephone* 01445 781280); and Mrs Lyndall Leet, 8 Burnside, Thurso, Caithness (*telephone* 01847 896989)

405 CLACHAN CHURCH, APPLECROSS, ROSS-SHIRE

NG 712 459

Standing on the ancient site of St Maelrubha's church (673 AD), the present church was built in 1817. The beauty and tranquillity of the surroundings complement the quiet simplicity of the plain stone building. To the left of the gate stands a tall, plain slab with an incised Celtic cross, said to mark the grave of Ruairidh Mor MacAogan, abbot of Applecross, who died in 801 AD. The remains of carved Celtic crosses, dating from eighth century, are in glass cases. The church is recommended for its simplicity and peace, a fitting heritor of the old Gaelic name of *A'Chomraich* - the Sanctuary. No regular services, but used for weddings, funerals and memorial services. Location for Pilgrimage 26 August 2000.

Open daily

INTERDENOMINATIONAL **B**

406 ST MUN'S, BALLACHULISH, INVERNESS-SHIRE

NN 083 579

Built 1837 by Bishop Scott, Vicar-Apostolic for West of Scotland. Simple Highland church in good condition. Adjacent building was originally the Priest's house. Sunday Service 11.00am, daily as announced

Open at all times

ROMAN CATHOLIC WC

ST MUN'S, BALLACHULISH, INVERNESS-SHIRE

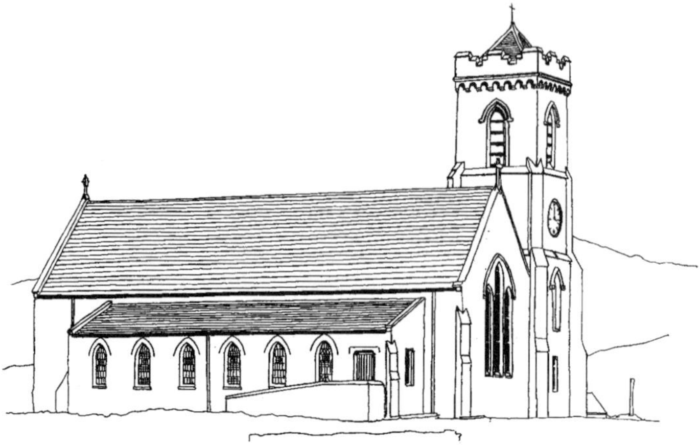

OUR LADY STAR OF THE SEA, CASTLEBAY, BARRA

407 OUR LADY STAR OF THE SEA, CASTLEBAY, BARRA

NL 667 983

Castlebay, Barra

Opened Christmas 1886, architect Woulfe Brenan of Oban. Statue by Dupon of Bruges of Our Lady Star of the Sea. Stained glass of crucifixion in Sanctuary, and of Our Lady Star of the Sea installed as war memorial in early 1950s. Bell in tower; the clock chimes the hour during day and night. Sunday Service: 11am

Open at all times

ROMAN CATHOLIC (wheelchair access) (ramp access available) (hearing loop) **B**

408 ST BRENDAN, CRAIGSTON, BARRA

NF 657 018

Craigston, Barra

Dating from 1805, the oldest church in the Isles of Barra. Restored 1858. Two etchings (scraperboard white on black) of St Brendan and St Barr, by Fr Calum MacNeill, retired priest of the diocese. Saturday Vigil 7pm

Open at all times

ROMAN CATHOLIC (wheelchair access)

409 ST VINCENT DE PAUL, EOLIGARRY, BARRA

NF 703 076

Built in 1964, the church has a tall roof with swept eaves. Small cemetery at Cille Bharra, burial place of MacNeil chieftans. Sunday: Mass 11am

Open at all times

ROMAN CATHOLIC

ST VINCENT DE PAUL, EOLIGARRY, BARRA

410 NORTH CHAPEL, CILLE BHARRA, EOLIGARRY, BARRA

NF 705 074

Twelfth-century church built on site of seventh-century foundation dedicated to St Finbarr of Cork, Eire. Re-roofed with help from the Scottish Development Department. Contains notable twelfth-century runic stone (original now in the Royal Museum, Edinburgh) and 16th-century grave-slabs with carvings of animals and foliage. Mass on the feasts of the Celtic saints

Open at all times

ROMAN CATHOLIC

411 ST BARR'S, NORTHBAY, BARRA

NF 707 031

A simple lancet-windowed building by G Woulfe Brenan, 1906, with porch and vestry added 1919. Small bellcote on porch. Services daily: Mass 7.30pm, Sunday 11am

Open at all times

ROMAN CATHOLIC

412 ST MARY'S CHURCH, BEAULY, INVERNESS-SHIRE

NH 528 467

High Street, Beauly

Nave, chancel and north aisle, and adjoining house, built as a unit in red sandstone 1864, probably by Joseph A Hansom. Nearby the ruins of Beauly Priory, founded for Valliscaulian monks in 1230, maintained by Historic Scotland. Also serves St Mary's, Eskadale and Our Lady and St Bean, Marydale. Sunday Mass 11am

Open Easter to September. Other times, call at Priest's house adjoining

ROMAN CATHOLIC **B**

413 BERNERAY CHURCH, ISLE OF BERNERAY

NL 552 801

Opposite war memorial

Built 1887, architect Thomas Binnie of Glasgow, for the United Free Church. By uniting with the Established Church, now in ruins, it became the Church of Scotland and still flourishes as such. HRH the Prince of Wales worshipped here on a private visit in 1991. Berneray is now accessible by a causeway across Sound of Harris. Sunday Services: 12noon in English, 6pm in Gaelic

Open by arrangement, with Mr MacLean telephone 01876 540249

CHURCH OF SCOTLAND WC

414 BOWER PARISH CHURCH, CAITHNESS

ND 238 622

midway between Thurso and Wick on B876

Built 1847, architect William Davidson. Re-casting and alterations, architect Donald Leed 1902. Finialled and panelled Gothic screen flanks pulpit. Unusual in that two long windows which formerly flanked the pulpit are in the north, not south, wall. Stained glass window dedicated to Sir John Sinclair, seventh Baronet of Dunbeath. Mural memorials to members of Henderson and Sinclair families and plaque in memory of Zachary Pont, minister 1605-13, and his wife Margaret, daughter of John Knox. Ongoing restoration work has uncovered bronze bell from pre-Reformation church. Sunday Service 12.15pm

Open by arrangement, telephone Mrs McAdie 01955 661252

CHURCH OF SCOTLAND **B**

415 EAST CHURCH, CROMARTY, ROSS-SHIRE

NH 791 673

Church Street, Cromarty

Described by John Hume as 'unquestionably one of the finest 18th-century parish churches in Scotland'. Starting as a simple east-west rectangle in the late 16th century, the north aisle was added 1739 to create a T-plan church. Further alterations in 1756 and 1798. The interior dates principally from the 18th century with galleries added to accommodate the growing congregation, the most elaborate being the Cromartie loft of 1756. Several fine monuments. Owned and maintained by the Scottish Redundant Churches Trust. Four services during summer months plus occasional services by arrangement

Open 8.30am-5pm (4pm in winter)

CHURCH OF SCOTLAND **A**

EAST CHURCH, CROMARTY, ROSS-SHIRE

416 CROICK CHURCH, ARDGAY, SUTHERLAND

NH 457 915

Ardgay, Strathcarron

Harled T-plan 'Parliamentary' Church built by James Smith 1827 from a Thomas Telford design. One of the few Parliamentary churches still in use in its original form. Furnishings virtually unchanged since first built; old-style long communion table and original pulpit. East window has messages scratched in 1845 by evicted inhabitants of Glencalvie. Pictish broch in church glebe. Ardgay is ten miles west of A9/A836 (signed). Sunday Services: second Sunday May to September 3pm, Communion second Sunday in July 3pm

Open during daylight hours

CHURCH OF SCOTLAND **A**

CROICK CHURCH, ARDGAY, SUTHERLAND

DALAROSSIE CHURCH, INVERNESS-SHIRE

417 DALAROSSIE CHURCH, INVERNESS-SHIRE

NH 767 242

3 miles from old A9

Dalarossie Church, on the River Findhorn, is an ancient place of worship dating back to the eighth century - St Fergus. The present building, set within the walled graveyard, dates from 1790 and features an ancient baptismal font as well as a 'covenant stone'. Services April–October first and third Sundays, 10.30am, November–March first Sunday, 10.30am

Open by arrangement, telephone Rev Lilian M Bruce 01463 772242 or Mrs Vivian Roden 01808 511355

CHURCH OF SCOTLAND (by arrangement) **B**

418 DAVIOT CHURCH, INVERNESS-SHIRE

NH 722 394

on A9, 6 miles south of Inverness

Built in 1826 and restored 1991. There has been a place of worship on the site since early times, long before its charter was granted in the 13th century. The surrounding graveyard tells of the changing history of this interesting parish. Sunday Service 12noon

Open by arrangement telephone Rev Lilian M Bruce 01463 772242

CHURCH OF SCOTLAND

(guides by arrangement) **B**

DAVIOT CHURCH, INVERNESS-SHIRE

419 ST JAMES THE GREAT CHURCH, DINGWALL, ROSS-SHIRE

NH 552 588

Castle Street, Dingwall

The building is on the site of an earlier chapel (1806) which was demolished in 1851 and the new building erected to a New Gothic design by J L Pearson. It was consecrated in 1854 but gutted by fire in 1871. Restoration, by Alexander Ross, Inverness, began immediately, following the original design. Sunday Services: 8.30 and 11.30am (except 1st Sunday); 11am October to March (except 1st Sunday). April to September 1st Sunday, Strathpeffer

Open daily during daylight hours

SCOTTISH EPISCOPAL ♿ WC

ST JAMES THE GREAT CHURCH, DINGWALL

420 ST DUTHAC'S CHURCH, DORNIE, ROSS-SHIRE

NG 884 268

Dornie, by Kyle of Lochalsh (beside Eilean Donan Castle)

The first Catholic church on the site was built in 1703. The present building dates from 1860, architect Joseph A Hansom. It is in simple Gothic style with nave and chancel. The stone reredos has polished granite shafts, while similar columns support the altar. The simplicity continues with the demi-octagonal stone pulpit and braced rafter roof. Sunday Service 10.30am; Saturday Vigil 7.30pm

Open daily

ROMAN CATHOLIC **B**

421 DORNOCH CATHEDRAL, DORNOCH, SUTHERLAND

NH 797 897

Dornoch

Cathedral founded by Bishop Gilbert de Moravia in 13th century, the first service in the building was held in 1239. The medieval masonry of the chancel and the crossing piers remains mostly intact today. The nave was destroyed by fire in 1570, the transepts and choir were reroofed 1616, and the nave rebuilt 1837. In 1924 the interior stonework was exposed. Lavish display of stained glass, including several windows by James Ballantine, others by Percy Bacon, and the St Gilbert window by Crear McCartney 1989. Sunday Services: 11am all year, 8.30pm summer months

Open during daylight hours

CHURCH OF SCOTLAND ♿ **A**

422 DUNLICHITY CHURCH, DUNLICHITY, INVERNESS-SHIRE

NH 659 327

near Loch Duntelchaig

An ancient place of worship, much earlier than the present building which dates back in part to the 16th century. Many interesting features, including a 1702 handbell, and surrounded by a graveyard of much historical interest, with its own 1759 watch-house. Services: April-October first Sunday, 7pm; November-March first Sunday, 10.45am

Open by arrangement telephone Rev Lilian M Bruce 01463 772242

CHURCH OF SCOTLAND (guides by arrangement) **B**

423 ST MARY'S CHURCH, ESKADALE, INVERNESS-SHIRE

NH 453 399

A spacious white-harled church in a picturesque woodland setting. Built 1826 by the 14th Lord Lovat. Alterations and additions by Peter Paul Pugin 1881. Founder's tomb in the chancel. Lovat family graveyard to the west of the church. The contemporary stable to accomodate horses ridden by those attending Mass, 50m to the west of the church, is an unusual feature. On a minor road on the south east side of the River Beauly. Served by St Mary's, Beauly. Sunday Mass 9am alternate Sundays

Open by arrangement, telephone Mr James Christie 01463 741536

ROMAN CATHOLIC **B**

424 FEARN ABBEY, ROSS-SHIRE

NH 837 773

Hill of Fearn

Known as 'The Lamp of the North', it is one of the oldest pre-Reformation Scottish churches still in use for worship. Rebuilt 1772 by James Rich and restored by Ian G Lindsay & Partners 1972. Originally a monastery of Premonstratensian monks of the Order of St Augustine. Patrick Hamilton, burnt for heresy at St Andrews in 1528, was the Commendatory Abbot from 1517 to 1528. A9, Hill of Fearn Village. Sunday Service 11am

Open May to September, Saturday and Sunday 10am-4.30pm.
Or by appointment, telephone Mr B Paterson 01862 832756

CHURCH OF SCOTLAND WC **A**

FEARN ABBEY

FORT GEORGE CHAPEL

425 FORT GEORGE CHAPEL, INVERNESS-SHIRE

NH 761 567

Fort George, Ardersier

The garrison chapel built in 1767, probably to a design by William Skinner. Interior, two-tiered arcade on three sides supported by Roman Doric columns. Eighteenth-century three-decker pulpit. Working garrison. Visitor displays, Historic Scotland. Off A96, north-east of Inverness

Open April to September, Monday to Saturday 9.30am-6.30pm, Sunday 9.30am-6.30pm; October to March, Monday to Saturday 9.30am-4.30pm, Sunday 2-4.30pm

NON-DENOMINATIONAL **A**

426 GAIRLOCH FREE CHURCH, GAIRLOCH, ROSS-SHIRE

NG 804 761

Gairloch

On a commanding site overlooking Loch Gairloch. Gothic in style, to a design by Matthews & Lawrie 1881. Simple interior with original fittings and Gothic panelled gallery across east end. Spandrels of roof trusses with cusped decoration. Fabric appeal. A832 to Gairloch. Sunday Services 11am and 5pm. Gaelic Service 12noon alternate Sunday

Open by arrangement, telephone the Minister 01445 712371

FREE CHURCH OF SCOTLAND WC **C**

427 ST MARY AND ST FINNAN CHURCH, GLENFINNAN, INVERNESS-SHIRE

NM 904 808

The church was consecrated in 1873. Designed by E Welby Pugin in the Gothic style, the church enjoys an elevated and commanding position overlooking Loch Shiel with a spectacular view of the loch and surrounding hills. The church is a memorial chapel to the MacDonalds of Glenaladale, the family with whom Bonnie Prince Charlie stayed prior to the raising of the Jacobite standard at Glenfinnan in August 1745. The church contains memorial stones to the Prince and to members of the MacDonald family. In the village, 15 miles west of Fort William on A830 to Mallaig. Sunday Mass 1pm

Open daily sunrise to sunset

ROMAN CATHOLIC **B**

428 INVER MEETING HOUSE, INVER, ROSS-SHIRE

NH 863 828

New Street, Inver, by Portmahomack

A meeting house in the style of cottages. Inver, largely in original form, originates as a settlement of persons displaced during clearances. Memorial, to north of village on the shore, marks common grave of cholera victims, a large proportion of the population. Sunday Service 10am

Open by appointment telephone Mr Skinner 01862 871522

CHURCH OF SCOTLAND ♿

429 OLD HIGH CHURCH, INVERNESS

NH665 455

Church Street, Inverness

Present building completed 1772 to a plan by George Fraser of Edinburgh on site of medieval church. Traditionally thought to be the site where St Columba converted Brude, King of the Picts to Christianity. Porches, apse and chancel arch date from 1891, to designs by Ross & Macbeth. Lowest portion of the west bell tower is 15th or 16th century. The colours of the Queen's Own Cameron Highlanders are hung and the Regiment's Books of Remembrance are housed in the church. Two-manual organ by Henry Willis & Sons 1895, rebuilt by H Hilsdon 1923. Stained glass by, amongst others, Douglas Strachan 1925, Stephen Adam & Co 1893, and A Ballantine & Gardiner 1899. Sunday Service 11.15am all year; mid-June to mid-September Fridays 1pm

Open June, July and August, Fridays noon-2pm. Guided tour at 12.30pm

CHURCH OF SCOTLAND **A**

OLD HIGH CHURCH, INVERNESS

430 ST ANDREW'S CATHEDRAL, INVERNESS

NH 664 450

Ardross Street, Inverness

First new cathedral completed in Great Britain after the Reformation. 1869 by local architect Alexander Ross. Polished granite pillars, stained glass, fine furnishings. Angel font after Thorvaldsen. Founder's memorial, ikons presented by Tsar of Russia. Peal of bells. Fine choir. On west bank of River Ness, just above Ness Bridge, A862, close to town centre. Sunday Services: Eucharist 8.15am, Family Eucharist 9.30am, Sung Eucharist 11am, Choral Evensong 6.30pm; Matins, Eucharist and Evensong daily

Open daily 8.30am–6pm (later June to September)

SCOTTISH EPISCOPAL May–Sept WC **A**

431 ST MARY'S CHURCH, INVERNESS

NH 662 455

30 Huntly Street, Inverness

On the west bank of the River Ness, very close to the town centre. Built 1837 by William Robertson in Gothic Revival manner. Between pedestrian bridge and traffic bridge.

Sunday Services: Mass 10am and 6.30pm; Vigil Mass Saturday 7pm

Open daily, summer 8am–9pm, winter 9am–5pm

ROMAN CATHOLIC **A**

432 ST MICHAEL & ALL ANGELS, INVERNESS

NH 659 457

Abban Street/Lochalsh Road, Inverness

In 1877 Canon Edward Medley established a mission in the thatched cottage at Maggot Green, close to River Ness: a church was built in 1886 to a design by Alexander Ross. As the site proved liable to flooding, it was re-built in extended form in Abban Street in 1903–4, also by Ross. Many interior fittings, altar with gilded angels and tester, font with lofty steeple cover and archangel east window were designed by Sir Ninian Comper and installed between 1904–1928. Situated close to the town centre, by the riverside, to the north-west of Friar's Bridge. Sunday Services: Sunday Low Mass 8am, Parish Mass 11am, Low Mass daily

Open daily 9am–4pm Other times, telephone Canon Black: 01463 233797

SCOTTISH EPISCOPAL WC **B**

433 ST STEPHEN'S, INVERNESS

NH 672 449

Southside Road, Inverness

By W L Carruthers 1897 in Arts and Crafts Gothic, the hall added later. The church consists of a nave, single north transept and an apsidal chancel. Square tower with a delicate needle spire. High open roof, pulpit of locally grown native oak. Noteworthy stained glass of 1897 and 1906 by A Ballantine & Son. Two-manual organ by Wadsworth Bros 1902. At junction of Old Edinburgh Road and Southside Road. Sunday Service 10am; Evening Communion 8pm, fourth Sunday of June and last Sunday of January, April and September

Open by arrangement, telephone the Minister 01463 237129

CHURCH OF SCOTLAND B

ST STEPHEN'S, INVERNESS

434 TWEEDMOUTH MEMORIAL CHAPEL, INVERNESS

NM 663 445

Royal Northern Infirmary, Ness Walk, Inverness

Earliest example of purpose-built ecumencial worship space in Scotland, built in 1898, architects A Ross and R B MacBeth. Three sanctuary areas for Reformed, Roman Catholic and Episcopalian worship. Sunday Service 2.30pm, Monday 3.30pm

Keys available from Hospital Porters

INTERDENOMINATIONAL A

435 KINLOCHLEVEN PARISH CHURCH, INVERNESS-SHIRE

NS 187 621

Riverside Road, Kinlochleven

Built 1930 to a simple but elegant design by J Jeffrey Waddell with a high arch at the chancel end. Chancel area is a round bell-shape with stained glass windows depicting biblical scenes. Two stained glass windows in the south wall of the nave depicting St Andrew and St George. Linked with Nether Lochaber in 1981. A82 from Glencoe. Sunday Services 10am and 6.30pm

Keys available from 15 Wades Road, Kinlochleven

CHURCH OF SCOTLAND

KINLOCHLEVEN PARISH CHURCH

436 ST FINAN'S CHURCH, KINLOCHMOIDART, INVERNESS-SHIRE

NM 710 728

The church stands on a ledge of level ground in woodland above the mouth of the River Moidart and below an impressively steep hillside. It was built in 1857 to a design by Alexander Ross in simple Early English style, with crow stepped gables, a small belfry and a porch. There are two unusual stained glass windows by the Victorian artist Jemima Blackburn. Up a track leading off the A861, half mile north of the bridge over the River Moidart. Sunday Service, Easter and May to September 5.30pm

Open daily

SCOTTISH EPISCOPAL **C**

437 LAIRG PARISH CHURCH, SUTHERLAND

NC 583 065

Church Hill Road, Lairg

A simple Gothic church, built of local granite, 1847, designed by William Leslie. The graveyard, one and a half miles away, served the original church and contains some interesting monuments, including a large marble monument to Sir James Matheson of Achany. Linked with St Callan's, Rogart and Pitfure. Sunday Service 10.45am, also 6.30pm on first Sunday of month

Open by arrangement, telephone Rev J Goskirk 01549 402373

Adjacent church hall (built 1998) has level access and adapted toilets

CHURCH OF SCOTLAND WC

438 KIEL CHURCH, LOCHALINE, INVERNESS-SHIRE

NM 972 538

Lochaline, Morvern

The present church is the third on this site. Ruins of a medieval church are on the site of the original and much earlier building which, according to legend, was erected at the command of St Columba. Today's church was designed by P MacGregor Chalmers 1898. Interesting stained glass. Memorial plaque to the MacLeods, father and son, whose ministry here spanned more than a century. Fifteenth-century cross outside the front of the church. The nearby 18th-century Session House contains a collection of carved stones eighth to 16th centuries. One mile out of the village on the Drimnin road. Sunday Service 11am

Open daily all year

CHURCH OF SCOTLAND **C**

439 LOCHCARRON PARISH CHURCH (WEST CHURCH), ROSS-SHIRE

NG 893 391

Former United Free Church designed by William Mackenzie, 1910, sited in centre of Lochcarron. Crisply painted; standard UF layout. Also of interest the burial ground a mile east of the village with roofless former parish church (1751), superseded by neighbouring big, white-harled East Church (1834-36), James Smith, architect. Open during summer months. Services (West church only) every Sunday 11am, and second and fourth Sunday 6pm

Open during daylight hours

CHURCH OF SCOTLAND (after services) WC

440 OUR LADY AND ST BEAN, CANNICH, MARYDALE, INVERNESS-SHIRE

NH 342 317

Simple stone church in Gothic style, with adjoining presbytery, walled garden, school and schoolhouse, designed as a unit by Joseph A Hansom 1868. The church has nave and apse with a porch and circular bell tower. St Bean is said to have been a monk of Iona, a cousin of St Columba, and the first to evangelise Strathglass. Sputan Bhain (NH 334 305) was the spring at which he baptised. On the other side of the road is Clachan Comair, a walled graveyard with the ruins of a small 17th-century church, on the site of an early tenth-century chapel dedicated to St Bean. In 1998 a new altar was installed made from solid 300-year-old oak, designed by local artist Alistair MacPherson. The former presbytery is being developed as a monastic retreat, with an icon painting workshop. Served by St Mary's, Beauly. On the north side of the A831, between Cannich Bridge and Comar Bridge.

Mass 9am alternate Sundays.

Open daily

ROMAN CATHOLIC WC **B**

441 MELNESS CHURCH, SUTHERLAND

NC 586 634

near Talmine, 4 miles from junction with A838 (Tongue-Durness)

Built at the turn of the 20th century by local craftsmen to replace an earlier building at an adjacent site. Interior totally wood lined. Local feeling was that it should have been called the 'Kerr Memorial Church' as it was due to the Minister at the time, Rev Cathel Kerr, that the church was completed. Sunday Service 12.30pm (Holy Communion held twice yearly)

Open at all times

CHURCH OF SCOTLAND WC

442 MOY CHURCH, INVERNESS-SHIRE

NH 772 342

on old A9, 13 miles south of Inverness

Built in 1765, on a previous site, and surrounded by an interesting graveyard with its own watch-house. Memorial stone to Donald Fraser, the hero of the 'Rout of Moy', just before the Battle of Culloden in 1746. Services: April-October fourth Sunday, 10.45am, November-March third and fifth Sunday, 10.45am

Open by arrangement telephone Rev Lilian M Bruce 01463 772242 or Mrs Vivian Roden 01808 511355

CHURCH OF SCOTLAND (by arrangement) **B**

MOY CHURCH, INVERNESS-SHIRE

443 NAIRN OLD PARISH CHURCH, NAIRN

NH 879 564

Academy Street/Inverness Road, Nairn

Considered the finest structure in the area, 1897 by John Starforth. Architecture of Early English Transition period, Gothic reminiscences are abundant. Transeptal in form but almost circular in shape. Square tower is almost 100 ft high. Lovely light interior. Glorious stained glass. Sunday Service 11am, also June to August 9.30am

Open weekdays 9.30am-12.30pm

CHURCH OF SCOTLAND WC **A**

NETHER LOCHABER PARISH CHURCH, ONICH, INVERNESS-SHIRE

444 NETHER LOCHABER PARISH CHURCH, ONICH, INVERNESS-SHIRE

NN 031 614

Onich, near Fort William

Built in 1911 to replace original Telford church at Creag Mhor, using some of the original stone. Known as one of the finest rural churches in the Highlands. Most illustrious minister was Dr Alexander Stewart 1851-1901, known as 'Nether Lochaber' and renowned throughout the Celtic world for his wide-ranging learning and writing. Twenty ft Celtic cross erected by the Stewart Society at Innis-na Bhirlin cemetery off A82 five miles north of Onich. Linked with Kinlochleven 1981. Church located on A82 in Onich village eleven miles south of Fort William. Sunday Service 12 noon

Keys available from Glenmorven Guest House, Onich

CHURCH OF SCOTLAND

445 ST MOLUAG, EORROPAIDH, NESS, ISLE OF LEWIS

NB 519 651

The building probably dates from the twelfth century, but the site is believed to have been consecrated in the sixth century and is probably the place where Christianity was first preached to the people of Lewis. The church was restored in 1912 by Norman Forbes of Stornoway, under the guidance of the architect J S Richardson; the altars date from this restoration. The side chapel is connected to the main church only through a squint. The church has no heating, electricity or water; lighting is by candles and oil lamps. Two hundred yards from B8013 (signed Eorropaidh from A857). Services 11am Easter Day, and on 1st Sunday of May to September

Open during daylight hours, Easter to 1st Sunday in September. Vehicular access impossible. In wet weather, path to church can be muddy

SCOTTISH EPISCOPAL **A**

446 CARINISH CHURCH, NORTH UIST

NF 820 604

Clachan an Luib, North Uist

The original Church of Scotland for North Uist. The main feature is that the communion pews run down the length of the church so that those taking communion would sit side-on to the pulpit. Sunday Service: 6pm, Gaelic once a month

Open by arrangement, telephone 01875 580219

CHURCH OF SCOTLAND wc **B**

447 CLACHAN CHURCH, NORTH UIST

NF 874 760

Built 1889 for the United Free Church, architect Thomas Bennie of Glasgow. Considerable difficulty was experienced procuring the site from Sir William Powlet Campbell Orde, Bart. After lengthy negotiations he reluctantly gave the present site at an annual rental of £3/9/-. Sunday Service: 12noon in English

Open by arrangement, telephone 01875 580219

CHURCH OF SCOTLAND wc

CLACHAN CHURCH, NORTH UIST

448 KILMUIR CHURCH, NORTH UIST

NF 708 706

west side of North Uist, close to Balranald RSPB Reserve

Originally North Uist Parish Church. Gothic T-plan by Alexander Sharp, 1892-4. In the south-west inner angle is a two-stage tower, its battlemented parapet enclosing a slated pyramidal spire. Inside, a wealth of pitch-pine. One of the few remaining Gaelic-essential charges; during the morning Gaelic service one can hear, and participate in, the precenting of Gaelic psalms. Sunday Services: 10am (Gaelic), 6pm (English).

Open by arrangement, contact Mr Macbain telephone 01876 510241

CHURCH OF SCOTLAND wc

KILMUIR CHURCH, NORTH UIST

449 PITFURE CHURCH, SUTHERLAND

NC 710 038

Pitfure

A simple, pleasant place to worship. Built by the United Free congregation in 1910, architect Robert J Macbeth, Inverness. Linked with Lairg and St Callan's Rogart. Sunday Service first, third and fifth Sundays of month, October to May, 12.15pm; June to September 11.30am. Second Sunday of month 6.30pm

Open daily

CHURCH OF SCOTLAND

450 ST MAELRUBHA'S, POOLEWE, ROSS-SHIRE

NG 857 807

St Maelrubha's Close, Poolewe

The first Episcopal church to be built on the north-west coast of Scotland since the Jacobite rebellion of 1745, St Maelrubha's (a former cow byre) was dedicated in 1965. Tiny, simple and made of local stone, it houses a fragment of the Celtic cross erected as a monument to the Saint and brought from Applecross. Memorial to the Highland Fieldcraft Training Centre. Visiting clergy take Sunday services during the summer. Close to Inverewe Gardens (National Trust for Scotland). Sunday Service 11am, Wednesday 10am

Open during daylight hours

SCOTTISH EPISCOPAL

451 PORTMAHOMACK PARISH CHURCH, ROSS-SHIRE

NH 917 846

off Main Street

Simple rectangular former United Free Church building, architects Andrew Maitland & Sons 1908. Flower Festival during Gala Week (last in July). Tarbat Discovery Centre (former Tarbat Old Parish Church) has displays of church and archaeology, including Pictish stones, and place for private prayer in crypt. Adjacent archaeological dig ongoing. Sunday Service 11.30am

Please ask for key at Village Shop (50m), shop hours only

CHURCH OF SCOTLAND

PORTMAHOMACK PARISH CHURCH, ROSS-SHIRE

452 ST CALLAN'S CHURCH, ROGART, SUTHERLAND

NC 715 038

Rebuilt in 1777 on the site of a medieval church. The austere whitewashed exterior with its plain sash windows gives little hint of the warm, gleaming interior. A high canopied pulpit stands against the east wall. Long communion table and pews. Other pews are tiered from the entrance to the west end. Two small stained glass memorial windows on either side of the pulpit – Nativity and Penitence by Margaret Chilton and Marjorie Kemp 1929. Modern vestry wing built in 1984. From crossroads at Pittentrail, take Rhilochan/Balnacoil road. Church on right approximately two miles. Linked with Lairg and Pitfure. Sunday Service second and fourth Sundays of month, October to May, 12.15pm; June to September 11.30am

Open daily

CHURCH OF SCOTLAND WC **B**

453 ST JOHN THE BAPTIST CHURCH, ROTHIEMURCHUS INVERNESS-SHIRE

NH 900 111

Rothiemurchus

Church founded by John Peter Grant, 11th Laird of Rothiemurchus 1930. Architect, Sir Ninian Comper. A simple white interior with a groin vaulted ceiling and a rose damask baldacchino. Simple burial ground surrounds the church. Approximately one mile from the centre of Aviemore, 'the little white church on the ski road'. Sunday Service Holy Eucharist 10.30am

Open by arrangement, contact the Rectory, Inverdruie 01479 811433

SCOTTISH EPISCOPAL **B**

454 DALIBURGH/DALABROG, SOUTH UIST

NF 754 214

Built originally as South Uist Free Church in 1862-3, now Church of Scotland. Manse completed 1880 and vestry/hall behind low wall added later. All harled. Church rectangular in plan with three bays with round-headed openings and a single window in either gable. Door and apex belfry to south gable. Pulpit with panelled front. Communion table and war memorial based on design of that at Howmore by Archibald Scott. Sunday Service: 11.00am

Open at all times

CHURCH OF SCOTLAND WC **B**

HOWMORE CHURCH, SOUTH UIST

455 HOWMORE CHURCH, SOUTH UIST

NF 758 364

Simple austere building by John McDearmid, 1858, set in open land overlooking the Atlantic. Acts as landmark for west coast fishermen. One of few churches in Scotland with central Communion table. Nearby are remains of 13th century church. Sunday Service: 12.30pm

Open at all times

CHURCH OF SCOTLAND ♿ WC **B**

456 IOCHDAR CHURCH, EOCHAR, SOUTH UIST

Built 1889 as a Mission House by David MacIntosh, a small, compact church with traditional pews and central pulpit. The church particularly lends itself to be a place for quiet prayer and meditation. Sunday Service: 6pm first Sunday of the month

Open by arrangement, telephone Mrs Stephenson on 01870 610401

CHURCH OF SCOTLAND

457 FODDERTY & STRATHPEFFER PARISH CHURCH

NH 482 480

Strathpeffer

Designed by William C Joass and built 1888-90 as part of the development of Strathpeffer as Britain's most northerly spa town. A rectangular building with side aisles and balcony to the rear; the chancel extends from the nave under a low roof. Services: Sunday 11.00am, also last Sunday in the month April-October 8.00pm

Open 25-27 July 2000 for a Flower Festival, other times by arrangement, telephone the Minister on 01997 421398

CHURCH OF SCOTLAND WC

458 ST ANNE'S CHURCH, STRATHPEFFER, ROSS-SHIRE

NH 483 580

Strathpeffer

Designed by John Robertson as a memorial to Anne, Duchess of Sutherland and Countess of Cromartie, it was constructed between 1890 and 1892 with the chancel added in 1899. The pulpit is of Caen stone and alabaster, the altar and reredos of marble and alabaster showing carved reliefs. Stained glass windows are by J Powell & Sons 1891 and Heaton, Butler & Bayne 1892–c.1910. Sunday Service 10am, except 1st Sunday at 11am (April to September). No service first Sunday, October to March

Open daily, Easter–September

SCOTTISH EPISCOPAL B

ST ANNE'S CHURCH, STRATHPEFFER, ROSS-SHIRE

459 ST ANDREWS, TAIN, ROSS-SHIRE

NH 777 822

Manse Street, Tain

Designed 1887 by Ross & Macbeth, replacing an earlier corrugated iron structure. The earliest stained glass, by Ballantyne and Gardner, was moved from the earlier church. Other glass by A L Ward 1910, and W Wilson 1955 and 1961. Fine organ by Hamilton & Muller, restored 1986. Forward altar designed and carved from American oak by Peter Bailey of Skye, 1995. Services: Sunday Eucharist 11am; first Sunday of every month: Matins 10am; Thursday Eucharist 10am and 6.30pm

Open 10am–4 pm

SCOTTISH EPISCOPAL WC B

ST ANNE'S CHURCH, STRATHPEFFER, ROSS-SHIRE

460 ST PETER'S & ST ANDREW'S CHURCH, THURSO, CAITHNESS

ND 115 684

Princes Street, Thurso

Built in 1832 to a design by William Burn, the church is the centre point of the town, fronted by town square garden and war memorial. U-plan gallery. Pipe organ, Norman & Beard 1914. Stained glass includes 'The Sower' by Oscar Paterson 1922. Sunday Services 11am and 6.30pm

Open July to August daily, 2-4pm, 7-8pm

CHURCH OF SCOTLAND WC **B**

ST PETER'S & ST ANDREW'S CHURCH, THURSO, CAITHNESS

461 TOMATIN CHURCH, INVERNESS-SHIRE

NH 803 290

on east side of old A9 in village of Tomatin

A fine example of the 'tin churches' erected c1910 by the United Free Church to serve as mission churches and halls in areas of new population. Services: April-October: second and fifth Sundays, 10.30am, November-March: second and fourth Sundays: 10.30am

Open by arrangement telephone Rev Lilian M Bruce 01463 772242 or Mrs Vivian Roden 01808 511355

CHURCH OF SCOTLAND (by arrangement)

TOMATIN CHURCH, INVERNESS-SHIRE

ST ANDREW'S PARISH CHURCH, TONGUE, SUTHERLAND

462 ST ANDREW'S PARISH CHURCH, TONGUE, SUTHERLAND

NC 591 570

Tongue

Rebuilt by Donald Mackay, Master of Reay, in 1680 following the Reay family's conversion to Protestantism (c.1600). The site was that of the ancient Celtic and latterly Roman Catholic Church (St Peter's Chapel). During a renovation in 1729, a vault was built covering the graves of earlier members of the MacKay family. Information leaflets are available free in the church. The church is on the Durness road (A838) past Tongue Hotel. Sunday Service 11.00am

Open all year, daylight hours

CHURCH OF SCOTLAND A

463 OUR LADY OF THE WAVES & ST JOHN, VATERSAY, WESTERN ISLES

NL 646 961

Uidh, Vatersay

Small functional church for celebration of Mass and other church services. reached by causeway from Barra. Sunday Service: 3.30pm

Open at all times

ROMAN CATHOLIC WC

464 ST JOHN THE EVANGELIST, WICK, CAITHNESS

ND 363 505

Francis Street/Moray Street

Built 1870 to a design Alexander Ross of Inverness, St John's is especially attractive with a warm friendly atmosphere. Four-light windows known affectionately as the 'I am' windows ('I am the Good Shepherd, ...the Resurrection and the Life, ...the True Vine, ...the Bread of Life), by David Gulland, a former member of the vestry of St John's and a recognised expert in glass. Sunday Service 11.30am Sung Eucharist

Open by arrangement with Peter MacDougall telephone 01955 602914

SCOTTISH EPISCOPAL **B**

465 CHRIST CHURCH, ST KILDA, WESTERN ISLES

NF 100 994

Village Bay, St Kilda

The stimulus for the kirk, designed by Robert Stevenson, came from the Rev Dr John Macdonald who visited St Kilda several times in the early 19th century. The church fell into disrepair after evacuation in 1930. Renovated over a period of 20 years since coming into the care of the National Trust for Scotland in 1957. Services by arrangement. St Kilda is Scotland's first World Heritage Site.

Open by arrangement contact The National Trust for Scotland telephone 01631 570000

INTERDENOMINATIONAL

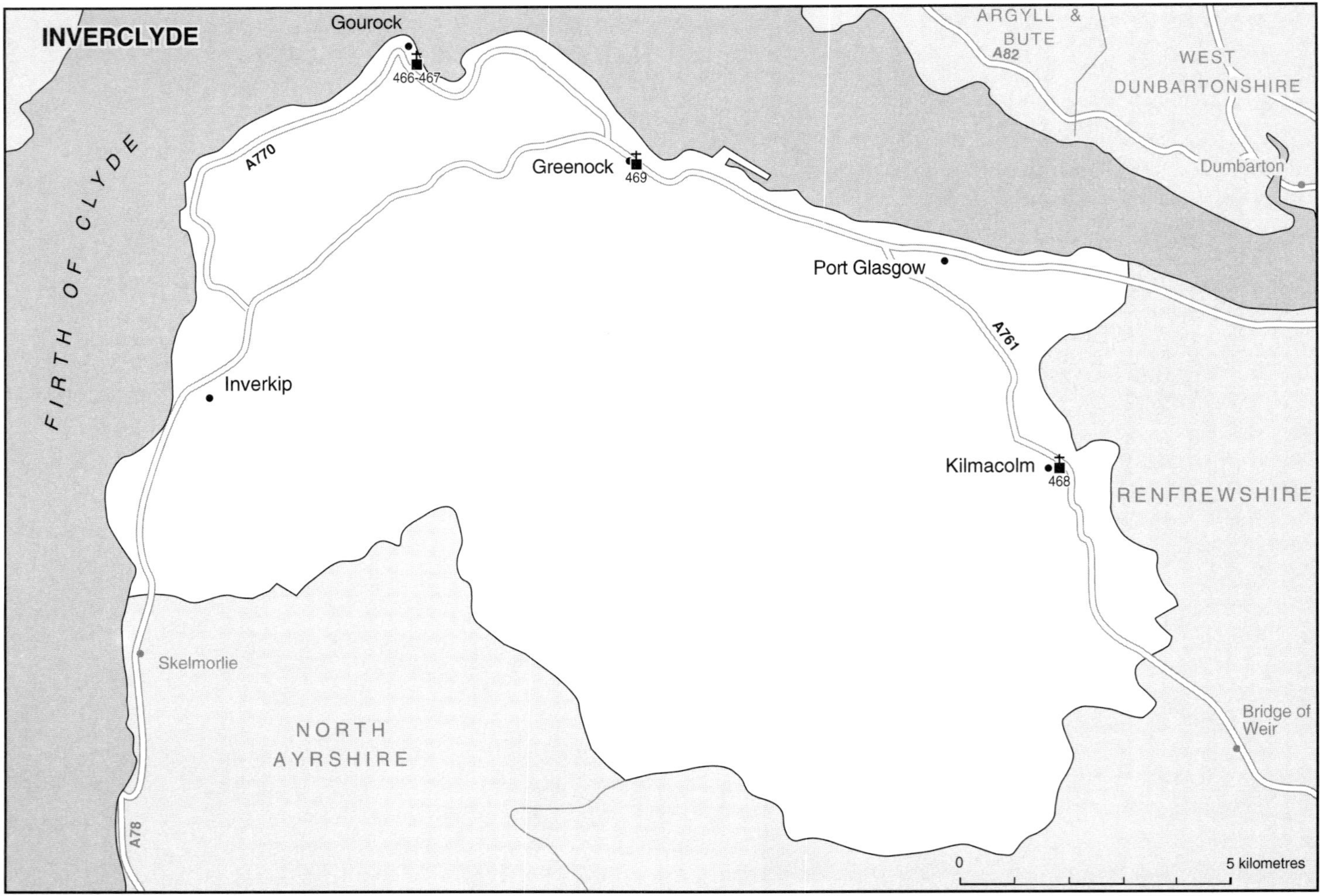
INVERCLYDE
Gourock
466-467
A770
Greenock
469
FIRTH OF CLYDE
ARGYLL &
BUTE
A82
WEST
DUNBARTONSHIRE
Dumbarton
Port Glasgow
A761
Inverkip
Kilmacolm
468
RENFREWSHIRE
Skelmorlie
NORTH
AYRSHIRE
Bridge of
Weir
A78
0
5 kilometres

INVERCLYDE

ST BARTHOLOMEW'S, GOUROCK

466 ST BARTHOLOMEW'S, GOUROCK

NS 239 777

Barrhill Road, Gourock

This beautiful little church sits on a cliff overlooking the River Clyde. 1867, designed by J C Sharp of Gourock. Chancel extension enhanced by a beautiful window depicting the Ascension designed by George Walton. Mural of the Nativity on the west wall. Memorial lectern and font. Plaque of Dutch tiles in remembrance of the hospitality given to Dutch soldiers, sailors and airmen during the Second World War. Sunday Service 10.30am Sung Eucharist, Wednesday 10.30am Holy Eucharist

Open by arrangement contact Mrs Boeker telephone 01475 521411

SCOTTISH EPISCOPAL WC **B**

467 ST NINIAN'S CHURCH, GOUROCK

NS 242 777

18 Royal Street, Gourock

Gourock formed part of the pre-Reformation parish of Inverkip, mentioned in Papal registers of 1216-27. In 1878 Archbishop Eyre of Glasgow arranged for the construction of a chapel-school to be dedicated to St Ninian. The foundation stone was laid in 1879. Extension carried out in 1982 for the visit to Scotland of Pope John Paul II. The altar contains marble from the papal altar at Bellahouston. Mosaics by Frank Tritschler, stained glass by Dom Ninian Sloan of Pluscarden Abbey, and a chasuble fashioned from an original Paisley shawl by Debbie Gonet. Small museum. Sunday Mass 9.30am and 11.30am; Daily 10am and Vigil Mass Saturday 5.30pm

Open daily 9am-4pm. Information leaflets in French, Spanish, Italian and German – children's worksheets also available. For access to museum, telephone Parish Priest 01475 632078 or fax 01475 631984. Website: //website.lineone.net/~st.ninians

ROMAN CATHOLIC

468 KILMACOLM OLD KIRK

NS 359 670

Kilmacolm

Built in 1830 James Dempster, Greenock, on the site of thirteenth and 16th-century churches. Thirteenth-century chancel is incorporated as the Murray Chapel. South aisle, J B Wilson, Glasgow, added 1903 contains stained glass window by C E Moira. Other stained glass by Norman Macdougall. Near centre of village, west of junction of B786 with A761. Sunday Service 11am, July and August 10am

Open daily 10am-4pm

CHURCH OF SCOTLAND **B**

KILMACOLM OLD KIRK

469 THE OLD WEST KIRK

NS 279 765

Esplanade, Greenock

Cruciform church first built 1591 at Westburn but rebuilt here (1926-28) with a new tower designed by James Miller. The masonry, window tracery and balustraded forestair are all original. Also brought from the old site are the surrounding headstones and graveslabs, some bearing trade emblems or coats of arms. Inside the church are galleries originally intended to be occupied by the laird, the sailors and the farmers of the parish. Notable collection of stained glass including windows by Morris & Co and Daniel Cottier. Behind the octagonal pulpit is a mural panel by the local artist Ian Philips, 1991. Sunday Service 11am

Open Wednesdays mid-May to mid-September from 10.30am-12noon. Second Saturday September 10am-4pm (Inverclyde Doors Open Day), other times by contacting Rev Ian Johnson 01475 888277

CHURCH OF SCOTLAND WC **B**

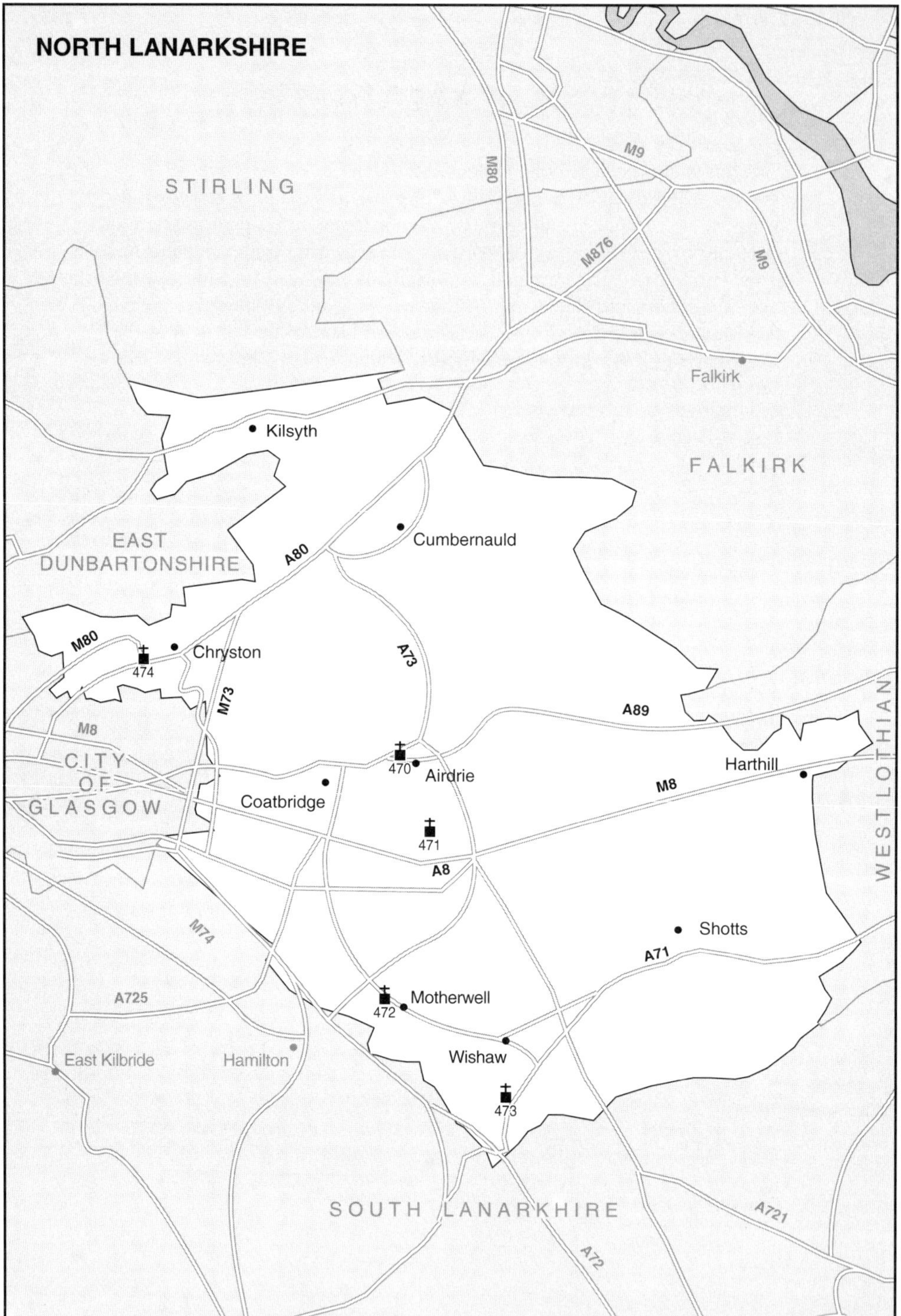

NORTH LANARKSHIRE
STIRLING
M80
M9
M876
Falkirk
Kilsyth
FALKIRK
Cumbernauld
EAST DUNBARTONSHIRE
A80
M80
Chryston
474
A73
M73
A89
M8
CITY OF GLASGOW
470
Airdrie
Harthill
Coatbridge
M8
471
A8
WEST LOTHIAN
M74
Shotts
A71
A725
472
Motherwell
Wishaw
East Kilbride
Hamilton
473
SOUTH LANARKHIRE
A721
A72

NORTH LANARKSHIRE

Local Representativs: Sheriff and Mrs V Canavan, 60 Alexander Street, Airdrie (*telephone* 01236 750493)

470 NEW MONKLAND PARISH CHURCH, AIRDRIE

NS 753 678

Condorrat Road, Glenmavis, Airdrie

A fine old Scots plain kirk which hides an attractive interior, Andrew Bell of Airdrie 1776. It holds a commanding position at the highest point in the village, and incorporates the bell tower of an earlier church (1698) which housed a cell for minor offenders. The old church was replaced when it 'suffered so badly from overcrowding that youthful members of the congregation colonised the exposed joists to roost!' The apse was added in 1904 by John Arthur. Extensive restoration 1997. Simple watchhouse by the cemetery. Sunday Service 10.30am

Open by arrangement, telephone Mr John Blades 01236 766511

CHURCH OF SCOTLAND WC **B**

471 CORPUS CHRISTI, CALDERBANK

NS 768 630

in the middle of Calderbank village

The Parish was founded in 1948 and the church was opened in 1952. It has undergone several renovations inside to accommodate liturgical changes. Stained glass window of the Sacraments, 1985, designed by Shona McInnis. New church furnishings by J McNally, made by a local craftsman. Sunday Services 9am, 11am, weekdays: 10 am, Saturday: 8.45am and Vigil 6pm.

Open 8am-8pm (if main door closed, use right-hand side door)

ROMAN CATHOLIC

472 DALZIEL ST ANDREW'S, MOTHERWELL

NS 752 571

Motherwell Cross

Union of the former Dalziel and St Andrew's Church of Scotland congregations in 1996. The parish of Dalziel has a history stretching back to the twelfth century, while St Andrew's was a daughter church of Dalziel. Erected in 1874, the building houses a Walker organ of 1900, recently restored. Worship is a sensitive mixture of traditional and modern with a warm welcome for all ages. Sunday Services 11am in the Main Sanctuary, Evening worship 6.30pm in the Mission Hall, Jupiter Street (except July and August)

Open Saturday 10am-12noon or by arrangement with the Church Officer 01698 266 284

CHURCH OF SCOTLAND WC

DALZIEL ST ANDREW'S, MOTHERWELL

473 OVERTOWN PARISH CHURCH

NS 801 527

Main Street, Overtown, by Wishaw

Village church built in 1876. Near picturesque Clyde Valley, Strathclyde Country Park and many other places of interest. A71, Edinburgh to Kilmarnock, 35 miles from Edinburgh

Open 13 and 20 May 2000 for sale of plants, with guided tours and café

CHURCH OF SCOTLAND

474 STEPPS PARISH CHURCH

NS 657 686

17 Whitehill Avenue, Stepps

Fine example of the neo-Gothic style favoured by ecclesiastical architect P MacGregor Chalmers 1900. Designed to reflect scale and simplicity of a village church. Interesting stained glass including works by Stephen Adam (1900). Pipe organ, Joseph Brook 1884, rebuilt James MacKenzie 1976. On rail and bus routes Glasgow–Cumbernauld. Sunday Service 10am mid June to mid August, 11am mid August to mid June

Open Tuesday, Thursday 10am-12 noon all year. Other times, telephone 0141 779 9556

CHURCH OF SCOTLAND

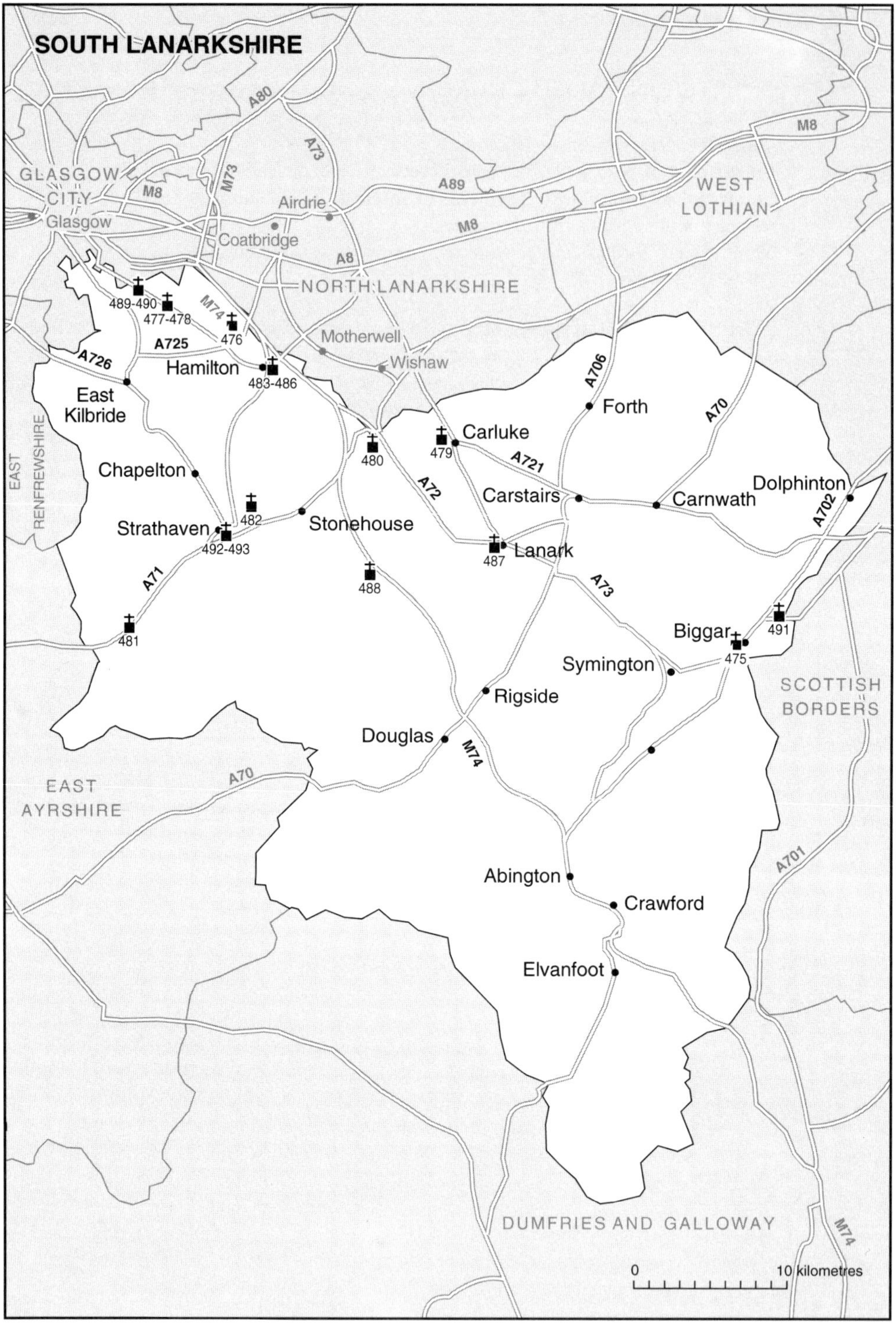

SOUTH LANARKSHIRE
GLASGOW CITY
Glasgow
Airdrie
Coatbridge
WEST LOTHIAN
NORTH LANARKSHIRE
Motherwell
Wishaw
EAST RENFREWSHIRE
A80
A73
M73
M8
A89
A8
M74
A725
A726
489-490
477-478
476
Hamilton
483-486
East Kilbride
Chapelton
Strathaven
492-493
482
Stonehouse
480
479
Carluke
A706
Forth
A70
A721
A72
Carstairs
Carnwath
Dolphinton
A702
Lanark
487
488
A71
481
A73
Biggar
491
475
Symington
Rigside
Douglas
SCOTTISH BORDERS
EAST AYRSHIRE
A70
Abington
Crawford
Elvanfoot
A701
DUMFRIES AND GALLOWAY
M74
0
10 kilometres

SOUTH LANARKSHIRE

Local Representativs: Mr Sandy Gilchrist, 11 Mercat Loan, Biggar (*telephone* 01899 221350)

475 BIGGAR KIRK

NT 040 379

Kirkstyle, Biggar

Rebuilt 1546, the last collegiate church to be founded before the Reformation in Scotland. A cruciform building with fine stained glass, including work by William Wilson and Crear McCartney. In the kirkyard are memorials to the forebears of William Ewart Gladstone and also Thomas Blackwood Murray, the Scottish motor pioneer of 'Albion'. From M74, A702, twelve miles from Abington. Sunday Services 11am also 9.30am June, July and August

Open daily in summer 9am–5pm.

In winter, key from Moat Park Heritage Centre opposite

CHURCH OF SCOTLAND **B**

476 BOTHWELL PARISH CHURCH

NS 705 586

Main Street, Bothwell

Scotland's oldest collegiate church still in use for worship and dedicated to St Bride, occupies the site of a former sixth-century church. Medieval choir. Nave and tower, 1833, David Hamilton, altered 1933. Monuments to the Earls of Douglas and the Duke of Hamilton. Stained glass by Gordon Webster, Douglas Strachan and Sir Edward Burne-Jones. Fascinating tales of an outstanding royal wedding and link with Bothwell Castle. Graveyard. Off A725 near Hamilton. Sunday Service 10.30am

Open daily Easter to September.

Bus parties welcome by arrangement, telephone 01698 853189

CHURCH OF SCOTLAND WC **A**

477 CAMBUSLANG OLD PARISH CHURCH

NS 646 600

3 Cairns Road, Kirkhill, Cambuslang

St Cadoc is believed to have had a holy site here c. AD 550, and early buildings have been recorded from twelfth century. The present building is by David Cousin 1841. Steeple with clock and bell. The chancel is by P MacGregor Chalmers 1922. Stained glass and tapestries by Sadie McLennan 1957. Heraldic shields of heritors decorate the ceiling. Interesting gravestones in churchyard including one to Rev William McCulloch, Minister at Scotland's largest ever revival 'The Cambuslang Wark' in 1742. Near Greenlees Road B759. Sunday Services September to June 11am and 6.30pm; July and August 9.30am and 11am

Open by arrangement, telephone Mr A Smith 0141 641 3585

CHURCH OF SCOTLAND WC **B**

478 ST BRIDE'S, CAMBUSLANG

NS 643 604

21 Greenlees Road, Cambuslang (opposite Police Station)

The church, which opened in 1960, has a Crucifixion window, an example of the early work of stained glass artist Gordon M Webster, and another free-standing window also by Webster. Services: Saturday Vigil 6pm, Sunday 8.30 and 10am, 12noon and 6pm

Open 8am–8pm every day

ROMAN CATHOLIC

479 ST ANDREW'S PARISH CHURCH, CARLUKE

NS 843 508

Mount Stewart Street, Carluke

The original church was replaced by the present building in 1799 following designs by Henry Bell (of the steamship 'Comet' fame). It incorporates an arch inside the porch and a window with slender fluted pillars in the front of tower from the old church. The tower of the old church has been retained as a monument in its original site in the old graveyard at the bottom of the town. Within the church are an organ made by H Willis and Sons and installed in 1903, stained glass windows including one made by Gordon McWhirter Webster (1932) and a pulpit fall and companion communion table runner by Marilyn E W McGregor DA (1999). Sunday Service 11.00am

Open by arrangement, telephone Mrs Jennifer Johnstone 01555 750155.

Flower Festival, 9 to 11 September 2000

CHURCH OF SCOTLAND **B**

ST ANDREW'S PARISH CHURCH, CARLUKE

480 DALSERF PARISH CHURCH

NS 800 507

Dalserf

Built 1655, centre transept added 1892. Oblong building with pulpit on long side. Outside stairs to three galleries. Belfry. Two large memorial windows on either side of pulpit by Douglas Hogg. The graveyard contains a pre-Norman hogback stone and an outstanding Covenanting memorial, 1753, to Rev John MacMillan, founder of the Reformed Presbyterian Church. Off A72 between Garrion Bridge and Rosebank. Sunday Service 12 noon

Open by arrangement, telephone Church Officer, Mr W Knox 01698 883770

CHURCH OF SCOTLAND **A**

DALSERF PARISH CHURCH

481 DRUMCLOG MEMORIAL KIRK

NS 640 389

Drumclog

1912 by J McLellan Fairley. The church has strong associations with the covenanters. A71, five miles west on Darvel road. Part of Avendale Old Church. Sunday Service 9.30am. All-age communion on the first Sunday of each month, except January, July and August. There is also an open-air Conventicle Service at the Battle of Drumclog Monument on the first Sunday of June

Open by arrangement, telephone Mr J Spence 01357 521939.

Website: www.garrion.co.uk/avendale

CHURCH OF SCOTLAND

DRUMCLOG MEMORIAL KIRK

482 GLASSFORD PARISH CHURCH

NS 726 470

Jackson Street, Glassford

Built 1820. Memorial stained glass windows to Rev Gavin Lang, grandfather of Cosmo Lang, Archbishop of Canterbury. Ruins of 1633 church and Covenanter's stone. Off A71 Stonehouse–Strathaven or A723 Hamilton–Strathaven. Linked with Strathaven East. Sunday Service 10am

Open by arrangement.
Also Doors Open Day, telephone Rev W Stewart 01357 521138

CHURCH OF SCOTLAND WC **B**

483 HAMILTON OLD PARISH CHURCH

NS 723 555

Strathmore Road, Hamilton

The present building is a Georgian gem. The only church designed and built by William Adam, 1734. Samples from the roof timbers found to be full of lead shot – Adam used wood from an old man-of-war! Chancel furnishings include embroidery by Hannah Frew Paterson. Exceptionally detailed engraved glass windows by Anita Pate depict the history of the church back to the sixth century. Memorial stained glass window of African animals to John Stevenson Hamilton, founder of Kruger National Park. Eleventh-century Netherton Cross and Covenanting memorials in graveyard. In centre of town. Sunday Service 10.45am, July and August 10am

Open Monday to Friday, 10.30am-3.30pm. Or by arrangement, telephone 01698 281905, Monday to Friday 9am-2pm. Easter Sunday, Church decorated with thousands of daffodils. E-mail: hamilton_old_parish@churchh.freeserve.com Website: www.churchh.freeserve.co.uk

CHURCH OF SCOTLAND (by arrangement on weekdays) WC **A**

HAMILTON OLD PARISH CHURCH

HAMILTON WEST PARISH CHURCH

484 HAMILTON WEST PARISH CHURCH

NS 712 558

Peacock Cross, Burnbank Road, Hamilton

The church was originally founded in 1874 as the 'Burnbank Mission Station' of St John's Free Church. Having been raised to full status in 1875, the church was rebuilt in 1880 and the Glasgow architect John Hutchison was commissioned. The result is the present building, whose design exhibits many features in the 13th-century Gothic style. The interior has one of the best examples in Scotland of a wooden hammerbeam roof. The organ was built by Hill & Son of London 1902 and is still in use today. The exterior is floodlit, highlighting the stonework which was restored in 1988. Sunday Service 10.45am, except July 10.00am

Open by arrangement, telephone Mr James Murdie 01698 425237

CHURCH OF SCOTLAND WC **B**

485 ST JOHN'S CHURCH, HAMILTON

NS 724 523

Duke Street, Hamilton

Idiosyncratic classical building (originally a chapel of ease) 1835. The interior was renovated in 1971 by Cullen Lochead & Brown who also completed the St John's Centre, opened 1970, and incorporating the former St John's Grammar School of 1836 and the Centenary Hall of 1934. In the St John's Centre Chapel stained glass ('Wings') by Susan Bradbury. Located at the 'Top Cross' opposite Marks & Spencer. Sunday Services 10.45am and 6.30pm (summer 10am and 9pm)

Open Mon to Saturday, 10am-12 noon and 2-4pm. St John's Centre open to public

CHURCH OF SCOTLAND **C**

ST JOHN'S CHURCH, HAMILTON

486 ST MARY THE VIRGIN, HAMILTON

NS 721 567

Auchingramont Road, Hamilton

The building designed by John Henderson was opened for worship in 1847 and is early English in style. Chancel ceiling panels were painted by Mabel Royds (1874-1941). There are fine stained glass commemorative windows with several memorials in marble and stone reflecting the links with the town's military history. Sunday Services 8.30 and 10am, 1st and 3rd Sunday 6pm; Wednesday 10am.

Open daily during March to September (key at Rectory)

SCOTTISH EPISCOPAL WC **B**

487 ST NICHOLAS PARISH CHURCH, LANARK

NS 881 437

The Cross, Lanark

By John Reid of Nemphlar 1774. Stained glass, baptismal font in Caen stone. Fine pipe organ. On A73, 30 miles south of Glasgow, follow signs for New Lanark. Sunday Service 11am, Wednesday 10.15am

Open during Doors Open Day and by arrangement, telephone Rev J Thomson 01555 662600. Kirkin' of Lord Cornet, 2 June, 12 noon 2000

CHURCH OF SCOTLAND

WC **B**

ST NICHOLAS PARISH CHURCH, LANARK

488 LESMAHAGOW OLD PARISH CHURCH

NS 814 399

David I granted a church and lands to the Tironensian monks in 1144. He also granted the right of sanctuary, violated in 1335 when the church was burned, with villagers inside, by John Eltham, brother of Edward I. The present church was built in 1803 and the apse added in the 1890s. Pipe organ 1889. Several stained glass windows including one whose central panel, 'The Descent from the Cross', is a copy of that in Antwerp Cathedral. The bell is dated 1625. Display in the Chapter House. Lesmahagow on M74, 23 miles south of Glasgow. A conservation village. Sunday Service 10am

Open by arrangement, telephone Rev Sheila Mitchell 01555 892425 or Church Officer Mr Alex McInnes 01555 892697

CHURCH OF SCOTLAND

489 RUTHERGLEN OLD PARISH CHURCH

NS 613 617

Main Street x Queen Street, Rutherglen

The present church was designed by the architect J J Burnet 1902 in Gothic style, the fourth on this site since the original foundation in the sixth century. The gable end of an eleventh-century church still stands in the graveyard supporting St Mary's steeple (15th century). It contains the church bell, 1635. Stained glass including a First World War memorial. Communion cups dated 1665 are still in use. The churchyard occupies an ancient site, at its gateway two stone offertory shelters, and a sundial set above its entrance dated 1679.
Sunday Service 11am

Open second Saturday of every month, 10am-12 noon

CHURCH OF SCOTLAND B

490 ST COLUMBKILLE'S CHURCH, RUTHERGLEN

NS 614 616

Main Street, Rutherglen

Magnificent church, Coia 1940, replacing original church founded in 1851. Modern adaptation of an Italian basilica. Between A724 and A731. Trains and city buses. Sunday Masses 9am, 10.30am, 12 noon and 7pm. Vigil Mass Saturday 5.30pm

Open Monday to Thursday 9am-5pm, Friday 9am-2pm

ROMAN CATHOLIC

491 SKIRLING PARISH CHURCH

NT 075 390

by Biggar

The earliest reference to a church in Skirling is in 1275. It was probably situated near to the present war memorial. It is not known when a church was built on the present site. However records show that the church was virtually rebuilt in 1720. Further significant alterations were made in 1891. The bellcote is of particular interest, as is the sundial on the tower. The floral design of the stained glass east window forms a backdrop to the communion table and matching chairs presented by the artist, Sir D Y Cameron, in 1948. Round churchyard enclosed by a ha-ha and entered through fine wrought-iron gates. Two miles east of Biggar on A72, approached from opposite village green by a steep metalled access road. Sunday Service 12 noon

Open by arrangement, telephone
A J Goodere 01899 860251

CHURCH OF SCOTLAND

SKIRLING PARISH CHURCH

492 AVENDALE OLD PARISH CHURCH, STRATHAVEN

NS 701 443

59a Kirk Street, Strathaven

Records show a church in Strathaven in 1288. This church was built in 1772 and the interior renovated 1879. The centre section of the south gallery was reserved for the family and tenants of the Duke of Hamilton and is known as 'The Duke's Gallery'. Stained glass window of the Last Supper, Crear McCartney 1996. In town centre A71. Sunday Service 11am; also first and third Sundays, except January, June and August 7pm. All-age communion is celebrated at the 11am service on the third Sunday of each month, except July and August.

Open Monday to Friday 9am-12 noon
(not school holidays). Other times,
telephone Session Clerk 01357 521939.
Website: www.garrion.co.uk/avendale

CHURCH OF SCOTLAND B

AVENDALE OLD PARISH CHURCH, STRATHAVEN

STRATHAVEN EAST PARISH CHURCH

493 STRATHAVEN EAST PARISH CHURCH

NS 702 446

Green Street, Strathaven

The white painted exterior is a local landmark. Built 1777 with clock tower added 1843. Major rebuilding 1877. Prominent pulpit and memorial windows. Linked with Glassford Church. Sunday Service 11.30am

Open by arrangement, telephone Rev W Stewart 01357 521138

CHURCH OF SCOTLAND

WC **A** (tower) **B** (church)

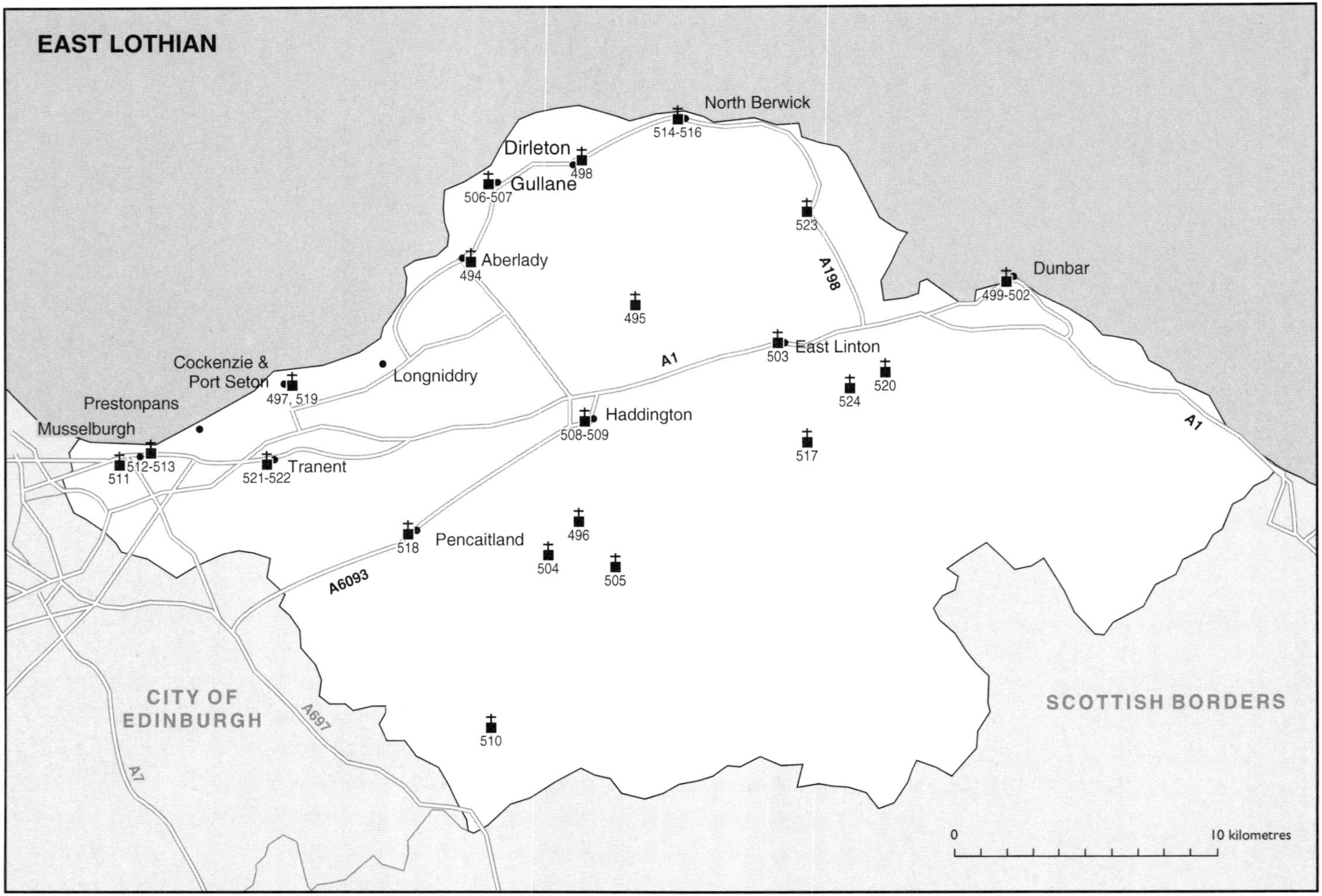
EAST LOTHIAN
North Berwick
514-516
Dirleton
498
Gullane
506-507
523
Aberlady
494
Dunbar
499-502
A198
495
East Linton
503
A1
Cockenzie &
Port Seton
497, 519
Longniddry
524
520
Prestonpans
Haddington
508-509
Musselburgh
517
511
512-513
521-522
Tranent
496
518
Pencaitland
504
505
A6093
CITY OF
EDINBURGH
A697
A7
510
SCOTTISH BORDERS
0
10 kilometres

EAST LOTHIAN

Local Representative: Mrs Margaret Beveridge, St Andrews, Duns Road, Gifford EH41 4QW (*telephone* 01620 810694)

494 ABERLADY PARISH CHURCH

NT 462 799

Main Street, Aberlady

Fifteenth-century tower, the body of the church recast in 1886 by William Young. Stained glass by Edward Frampton, London 1889. Eighth-century cross. Marble monument attributed to Canova. Tour guide boards in English, French, German, Spanish, Swedish. A198 Edinburgh–North Berwick. Sunday Service 11.15am

Open 1 May to 30 September, 8am-dusk. Other times, telephone Dr Hutchison 01875 870413, or F Burnett, 14 Rig Street, Aberlady 01875 870237

CHURCH OF SCOTLAND **A**

495 ATHELSTANEFORD PARISH CHURCH

NT 533 774

Athelstaneford

The original church 'Ecclesia de Elstaneford' on this site is said to have been founded in 1176 by the Countess Ada, mother of William the Lion. The present church dates from 1780. Cruciform design with central aisle, transepts and semi-octagonal chancel. Bellcote on the west gable. Three stained glass windows by C E Kempe. Doocot 1583. Church has historic link with the Scottish Saltire: commemorative plaque and Saltire floodlit. Heritage Centre to rear of church opened in 1997 with audio visual display (entry free). From A1, B1347. Sunday Service 10am

Open daily, dawn to dusk

CHURCH OF SCOTLAND **B**

496 BOLTON PARISH CHURCH

NT 507 701

Bolton

There has been a church on this site since before 1244. The present building dates from 1809 and remains structurally unchanged since that time. The architect was probably Archibald Elliot. The interior is plain and unspoiled, complete with carpenter's Gothic pulpit, and gallery on clustered iron posts. Robert Burns's mother, brother and sisters are buried in the churchyard. Graveguard and other items dating from the time of the 'Resurrection Men' displayed in the porch. Linked with Saltoun, Humbie and Yester. B6368 from Haddington. Sunday Service 10am, alternating with Saltoun

Open daily

CHURCH OF SCOTLAND **B**

BOLTON PARISH CHURCH

COCKENZIE METHODIST CHURCH

497 COCKENZIE METHODIST CHURCH

NT 398 756

28 Edinburgh Road, Cockenzie

The third of East Lothian's three Primitive Methodist Chapels, 1878. Simple and attractive. Original interior. South side of main road at west end of village. Sunday Service 2.30pm

Open by arrangement, telephone Church Office 01875 610388

METHODIST

498 DIRLETON KIRK

NT 513 842

Dirleton

Attractive stone building erected in 1612 to replace twelfth-century kirk in Gullane which was 'continewallie overblawin with sand'. Archerfield Aisle added 1650, first example of neo-classical design in Scotland. Tower crowned with Gothic pinnacles 1836. Stained glass window depicting St Francis and the Animals, Margaret Chilton 1936. Sunday Service 11.45am, 8-8.30pm July and August

Open daily 10am to dusk. Light lunches, snacks in Dirleton Gallery adjacent

CHURCH OF SCOTLAND WC **A**

DIRLETON KIRK

CHURCH OF OUR LADY OF THE WAVES, DUNBAR

499 CHURCH OF OUR LADY OF THE WAVES, DUNBAR

NT 678 791

Westgate, Dunbar

Built in 1877, the church has stained glass behind the altar and wood carvings showing the Way of the Cross

Open daily 9am-6pm, with further information from 01368 862701

ROMAN CATHOLIC

500 DUNBAR METHODIST CHURCH

NT 679 791

10 Victoria Street, Dunbar

Scotland's oldest Methodist Church, built in 1764. John and Charles Wesley were trustees and John often preached here. Enlarged 1857, renovated 1890. Fine interior, unexpected from plain exterior. Oak pulpit. Stained glass windows from St Giles, Edinburgh. South side of road leading from High Street to Harbour. Sunday Service 11am

Open by arrangement 01875 610388

METHODIST A

DUNBAR METHODIST CHURCH

501 DUNBAR PARISH CHURCH

NT 682 786

Queen's Road, Dunbar

The building, designed by Gillespie Graham in 1821, has been beautifully reconstructed by Campbell & Arnott 1990 following a devastating fire in 1987. The colourful and modern interior includes the early 17th-century monument to the Earl of Dunbar and some fine stained glass by Shona McInnes and Douglas Hogg 1990. Two hundred yards south of High Street south end. Intercity trains to Dunbar. Sunday Service 11am

Open daily 1.30pm-4pm. Sunday 2pm-4pm, June to September. Part of the John Muir exhibition will be held in the church from April to September 2000

CHURCH OF SCOTLAND WC **A**

502 ST ANNE'S CHURCH, DUNBAR

NT 678 791

Westgate, Dunbar

The church is by H M Wardrop and Sir R Rowand Anderson 1890. Built in the Gothic revival style and decorated with some Scots detail. Carved oak furnishings, Henry Willis organ, stained glass by Ballantine & Gardiner, Heaton, Butler & Bayne and the Abbey Studio. North end of Dunbar High Street. Sunday Service 11am

Open Saturday 19 June 10am-4pm.

Other times, telephone Rev P Allen 01368 865711

SCOTTISH EPISCOPAL WC (open day only) **B**

503 PARISH OF TRAPRAIN, PRESTONKIRK, EAST LINTON

NT 592 778

Preston Road, East Linton

Dedicated to St Baldred, the church possesses in its former chancel the best fragment of 13th-century church architecture in East Lothian. The tower dates from 1631, the main building from 1770, enlarged 1824, redesigned internally 1892 by James Jerdan. Organ by Vincent of Sutherland. St Baldred window 1959 and two Second World War memorial windows by William Wilson. Among the gravestones are those of Andrew Meikle, inventor of the threshing machine, and George Rennie, agriculturalist and brother of John Rennie, the civil engineer. Off A1, follow signs to Preston Mill. Sunday Service 11.30am, 24 December 11.30am, 25 December 10am. Please note times of services may be changed

Open by arrangement, telephone 01620 860598

CHURCH OF SCOTLAND

(by arrangement) WC (in Church Hall) **A**

PARISH OF TRAPRAIN, PRESTONKIRK, EAST LINTON

504 SALTOUN PARISH CHURCH, EAST SALTOUN

NT 474 678

East Saltoun

There has been a church on this site since before 1244. The present building is a T-plan Gothic kirk of 1805 which John Fletcher Campbell built 'as a monument to the virtues of his ancestors'. The actual designer is most likely to have been Robert Burn. The interior was recast in 1885, the architect was John Lessels. Beneath the church lies the Fletcher Vault, containing the remains of Andrew Fletcher 'The Patriot' and members of his family. Linked with Bolton, Humbie and Yester. Sunday Service 10am, alternating with Bolton

Open daily

CHURCH OF SCOTLAND **A**

SALTOUN PARISH CHURCH, EAST SALTOUN

505 YESTER PARISH CHURCH, GIFFORD

NT 535 681

Main Street, Gifford

By James Smith, finished 1710. A white harled T-plan church with square staged tower and slated spire. Weather vane in the form of a heron, William Brown, Edinburgh 1709. Church bell from the old Church of Bothans 1492. Pulpit 17th-century with bracket for baptismal basin. Memorial in village wall opposite to Rev John Witherspoon, son of the Manse, who signed the American Declaration of Independence 1784. B6369 from Haddington. Hourly bus service. Sunday Service 11.30am

Open daily, April to October, 9am to sunset. Village gala day June. Flower show August

CHURCH OF SCOTLAND WC **A**

YESTER PARISH CHURCH, GIFFORD

506 GULLANE PARISH CHURCH (ST ANDREW'S)

NT 480 827

East Links Road, Gullane

The church, designed by Glasgow architect John Honeyman and completed in 1888, replaced an earlier twelfth-century building vacated in 1612 when the congregation was rehoused in a new kirk at Dirleton. The Kirk Session of Dirleton decided to build the present parish church for the benefit of 'the large number of summer visitors annually residing in the village'. Simple Norman style with east apse. The zigzagged chancel arch is derived from the old parish church, as is the south doorway whose tympanum has a low relief of St Andrew. A198 to North Berwick. Sunday Service 9.45am

Open daily all year. Coffee on Tuesdays 10–11.30am

CHURCH OF SCOTLAND **A**

507 ST ADRIAN'S CHURCH, GULLANE

NT 480 838

Sandy Loan, Gullane

A simple aisleless church in Arts and Crafts style by Reginald Fairlie 1926. Built of stone from the Rattlebag quarry with a low tower and slated pyramidal spire. three-light chancel window by Douglas Strachan 1934. Sandy Loan is first right going westwards from Queen's Hotel. Sunday Services 9.30 Sung Eucharist; Said Eucharist first and third Sundays 8am

Open 10am–5pm, April to September

SCOTTISH EPISCOPAL **B**

508 HOLY TRINITY CHURCH, HADDINGTON

NT 518 739

Church Street, Haddington

Built 1770 on site of original 'Lamp of Lothian'. Chancel added 1930. Stations of the Cross, Bowman. Christ Crucified, Sutherland. Medieval walls of former priory and town defences. Sunday Services 8.30am, 10am Eucharist, 6pm Evensong (except July and August), Wednesday 10am Eucharist

Open Wednesday 10am–4pm, and in summer Saturday 10am–4pm. Other times, contact the Rectory adjacent

SCOTTISH EPISCOPAL WC **B**

509 ST MARY'S COLLEGIATE CHURCH, HADDINGTON

NT 519 736

Sidegate, Haddington

Dating back to the 14th century, one of the three great pre-Reformation churches of the Lothians. Known as 'The Lamp of Lothian', largest parish church in Scotland with fascinating history. Nave repaired for John Knox and the reformers after siege of Haddington 1548 and used as the parish church for almost 400 years. Transepts and choir restored, Ian G Lindsay & Partners 1973. Lauderdale Aisle, now The Chapel of the Three Kings, in regular ecumenical use. Fine stone carvings, especially west door. Notable stained glass. Modern tapestries. Fine pipe organ by Lammermuir Pipe Organs 1990. A peal of eight bells installed in the tower (and dedicated by the Moderator) in 1999.

ST MARY'S COLLEGIATE CHURCH, HADDINGTON

Sunday Services 9.30am Family Circle and 11am

Open 1 April to 30 September, daily, 11am-4.30pm, Sunday 2-4.30pm.
Annual ecumenical Whitekirk/Haddington Pilgrimage Saturday 13 May 2000.
Brass Rubbing Centre open Saturday throughout season 1-4pm, except weddings.
Regular concerts and recitals of international repute

CHURCH OF SCOTLAND **A**

510 HUMBIE KIRK

NT 461 637

Humbie

On the site of a pre-Reformation church, set in an ox-bow of Humbie Burn, a T-plan Gothic church by James Tod dated 1800. Vestry added 1846, and alterations by David Bryce 1866. The chancel added 1930, probably W J Walker Todd. Open scissor-braced timber roof. Stained glass. Organ by David Hamilton c.1840 with decorative Gothic dark wood case, from the Norwegian Seamen's Chapel at Granton. Fine gravestones with classical detail dating from earlier church. Broun Aisle, 1864 Bryce, sited at west gate, erected by Archibald Broun of Johnstonburn 'in lieu of the burial place of his family within the church, which in deference to the feelings of the parishioners, he has now closed'! Linked with Bolton, Saltoun and Yester. Sunday Service 10am

Open daily

CHURCH OF SCOTLAND **B**

511 PARISH CHURCH OF ST MICHAEL'S, INVERESK

NT 344 721

Musselburgh

There has been a church on the site since the sixth century. The present church was built in 1805 to the design of Robert Nisbet, the steeple by William Sibbald. The interior was reorientated and remodelled in 1893 by J MacIntyre Henry. Known as the 'visible Kirk' because of its prominent position, it stands on the site of a Roman praetorium and replaces a medieval church. Fine Adam-style ceiling and some excellent stained glass. Magnificent pipe organ enlarged 1897 by Lewis & Co. of London. Surrounded by a fine graveyard with many interesting old stones. Sunday Service 11.15am

Open by arrangement, telephone Mr G Burnet 0131 665 2689.

Open when village gardens open under Scotland's Gardens Scheme

CHURCH OF SCOTLAND (two steps to door) WC **A**

512 MUSSELBURGH CONGREGATIONAL CHURCH

NT 341 729

6 Links Street, Musselburgh

Simple but charming Georgian building completed in 1801, built with stone carried by fishermen and sailors from the shores of the Forth at Fisherrow. Oldest church in Musselburgh and one of first Congregational churches in Scotland. Pipe organ, fine example of the work of George Holdich built 1860 for St Michael's, Appleby. Rebuilt for Musselburgh Congregational church 1977. Church sits behind Brunton Hall. Sunday Service 11am

Open by arrangement, telephone Mr J Brown, 11 Links Street 0131 665 3768

CONGREGATIONAL WC **C**

MUSSELBURGH CONGREGATIONAL CHURCH

513 OUR LADY OF LORETTO AND ST MICHAEL, MUSSELBURGH

NT 346 753

17 Newbigging, Musselburgh

Stone building opened in 1905. Sanctuary recently modernised. All windows are of stained glass and the walls of the sanctuary are covered in fine art work, in gold leaf, depicting the events in the life of our Lord, corresponding to the Joyful Mysteries of the Rosary. Sunday Services 9 and 11.30 am; Saturday Vigil 6pm

Open daily

ROMAN CATHOLIC **B**

ABBEY CHURCH, NORTH BERWICK

514 ABBEY CHURCH, NORTH BERWICK

NT 551 853

High Street, North Berwick

Built 1868 as United Presbyterian by Robert R Raeburn in Early English style. A complete early 20th-century scheme of stained glass with, superimposed on one window, an arrangement of suspended planes representing an ascent of doves, by Sax Shaw 1972. Sunday Services 10.15am and 6pm

Open 9am-6pm, Mondays to Fridays, July and August

CHURCH OF SCOTLAND WC

515 CHURCH OF OUR LADY STAR OF THE SEA, NORTH BERWICK

NT 553 850

Law Road, North Berwick

Built in 1879, it is a simple Victorian church by Dunn & Hansom with seating for 200 people. The chancel was added by Basil Chanpreys in 1889 and the Lady Chapel by Sir Robert Lorimer in 1901. The interior contains a number of pictures after Benezzo Gozzoli and Botticelli and a Della Robbia (probably a copy). Sunday Services 9 and 11am; Saturday Vigil 7pm

Open daily, 8am-8pm

ROMAN CATHOLIC **B**

516 ST BALDRED'S CHURCH, NORTH BERWICK

NT 556 853

Dirleton Avenue, North Berwick

The original Norman-style church by John Henderson 1861, was cleverly extended in 1863 incorporating the old masonry by Seymour & Kinross, who also designed the altar. The porch with its magnificent carved doors was added by Robert Lorimer in 1916. Choir stalls by H O Tarbolton, porch doors by Mrs Meredith-Williams. Stained glass by Ballantine & Son. Convenient for North Berwick railway station. Sunday Services: Sung Eucharist 11am; second and fourth Sunday, Said Eucharist 8am

Open all year, 10am-4pm

SCOTTISH EPISCOPAL **B**

517 NUNRAW ABBEY

NT 593 700

Garvald, by Haddington

Modern Monastery of Cistercian Monks built 1952-70 (but unfinished), architect Peter Whiston. Nunraw House is an historic building and functions as the Abbey guest house where people may stay for a few days of retreat in the monastic atmosphere. Sunday Services Mass, 11am, Vespers 4pm, Compline 7.30pm; Weekday Services: Lauds and Mass 6.45pm, Vespers 6pm, Compline 7.30pm

Reception area and church open at all times

ROMAN CATHOLIC WC

518 PENCAITLAND PARISH CHURCH

NT 443 690

Consecrated in 1242, the earliest part of the church dates from the 12th century. The present building consists of nave, with a gallery at the west end, and two aisles on the north side, the older called the Winton Aisle and the other the Saltoun Aisle. Churchyard with many interesting gravestones, offering houses, renovated carriage house, stables, harness room and cottage. A1 from Edinburgh to Tranent, B6355 to Pencaitland. Bus 113 from Edinburgh. Sunday Service 10am; third Sunday 'Face-to-Face' celebration 6.30pm in the Carriage House; last Sunday Healing Service 6.30pm in the Winton Aisle

Open July and August, Sunday 2-5pm; September to June, Saturday 9.30am-1pm. Other times, telephone Rev C Donaldson 01875 340208

CHURCH OF SCOTLAND WC **A**

PENCAITLAND PARISH CHURCH

519 CHALMERS MEMORIAL CHURCH, PORT SETON

NT 403 757

Edinburgh Road, Port Seton

Built to a design by Sydney Mitchell for the United Free Church, the foundation stone was laid in 1904. It has a very elegant spire and bell tower and unique stencilled interior. Stained glass windows by Margaret Chilton and Marjorie Kemp 1924-50. Sunday Services 11.15am and 6.15 all year

The Church is open to visitors and for coffee at the end of both services every Sunday. Visitors are also welcome every third Wednesday of every month 2pm-4pm

CHURCH OF SCOTLAND

A

CHALMERS MEMORIAL CHURCH, PORT SETON

520 STENTON PARISH CHURCH

NT 641 753

Main Street, Stenton

By William Burn 1829, a T-plan kirk with a splendid east tower. Redesigned internally by James Jerdan in 1892. Stained glass by E C Kempe and Ballantine & Gardiner. In the graveyard is a fragment of the 16th-century kirk and a fine selection of monuments. Rood well in village. Follow signs to Stenton off A1. Sunday Service 10am. Please note time of service may be changed

Open daily dawn to dusk.

CHURCH OF SCOTLAND

(only available at services) **B**

STENTON PARISH CHURCH

TRANENT METHODIST CHURCH

521 TRANENT METHODIST CHURCH

NT 403 729

63 Bridge Street, Tranent

Built 1870, second of East Lothian's three Primitive Methodist Chapels. Subdivided 1958 to create church hall. Simple interior. Monument to Barnabas Wild, minister 1890s. North side of main road at west end of town. Sunday Service 11am

Open 1st Saturday of month for coffee morning

METHODIST **A**

522 ST MARTIN OF TOURS, TRANENT

NT 410 727

East end of High Street (opposite Co-op supermarket)

This is the third church building on the site in one hundred years and was built in 1969 in an octagonal shape using the Scandinavian compressed timber girder design. Contains two rough stained glass windows and an early 20th century Italian crucifix above the altar. Irish limestone statue of classical design of St Martin as a Roman soldier. Sunday Service 10.30am, weekdays 9am, Saturday: 10am and Vigil 6pm

Open by arrangement, telephone 01875 610232

ROMAN CATHOLIC

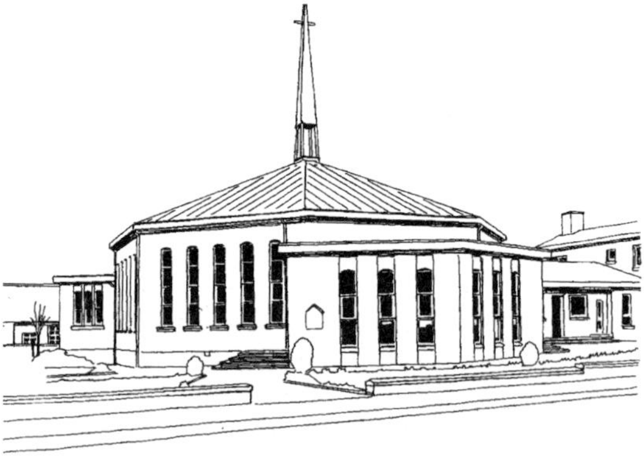

ST MARTIN OF TOURS, TRANENT

ST MARY'S PARISH CHURCH, WHITEKIRK

523 ST MARY'S PARISH CHURCH, WHITEKIRK

NT 596 815

Whitekirk

Dating from twelfth century, the original building was reconstructed during the 15th century starting with the vaulted stone choir, built in 1439 by Adam Hepburn of Hailes. In medieval times Whitekirk was an important place of pilgrimage. The church was set on fire in 1914 by suffragettes. Restored by Robert Lorimer. Ceiled wagon roof over nave and transepts, communion table, pulpit, lectern and font all by Lorimer. Stained glass by C E Kempe 1889 and Karl Parsons 1916. Tithe barn and historic graveyard. On A198. Sunday Service 11.30am

Open daily dawn to dusk

CHURCH OF SCOTLAND WC **A**

524 WHITTINGEHAME PARISH CHURCH

NT 603 737

Main Street, Stenton

Spiky battlemented Gothic T-plan church built 1722, and added to by Barclay and Lamb in 1820 for James Balfour, grandfather of A J Balfour, Prime Minister 1902-5. Eighteenth-century burial enclosure of Buchan Sydserfs of Ruchlaw and good late 17th-century headstones show that there was an earlier church on the site. Follow signs to Whittingehame off A1. No regular Church Services

Open daily dawn to dusk

CHURCH OF SCOTLAND **B**

WHITTINGEHAME PARISH CHURCH

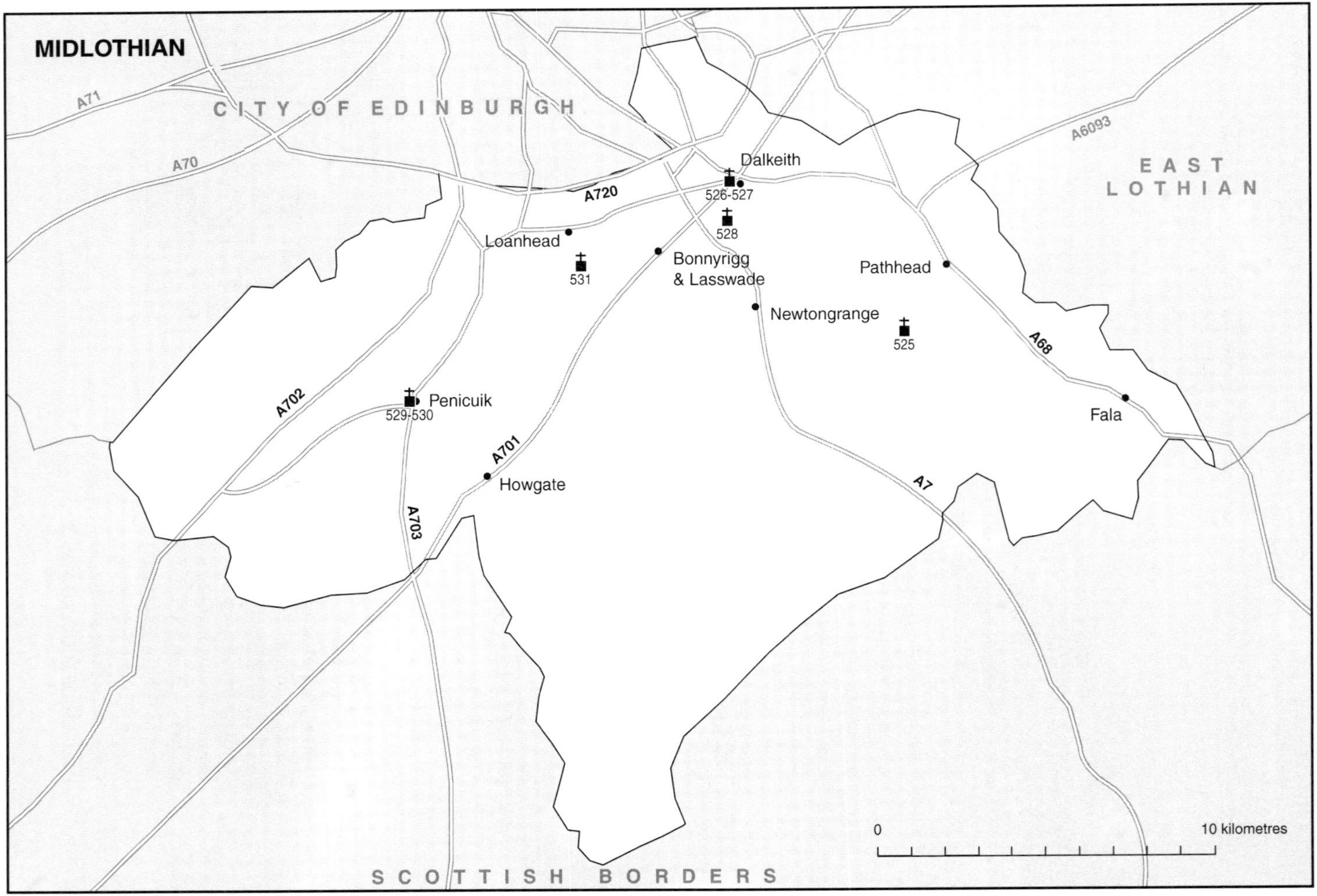

MIDLOTHIAN
CITY OF EDINBURGH
A71
A70
A720
A6093
EAST LOTHIAN
Dalkeith
526-527
528
Loanhead
531
Bonnyrigg & Lasswade
Pathhead
Newtongrange
525
A68
A702
Penicuik
529-530
Fala
A701
Howgate
A7
A703
0
10 kilometres
SCOTTISH BORDERS

MIDLOTHIAN

525 CRICHTON COLLEGIATE CHURCH

NT 381 616

Crichton, Pathhead

Collegiate church rebuilt in 1449 by William Crichton, Lord Chancellor of Scotland. Restored by Hardy & White 1898 and Benjamin Tindall 1998. Fine pointed barrel vaults over choir and transepts and splendid square tower over crossing. Organ by Joseph Brook & Co. Magnificent position at head of Tyne valley close to Crichton Castle. Signed road B6367 from A68 at Pathhead. Programme available of occasional services and concerts in summer months

Open May to September, Sunday 2-5pm. Or by appointment, telephone Mrs Tindall 01875 320341. Crichton Castle open 1 April to 30 September

NON-DENOMINATIONAL WC **A**

CRICHTON COLLEGIATE CHURCH

526 ST MARY'S CHURCH, DALKEITH

NT 335 677

Dalkeith Country Park, Dalkeith

Built as the chapel for Dalkeith Palace in 1843 by William Burn and David Bryce. Early English style with splendid features: double hammerbeam roof, stained glass windows, heraldic floor tiles by Minton, and the only working water-powered Hamilton organ in Scotland. Sunday Service 9.45am

Open most weekend afternoons in summer and by arrangement, telephone Mr Fiddes 0131 663 3359. Summer concerts. Fun Day in September.

SCOTTISH EPISCOPAL WC WC **A**

527 ST NICHOLAS BUCCLEUCH PARISH CHURCH, DALKEITH

NT 333 674

High Street, Dalkeith

Medieval church, became collegiate in 1406. Nave and transepts 1854 by David Bryce. James, first Earl of Morton and his wife Princess Joanna (the profoundly deaf third daughter of James I) are buried within the choir, c.1498. Memorial monument with their effigies mark the burial site. Two hundred yards east of A68/A6094 junction. Sunday Services 9.30am Family Worship, 11am Parish Worship

Open Easter Sunday to 30 September, weekdays, 10am-12 noon and 2-4pm, Sunday 10-11am. Or contact Mr A Brown, telephone 0131 663 0799

CHURCH OF SCOTLAND WC **A**

528 NEWBATTLE CHURCH

NT 331 661

Newbattle Road, Newbattle

Harled, T-plan church with belfry by Alexander McGill, 1727. Two galleries added 1851. A remarkable number of the original fittings survive including the upper part of the 17th century pulpit and the pilastered wooden frame of the Lothian Loft. A Millennium project to restore the Lothian Gallery to its original layout is projected for 2000. Good 17th century gravestones including the amazing, ornamented Welsh family monument. Sunday Service: 10am

Open by arrangement, telephone Mr Iain McCarter 0131 663 3896

CHURCH OF SCOTLAND WC **B**

NEWBATTLE CHURCH

529 PENICUIK SOUTH CHURCH

NT 236 595

Peebles Road, Penicuik

Designed in 1863 by Frederick T Pilkington. Open timber roof. Stained glass. Fully restored 1991. Short history available, models of church on sale. Sunday Services 11.15am and 7pm

Open Saturdays all year, 10am-12 noon

CHURCH OF SCOTLAND **B**

PENICUIK SOUTH CHURCH

530 ST JAMES SCOTTISH EPISCOPAL CHURCH, PENICUIK

NT 232 597

Broomhill Road, Penicuik

The original church which now forms the nave was designed by H Seymour of Seymour & Kinross 1882. The chancel, vestries, tower and bell were added by H O Tarbolton, 1899. An excellent lot of stained glass including one light by Shrigley & Hunt of Lancaster and four magnificent lights by C E Kempe. Rood screen designed by Tarbolton and carved by T Good, communion rails also designed by Tarbolton and carved by Scott Morton & Co. Reredos designed and executed by Mrs Meredith-Williams, 1921. Services every Sunday 8am and 10.15am, first Sundays Choral Evensong 6.30pm

Open by arrangement, telephone the Rector 01968 672862

SCOTTISH EPISCOPAL **B**

531 ROSSLYN CHAPEL (ST MATTHEW'S)

NT 275 631

Chapel Loan, Roslin

Built 1450 as the church of a college established by William Sinclair, third Earl of Orkney. Intended to be cruciform but only the choir was completed. Famous for its decorative stone carving that covers almost every part of the building. The 'Prentice Pillar' has spectacular decoration. Sunday Services 10.30am and 3.30pm in winter, 5.30pm summer

Open all year, Monday to Saturday 10am-5pm, Sunday 12 noon-4.45pm

SCOTTISH EPISCOPAL **A**

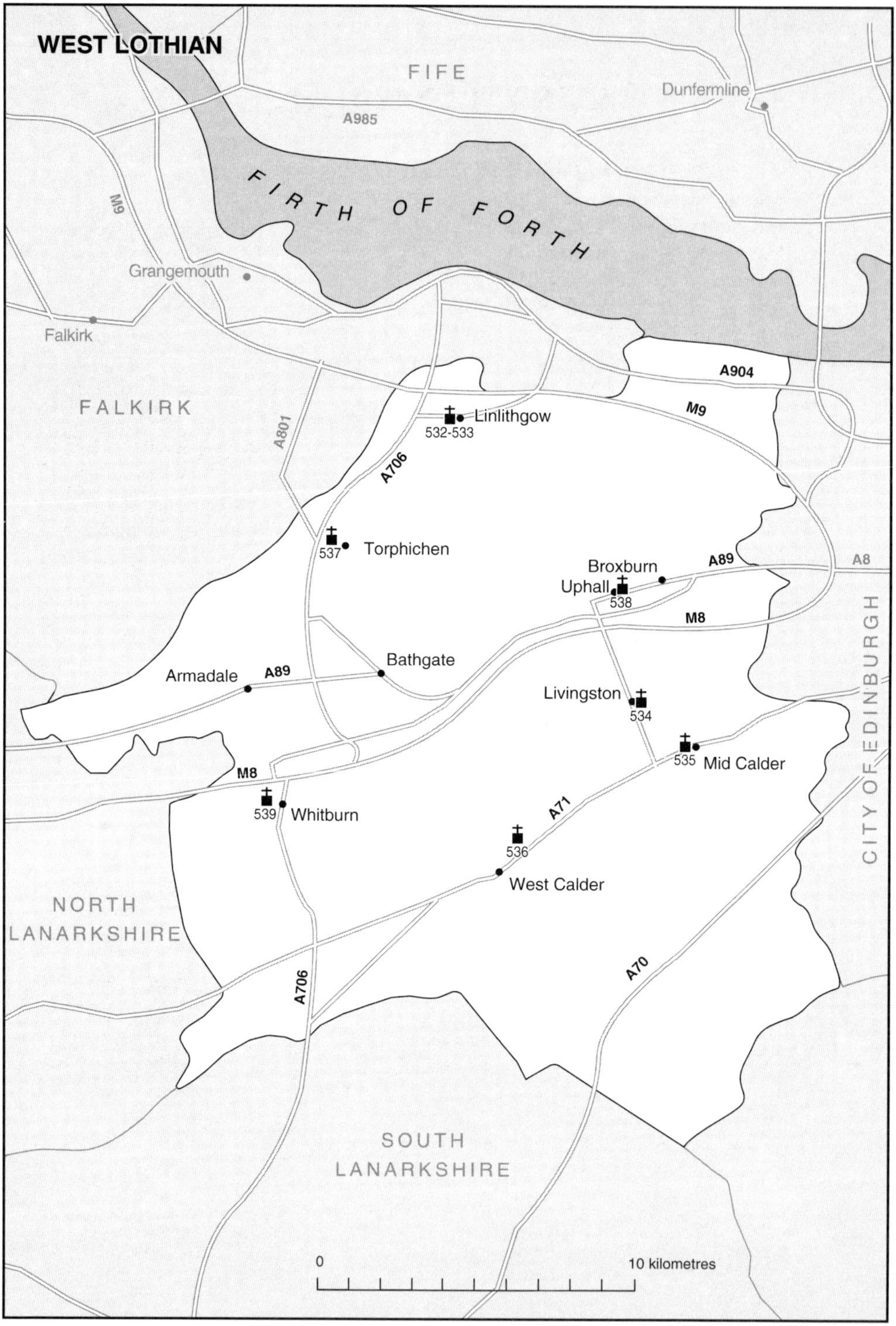
WEST LOTHIAN
FIFE
Dunfermline
A985
FIRTH OF FORTH
M9
Grangemouth
Falkirk
FALKIRK
A904
M9
Linlithgow
532-533
A801
A706
537
Torphichen
Broxburn
A89
A8
Uphall
538
M8
CITY OF EDINBURGH
Bathgate
Armadale
A89
Livingston
534
535
Mid Calder
M8
539
Whitburn
A71
536
West Calder
NORTH
LANARKSHIRE
A706
A70
SOUTH
LANARKSHIRE
0
10 kilometres

WEST LOTHIAN

532 ST MICHAEL'S PARISH CHURCH, LINLITHGOW

NT 002 773

Kirkgate, Linlithgow

One of the finest examples of a large medieval burgh church. Consecrated in 1242 on the site of an earlier church, most of the present building dates from the 15th century with some 19th-century restoration. Situated beside Linlithgow Palace, its history is intertwined with that of the royal house of Stewart. The modern aluminium crown, 1964, symbolises the Church's continuing witness to Christ's Kingship. Window commemorating 750th anniversary of the church, 1992, by Crear McCartney. The Peel, Linlithgow Palace and Loch adjacent. Sunday Services 9.30am and 11am

ST MICHAEL'S PARISH CHURCH, LINLITHGOW

Open all year, May to September, Monday to Saturday 10am-4pm; Sunday 12.30pm-4pm. October to April, Monday to Friday 10am-3pm

CHURCH OF SCOTLAND (on request) A

533 ST PETER'S EPISCOPAL CHURCH, LINLITHGOW

NS 000 770

High Street, Linlithgow

Built in 1928 as a memorial to George Walpole, Bishop of Edinburgh and his wife Mildred with assistance from missions in England and USA. Design by J Walker Todd of Dick Peddie & Todd is a Byzantine basilica with a 'cross in the square' plan form, a high central dome and half dome over the sanctuary apse. It is a small church located on south side of High Street, and is popular as a refuge from the main shopping area. Sunday Services 9.30am and 8.30am on 4th Sunday of month (to 1929 prayer book)

Open Saturdays from mid June to September, 2-4pm, or telephone Rev Stuart Bonney 01506 842384

ST PETER'S EPISCOPAL CHURCH, LINLITHGOW

SCOTTISH EPISCOPAL WC

534 LIVINGSTON VILLAGE KIRK

NT 037 669

Kirk Lane, Livingston

There has been a church on the site since twelfth century. The present building was rebuilt 1732. Late 18th-century pews and pulpit with Gothic sounding board and a pretty stair. Pewter communion vessels and old collecting shovels on display. Plaque in entrance commemorates Covenanters from village drowned off Orkney. Kirkyard has some fine monuments from 17th and 18th centuries, including some lively headstones featuring phoenixes and leafy cartouches. Close to Heritage Centre. Sunday Service 10am. Other services as advertised on notice board

Open by arrangement, telephone the Minister 01506 420227

CHURCH OF SCOTLAND WC **B**

535 KIRK OF CALDER, MID CALDER

NT 074 673

Main Street, Mid Calder

This 16th-century parish church, recently restored, won the West Lothian Award for Conservation in 1992. John Knox, James 'Paraffin' Young, David Livingston and Frederick Chopin have already visited here – we look forward to meeting you too! Admission free, donations welcome. 1995 restoration of stained glass windows. Off A71 on B7015 in village of Mid Calder. LRT bus 9, SMT buses 26, 27, 285, 271, from Edinburgh. Sunday Service 10.30am

Open May to September, Sunday 2-4pm.

Near to Almondell Country Park, open all year

CHURCH OF SCOTLAND WC **A**

Scottish Tourist Board COMMENDED

KIRK OF CALDER, MID CALDER

536 POLBETH HARWOOD PARISH CHURCH

NT 017 628

Chapelton Drive, Polbeth, West Calder

The congregation was formed in 1795 and the church completed in 1796 as Burgher Kirk. Congregation translated from West Calder to Polbeth, 1962. A71 between Livingston New Town and West Calder. Fifteen minutes walk from West Calder station. Sunday Service 11am

Open Monday and Wednesday during school term time 10am–12 noon, Thursday 6-8pm during summer

CHURCH OF SCOTLAND

537 TORPHICHEN KIRK

NS 969 725

The Bowyett, Torphichen

Built in 1756 on the site of the nave of the twelfth-century preceptory, it is a T-shaped building with three galleries including a laird's loft. Two centre pews can be tipped back to form extended communion tables. Sanctuary stone in the graveyard. Preceptory church adjoining in the care of Historic Scotland. Sunday Service 11.15am

Open parish church and preceptory Easter to end October, Saturday 11am-5pm, Sunday 2-5pm. Exhibition. Charge for entry to preceptory. Groups welcome for guided tours of both buildings, telephone Mrs Stirling 01506 654142

CHURCH OF SCOTLAND WC **A**

538 ST NICHOLAS, UPHALL

NT 060 722

Ecclesmachan Road, Uphall

Tower and nave with Romanesque doorway of 1187, Buchan stairs of the 17th century, aisles added 1590 and 1878. A picture shows the balconies that existed before the restoration of 1938. Buried in the tower are Erskines, Earls of Buchan and sons. Mixture of old and modern stained glass windows. The bell, one of the oldest in West Lothian, is inscribed *in onore sancte nicolae campana ecclegie de strabork anno dni mviii.* 'Judas' Bible of 1613. Sunday Service: 11.30am

Open by arrangement, telephone the Minister 01506 852550

CHURCH OF SCOTLAND WC **B**

539 WHITBURN SOUTH PARISH CHURCH

NS 947 646

Manse Road, Whitburn

Dating from 1729, the walls house a modern interior of the 1950s, the result of a fire. Crucifrom and typically Georgian though some earlier architectural features are evident. The graveyard is host to several local notables and is the last resting place of Robert Burns' eldest daughter, Elizabeth Paton (dear 'Bought' Bess) who married John Bishop, the overseer at Polkennet Estate. Sunday Service: 11am all year, September-Easter 6pm, 10am Christmas Day, 7pm Maundy Thursday.

Open by arrangement, telephone the church officer Mr John Tennant 01501 741627

CHURCH OF SCOTLAND WC **B**

WHITBURN SOUTH PARISH CHURCH

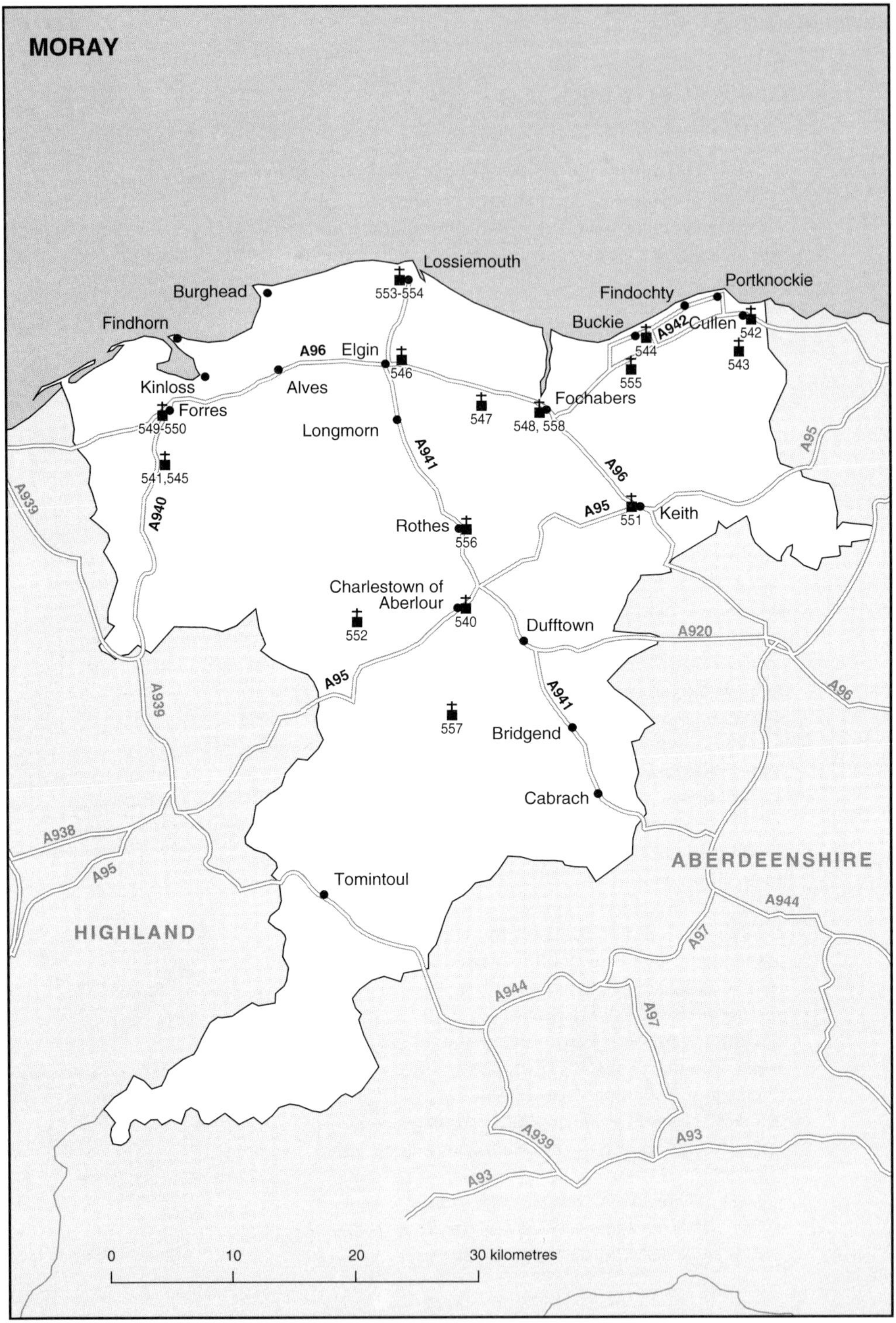

MORAY
Lossiemouth
Burghead
553-554
Findochty
Portknockie
Findhorn
Buckie
A942
Cullen
542
A96
Elgin
544
543
546
555
Kinloss
Alves
Forres
Fochabers
547
549-550
548, 558
Longmorn
A941
A95
A96
541,545
A939
A940
A95
551
Keith
Rothes
556
Charlestown of
Aberlour
552
540
Dufftown
A920
A95
A939
A96
A941
557
Bridgend
Cabrach
A938
ABERDEENSHIRE
A95
Tomintoul
A944
HIGHLAND
A97
A944
A97
A939
A93
A93
0
10
20
30 kilometres

MORAY

Local Representative: Mrs Elizabeth Beaton, Keam Schoolhouse, Hopeman, Moray (*telephone* 01343 830301)

540 ST MARGARET OF SCOTLAND, ABERLOUR

NJ 272 431

High Street, Aberlour

Designed by Alexander Ross and consecrated in 1879, the tall Gothic church retains its splendid original interior. Built for the orphanage 120 years ago, the feet of hundreds of children have worn down the Victorian tiled floor. Lovely carvings of flowers, birds and squirrels on pillar capitals and screen arch. Sunday Services 11am, first Sunday in the month; 9.15am other Sundays

Key from Aberlour Hotel (must be signed for)

SCOTTISH EPISCOPAL **A**

541 EDINKILLIE PARISH CHURCH

NJ 020 466

Edinkillie, Dunphail, near Forres

Small church built 1741 in traditional 18th-century style. Central pulpit and galleries on three sides. Fine pipe organ. Beautifully situated on the banks of the River Divie, nine miles south of Forres on the A940 from Forres to Grantown-on-Spey. Linked with Dyke. Sunday Service 12 noon

Open by arrangement, telephone Mr C J Falconer (Beadle) 01309 611220, or Mr W Reid 01309 611279

CHURCH OF SCOTLAND WC

542 OLD KIRK OF CULLEN

NJ 507 664

Cullen

This 13th-century church was originally dedicated to St Mary the Virgin and is the burial place of the 'interior parts' of Queen Elizabeth de Burgh (1327). A chaplaincy was endowed here by Robert I in 1327 and the church acquired collegiate status in 1543. Later additions include the St Anne's Aisle of 1539, while there is a fine example of a laird's loft (1602). Other features include a pre-Reformation aumbry or sacrament house, tombs and monuments including one to James, first Earl of Seafield, Chancellor of Scotland at the Treaty of Union of 1707, and 17th-century box pews. The churchyard has many interesting and imposing tombs, monuments and gravestones. The Church is at Old Cullen, three quarters of a mile south-west of the town centre. Sunday Service 10.30am.

Open summer 2-4pm, and by arrangement, telephone the Minister 01542 841851

CHURCH OF SCOTLAND WC **A**

OLD KIRK OF CULLEN

543 ST JOHN'S CHURCH, DESKFORD

NJ 509 617

Built in 1871 in the Victorian Gothic style, architect John Miller Cullen (architect and master of works to Seafield Estates, Cullen). It has unusual tracery detail in the transept window. Inside there is stencil work on the walls. The Old St John's Church (ruined) at Kirkton of Deskford incorporates a fine aumbry (1551) with inscriptions in English and Latin and carvings of angels supporting monstrance. B9018, 3 miles south of Cullen. Sunday Service 2nd and fourth of every month, 12 noon

Open by arrangement, telephone the Minister 01542 841851

CHURCH OF SCOTLAND ♿ **B**

544 ST PETER'S CHURCH, BUCKIE

NJ 419 653

St Andrew's Square, Buckie

To plans donated by Bishop Kyle and supervised by A and W Reid of Elgin. Dedicated on a site donated by Sir William Gordon. Rose window. Recent art work includes six murals of excellent quality in Church Hall and two canvases of David and Saul and of the 'Death of St Joseph' in the church, by local artist Lynn Thain. High altar of Italian marble surrounded by murals depicting 'The Calming of the Storm' and 'The Walking on the Water'. Reredos and baptistry, C J Menart 1907. Statue of Our Lady of Aberdeen, copy of original in Brussels. Saturday Vigil Mass 6.30pm; Sunday 10am; Weekdays 9.30am

Open daily, 9am-6pm

ROMAN CATHOLIC **A**

ST PETER'S CHURCH, BUCKIE

545 DYKE PARISH CHURCH

NH 990 584

Dyke, near Forres, Moray

Built 1781 in centre of village. Interesting crypt and triple pulpit (one of the only two in Scotland). Follow road to Brodie Castle, turning right to village before castle entrance. Linked with Edinkillie. Sunday Service 10.30am

Open by arrangement, key in village, telephone Minister 01309 641239

CHURCH OF SCOTLAND **A**

546 HOLY TRINITY, ELGIN

NJ 214 630

Trinity Place, Elgin

1826, Gothic style on a Greek cross ground-plan to a design by William Robertson. The crenellated and pinacled south entrance gable intended as an architectural feature visible from the High Street is now blocked by the ring-road. Chancel added 1852 and interior recast; nave lengthened 1879. Plain dignified interior with late 19th-century stained glass. Services: Sunday 8am Holy Communion, 11am Family Eucharist, 6.30pm Evensong, Holy Communion Tuesday 7pm, Wednesday 8am, Friday 11am, Saturday 9am.

Open 9am-5pm

SCOTTISH EPISCOPAL WC **B**

547 PLUSCARDEN ABBEY, ELGIN

NJ 143 576

Pluscarden, near Elgin

Founded in 1230 by Alexander II for Valiscaulian monks, it became Benedictine in 1454. Following the Reformation it was the property of various local families, culminating in the Dukes of Fife from whom it was bought by the Marquess of Bute, and whose son, Lord Colum, gave it to the monks in 1943. The buildings were eventually re-occupied in 1948. There are a number of interesting works by prominent artists and architects following the restoration. The Abbey offers retreat accommodation for men and women. Full details of this, together with Services and opening times, may be obtained by telephoning 01343 890257 (fax 01343 890258). Abbey is signposted from A96 and B1090

Open daily 4.45am–8.45pm

ROMAN CATHOLIC **A**

548 GORDON CHAPEL, FOCHABERS

NJ 346 589

Castle Street, Fochabers

Built in 1834 to a design by Archibald Simpson, restored in 1874. Stained glass designed by Sir Edward Burne-Jones. A fine Hill's organ. The church is upstairs with the rectory (originally a school) below. Sunday Services: Said Eucharist 8am. Family Service 10.30am weekly. First Sunday of month Choral Evensong 6.30pm

Open daily during daylight hours.

SCOTTISH EPISCOPAL **A**

GORDON CHAPEL, FOCHABERS

549 ST LAURENCE PARISH CHURCH, FORRES

NJ 035 588

High Street, Forres

Built on a site of Christian worship dating from mid 13th century, today's neo-Gothic building – designed by John Robertson and dedicated in 1906 – is a fine example of the stonemason's craft. The pitch pine ceiling and the stained glass windows by Douglas Strachan and Percy Bacon help to create the special atmosphere of peace and beauty. Font replica of one in Dryburgh Abbey. Information leaflets in English, French, German, Spanish and Italian are free. Welcomers on duty. Sunday Service 10am

Open May to September, Monday to Friday 10am-12 noon, 2-4pm

Other times by arrangement, telephone 01309 672260

CHURCH OF SCOTLAND **B**

550 ST JOHN'S CHURCH, FORRES

NJ 041 592

Victoria Road, Forres

Built in 1841, to a design by Patrick Wilson, remodelled in Italianate manner by Thomas Mackenzie, Elgin. The building has been beautified over the years including the laying of mosaic tiles throughout the chancel and aisles. The frontage is adorned with a wheel window, the entrance sheltered by an arcaded logia and flanked by a campanile. A large canvas in the apse (1906) and mural behind the font (1911) are the work of William Hole RSA. Sunday Services 8.00 am, 9.30am and 6.00pm

Open daylight hours (or key at Rectory)

SCOTTISH EPISCOPAL **A**

551 ST THOMAS' CHURCH, KEITH

NJ 430 502

Chapel Street, Keith

Built 1831, architect William Robertson, Elgin. Successor to 1785 chapel and cottage at Kempcairn, following planning and fund-raising by Father Lovi. Roman Doric pilastered exterior and 'plain' interior with nave and sanctuary. Enlarged with copper-clad dome, altar, communion rails, pulpit and oak pews 1915. Altar piece painting 'The Incredulity of St Thomas', commissioned by Charles X of France, 1828. Fine stained glass windows, 1970s. St John Ogilvie Chapel commemorating saint born nearby. Extensive restoration, 1996

Open daily, dawn to dusk

ROMAN CATHOLIC **A**

ST THOMAS' CHURCH, KEITH

552 KNOCKANDO PARISH CHURCH

NJ 186 429

Award winning design for new church by the Law & Dunbar-Nasmith Partnership 1993 on the site of an earlier building destroyed by fire in 1990. Sympathetic with the building which it has replaced. The Creation is symbolised in a new stained glass window by Andrew Lawson-Johnson. From A95 Aviemore–Elgin or A941 Dufftown–Elgin, take B9102 Archiestown Knockando. At Cardhu turn right. Church is signposted. Linked with Rothes. Sunday Service 10.30am

Open Wednesday only, 2pm-4pm July and August

CHURCH OF SCOTLAND

553 ST GERARDINE'S HIGH, LOSSIEMOUTH

NJ 233 706

St Gerardine's Road, Lossiemouth

The foundation stone was laid in 1898 and the building is of Norman Romanesque design by Sir J J Burnett. The plainness of the Norman Tower, white harled walls and red roof belie the magnificent interior. The features include many items of stained glass depicting various Biblical themes. Sunday Service 11.00am

Open by arrangement, telephone the Minister 01343 813146, or Mr James Cumming 01343 812194

CHURCH OF SCOTLAND B

ST GERARDINE'S HIGH, LOSSIEMOUTH

554 ST MARGARET OF SCOTLAND, LOSSIEMOUTH

NJ 227 706

Stotfield Road, Lossiemouth

Small church of 1922 with Gothic detailing built to a design by Alexander Ross of Inverness, responsible for Episcopal churches great and small throughout the north including Inverness Cathedral. Simple interior with open timber vaulted ceiling. Sunday Service: 9.30am Parish Eucharist, Thursday 10am Eucharist and 5 pm Eventide Prayer.

Open May-September Fridays 2pm-5pm

SCOTTISH EPISCOPAL

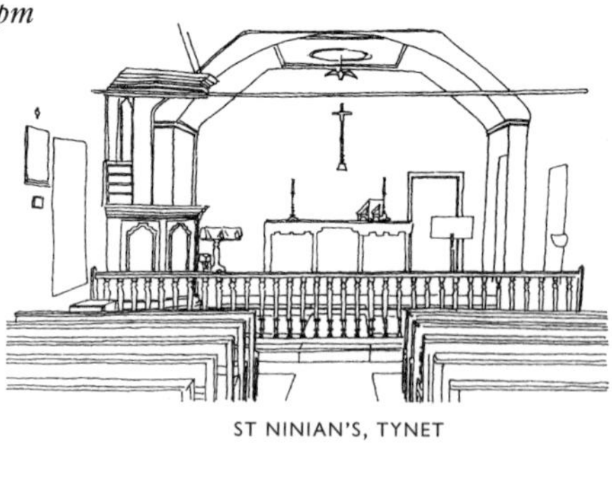

ST NINIAN'S, TYNET

555 ST GREGORY'S CHURCH, PRESHOME

NJ 409 615

Preshome, Clochan

Built in 1790, James Byres, architect. A wide rectangular church with harled walls and freestone dressing. The church is adorned with urn finials; its west end is a charming product of 18th-century taste, in which Italian Baroque has been skilfully naturalised to a Banffshire setting. Copy of a painting of St Gregory the Great by Annibale Caracci. Two holy water stoups of Portsoy marble. Sunday Mass occasionally at 6pm

Open by arrangement, telephone Mr G Gordon, St Gregory's Chapel House

ROMAN CATHOLIC **A**

556 ROTHES PARISH CHURCH

NJ 278 492

High Street x Seafield Square, Rothes

Built in 1781 with a steeple added in 1870. A traditional Scottish design of the Reformed tradition with the pulpit on the long wall, a three-sided gallery and apse. Pipe organ 1901 has recently been restored. Linked with Knockando. Sunday Service 12 noon

Open July to August, Tuesday to Friday 2-4.30pm

CHURCH OF SCOTLAND

557 OLD SEMINARY, SCALAN

NJ 246 195

Braes of Glenlivet, Ballindalloch, Banffshire

Scalan (Gaelic for a turf-roofed shelter) is a plain 18th-century house, the most significant relic of 'penal days'. Built in 1717 as a seminary for the training of priests. 1995 award of The Association for the Protection of Rural Scotland. Turn off B9008 Tomintoul–Dufftown at Pole Inn (signposted).
Annual Mass, first Sunday July 4pm

Open all year

ROMAN CATHOLIC **A**

558 ST NINIAN'S, TYNET

NJ 379 613

Mill of Tynet, Fochabers

The oldest post-Reformation Catholic church still in use in Scotland. At the request of the Duke of Gordon 1755, built to resemble a sheepcot in days when it was still an offence to celebrate Mass. Renovated 1957, Ian Lindsay, architect, the long low whitewashed building is still 'a church in disguise'. Sunday Service 8.30am; Saturday Vigil Mass 5.30pm

Open by arrangement, telephone Mr P Cromar, 'Golar', Newlands of Tynet (opposite church)

ROMAN CATHOLIC **A**

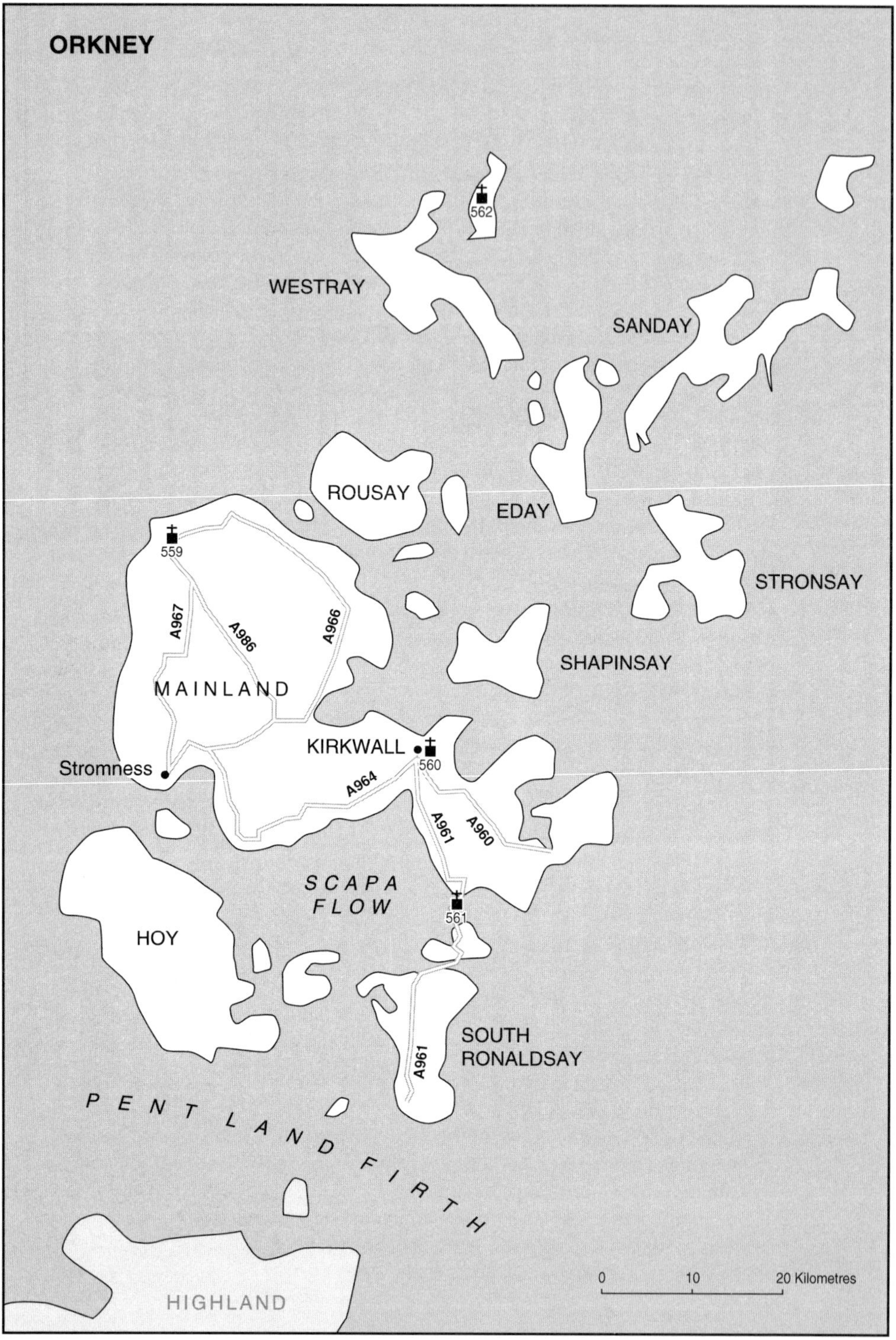
ORKNEY
562
WESTRAY
SANDAY
ROUSAY
EDAY
559
STRONSAY
A967
A986
A966
SHAPINSAY
MAINLAND
KIRKWALL
560
Stromness
A964
A961
A960
SCAPA FLOW
561
HOY
SOUTH RONALDSAY
A961
PENTLAND FIRTH
HIGHLAND
0
10
20 Kilometres

ORKNEY

559 ST MAGNUS CHURCH, BIRSAY

HY 248 277

The original church was built by Earl Thorfinn c.1060 and has been altered and restored several times, most recently in 1986. Stained glass window by Alexander Strachan showing scenes from the life of St Magnus. Inside the church are two 16th and 17th-century tombstones. Seventeenth-century belfry. The Mons Bellus stone is probably from the nearby Bishop's Palace. The church is now maintained by the St Magnus Church Birsay Trust. Twenty miles from Kirkwall, across the road from the Earl's Palace. Sunday Service once a month, details in church

Open daily, April to September. Key available all year from village shop

NON-DENOMINATIONAL (nearby) **B**

560 ST MAGNUS CATHEDRAL, KIRKWALL

HY 449 108

Broad Street, Kirkwall

The Cathedral Church of St Magnus the Martyr was founded in 1137 by Earl Rognval Kolson and dedicated to his uncle, Earl Magnus Erlendson. Completed c.1500. It contains many items of interest and ranks as one of the finest cathedrals in Scotland. Although it is owned and maintained by Orkney Islands Council, the Society of Friends of St Magnus was formed in 1958 to help raise funds for its preservation. Custodian on duty.

Sunday Service 11.15am

Open April to September, Monday to Saturday 9am-6pm, Sunday 2-6pm; October to March, Monday to Saturday 9am-1pm and 2-5pm. Closed public holidays and Christmas festive season, except for Church Services

CHURCH OF SCOTLAND

(side entrance) WC (public nearby) (braille and audio tape versions of guidebook available) **A**

ST MAGNUS CATHEDRAL, KIRKWALL

THE ITALIAN CHAPEL

561 THE ITALIAN CHAPEL

HY 488 006

Lambholm, Orkney

All that remains of the Italian Prisoner of War Camp 60, the famous Italian Chapel was created from two Nissen huts in 1943, using material from sunken blockships in Scapa Flow. Wonderful testimony to the artistic skills of Domenico Chiocchetti and his fellow prisoners who came to Orkney to work on the construction of the Churchill Barriers. Beautifully designed chancel, altar, altar-rail and holy water stoup. Painted glass windows depicting St Francis of Assisi and St Catherine of Siena. Restored 1960 and Preservation Committee is dedicated to upkeep of Chapel.

Service 3pm on first Sunday of summer months

Open daily

ROMAN CATHOLIC **B**

562 ST BONIFACE, PAPA WESTRAY

HY 488 527

Kirkhouse, Papa Westray

Founded in the eighth century, St Boniface was an important church in the early Middle Ages, possibly the seat of Orkney's first Bishopric. The present building is twelfth century, enlarged early 1700s and furnished with box pews, gallery and high pulpit. Restored 1993. Viking age hog-backed tombstone in the kirkyard, Pictish cross-slab now in the Orkney Museum, Kirkwall. Services: Wednesdays 8 pm mid-June to end-August, also Christmas, Holy Week and occasional services in winter

Open at all times

NON-DENOMINATIONAL

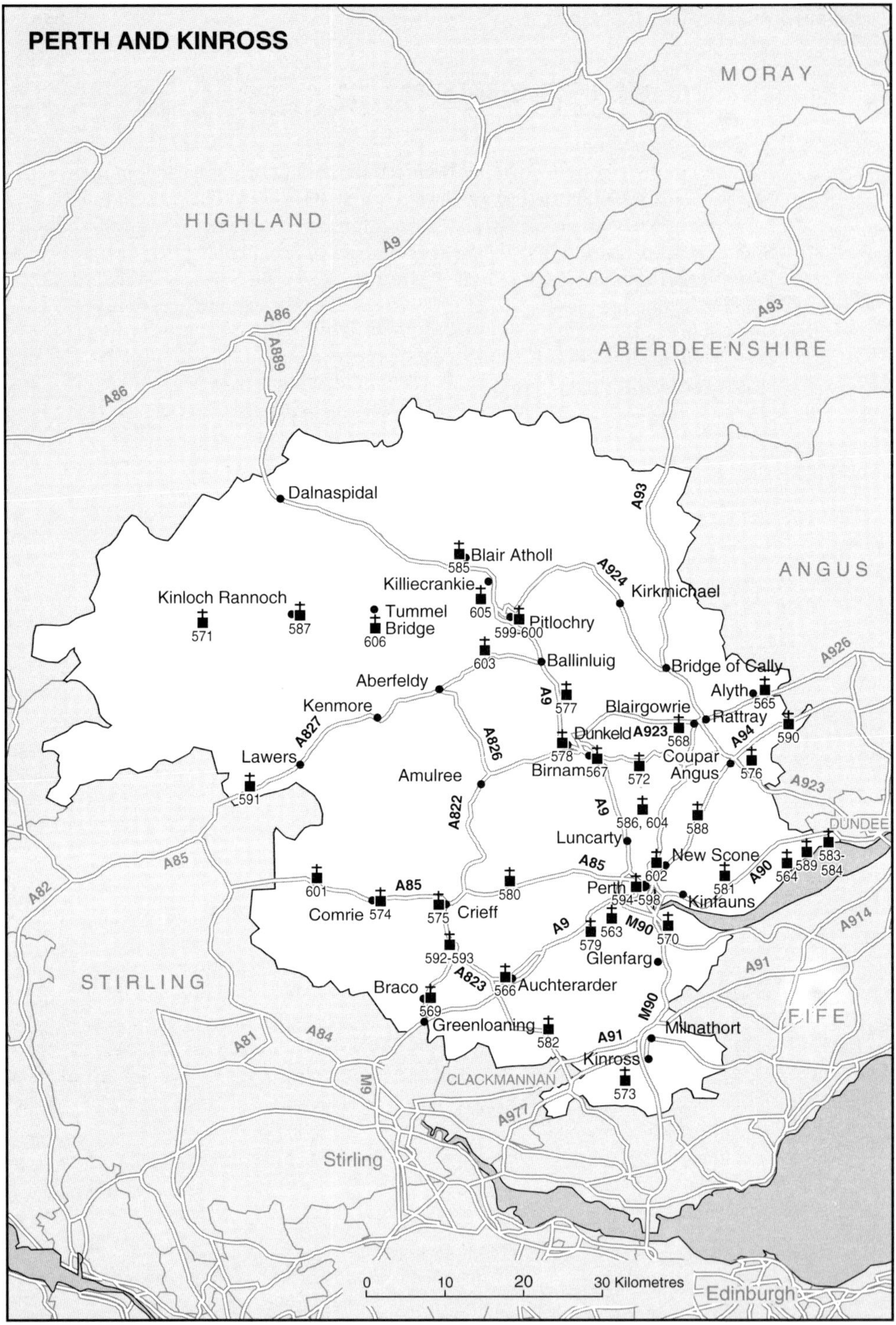
PERTH AND KINROSS
MORAY
HIGHLAND
ABERDEENSHIRE
ANGUS
STIRLING
FIFE
CLACKMANNAN
DUNDEE
Dalnaspidal
Blair Atholl
Killiecrankie
Kinloch Rannoch
Tummel Bridge
Pitlochry
Kirkmichael
Ballinluig
Aberfeldy
Kenmore
Lawers
Amulree
Bridge of Cally
Alyth
Blairgowrie
Rattray
Dunkeld
Birnam
Coupar Angus
Luncarty
New Scone
Perth
Kinfauns
Comrie
Crieff
Glenfarg
Braco
Auchterarder
Greenloaning
Milnathort
Kinross
Stirling
Edinburgh
0 10 20 30 Kilometres

PERTH & KINROSS

Local Representative: The Rev Malcolm Trew, 155 Park Road West, Rosyth
e-mail: malcolm.trew@virgin.net

563 ABERDALGIE AND DUPPLIN PARISH CHURCH

NO 064 194

Aberdalgie

Nestling in the Earn Valley on a site of enduring worship for centuries, the present church was built by the Earl of Kinnoull in 1773. A T-plan church of local sandstone features a fine laird's loft and Georgian retiring room. Fourteenth-century Tournai marble Oliphant monument. Sir Robert Lorimer remodelled the interior in 1929. Extensive use of Austrian oak gives the church a sense of peace and simple dignity. Renovations 1994. Signed off B9112, south of Aberdalgie village. Linked with Forteviot. Sunday Service 11.15am

Open by arrangement, telephone Rev Colin Williamson 01738 625854

CHURCH OF SCOTLAND WC **B**

564 ABERNYTE PARISH CHURCH

NO 267 311

Abernyte, by Inchture

The present church was built in 1736 to replace a building of pre-1400, although there may have been a Celtic church here much earlier. Major renovations in 1837 when the present cruciform shape was established. Intricate beams, stained glass and a modern wall hanging of 1992. Signposted from village. Linked with Longforgan and Inchture with Kinnaird. Sunday Service 11am

Open during daylight hours

CHURCH OF SCOTLAND **B**

565 ALYTH PARISH CHURCH

NO 243 488

Kirk Brae, Alyth

In a prominent position overlooking the town, Alyth Parish Church was completed in 1839 to a design by Thomas Hamilton. Gothic, with Romanesque influences, and an unusually high spire. Eighth- or ninth-century Pictish stone stands four ft high in the vestibule. All windows are stained glass and include work by Holliday, Adam and Webster. Large funeral escutcheon marks the death of Sir George Ramsay in a duel in 1790. Three-manual organ by Harrison & Harrison, 1890. Sunday Service 11am

Open July and August Saturday 10am-12noon, Sunday 2pm-4pm

CHURCH OF SCOTLAND WC **B**

566 ST KESSOG'S CHURCH, AUCHTERARDER

NN 942 128

High Street, Auchterarder

Built 1897, architect Alexander Ross of Inverness. Beautiful altar and reredos of Caen stone, both richly decorated with Florentine mosaic. Rood screen of white stone. East and west windows by Kempe of London. In quiet grounds and garden 50 yards off High Street. Linked with St James, Muthill. Sunday Service 11am

Open July and August, Monday to Friday 2pm-4pm or by arrangement, contact The Very Rev Randal MacAlister 01764 662525

SCOTTISH EPISCOPAL WC **C**

567 ST MARY'S CHURCH, BIRNAM

NO 032 418

Perth Road, Birnam

The main church and clock tower to a design by William Slater 1858 with north aisle by Norman & Beddoe 1883. Slater font and cover, Kempe east window, William Morris windows to Burne-Jones designs, three-bell chime, clock by James Ramsay of Dundee, 1882. Beautifully kept churchyard. On old A9 in centre of village. Sunday Service 9.45am; Wednesday 9.30am

Open Easter to Michaelmas 9.30am-6.30pm. Dunkeld & Birnam Arts Festival exhibition, summer concert and choral evensong last week in June

SCOTTISH EPISCOPAL (via Rectory) WC **B**

568 ST ANDREW'S, BLAIRGOWRIE

NO 177 454

James Street, Blairgowrie

The present building was completed in 1904 in Early English Gothic style with transepts, aisles, apse and a small back gallery. Five stained glass windows in the apse depict scenes from the life of Moses. Norman & Beard organ 1907, rebuilt 1989 by Mr A F Edmondstone. The first Free Church of Blaigowrie, 1843, is now the hall and back vestibule. Sunday Service: 11.15am.

Open June-August Thursday and Saturday 2pm-4pm

CHURCH OF SCOTLAND WC

569 ARDOCH PARISH CHURCH, BRACO

NO 839 098

Feddal Road, Braco

Officially opened for worship in 1781 as a chapel of ease, the church was originally a rectangular building. The bellcote being added in 1836 and a chancel built on the east end by William Simpson of Stirling in 1890. The most recent addition is the church hall, built 1985. Ardoch Church sits close by the famous Roman camp. Directions: A9 north of Dunblane, take A822 to Braco, turn onto B8033 to Kinbuck and church is on right. Sunday Service 11.30am in 2000. 10am in 2001

Open by arrangement, telephone 01786 880589

CHURCH OF SCOTLAND WC **C**

570 DUNBARNEY PARISH CHURCH, BRIDGE OF EARN

NO 130 185

Manse Road, Bridge of Earn

Built 1787. Pedimented bellcote added, interior recast and other alterations 1880. Rectangular plan with bow-ended west porch. Off the main street of Bridge of Earn. Sunday Service 9.30am

Annual Flower Festival, last weekend in September (Friday, Saturday and Sunday)

CHURCH OF SCOTLAND WC **C**

571 BRAES OF RANNOCH PARISH CHURCH, BRIDGE OF GAUR

NN 507 566

South Loch Road, Bridge of Gaur

Built in 1907 Peter MacGregor Chalmers. The bellcote is from an earlier building of 1776 and also borne by a church built in 1855 on this site. Granite-walled interior, unusual chancel and lovely woodwork give a special atmosphere of peace and beauty. Rothwell pipe organ from Urquhart Church, Elgin rebuilt 1991, David Loosley. This was the only charge of Rev Archibald Eneas Robertson (1907-20), first ascender of all 'Munros' in Scotland (283 peaks over 3000 ft). B846 Aberfeldy to Bridge of Gaur, and south Loch Rannoch road to Finnart. Sunday Service 9.45am

Open daily

CHURCH OF SCOTLAND **B**

572 CAPUTH PARISH CHURCH

NO 088 401

Caputh, near Dunkeld

Now into its third century, Caputh Church was built in 1798. There has been a church in Caputh since the ninth century, the present one being a fine stone building. The interior has oak furnishings, stained glass windows and a fairly rare pipe organ. On A984, four miles east of Dunkeld, Perthshire.
Sunday Service at 11.15am

Open by arrangement, telephone Mrs Easton 01738 710389

CHURCH OF SCOTLAND WC

CAPUTH PARISH CHURCH

573 CLEISH CHURCH

NT 095 981

Cleish

Built on 13th-century site in 1832 with additions 1897. Organ and lights from St Giles, Edinburgh. The hymn 'Jesus, tender Shepherd, hear me' written by former minister's wife in the manse. Interesting wall chart and graveyard. Exit 5 M90, Cleish two miles. Sunday Service 11.15am

Open daily, 10am-5pm

CHURCH OF SCOTLAND **B**

574 COMRIE AND STROWAN PARISH CHURCH, COMRIE

NN 770 221

Burrell Street, Comrie

Built in 1881 George T Ewing on a site surrounded by attractive grounds overlooking the River Earn. Sixteenth-century Flemish bell. Organ built 1910 for the London Exhibition. A85. Regular bus service from Perth. Linked with Dundurn. Sunday Service: 10am June to September; 10.30am October to May

Open daily

CHURCH OF SCOTLAND WC **C**

575 ST NINIAN'S, CRIEFF

NN 862 219

Comrie Road, Crieff

Placed on the Burrell Street axis, the rectangular church has a broad gabled façade with a centre tower with a gabled and pinnacled parapet. The old West Church has been refurbished to become a modern conference centre. Alterations carried out in 1970. Sunday Service 9.30am

Open all year during daylight hours (except Christmas Day)

CHURCH OF SCOTLAND WC **B**

576 KETTINS PARISH CHURCH

N0 238 390

Kettins, by Coupar Angus

On the site of one of six chapels established by a nearby Columban monastery, the present church dates from 1768, with the north wing added in 1870 and the tower in 1891. Sixteen stained glass windows dating from 1878 onwards. Belgian bell of 1519 now rests, complete with belfry, close to the west gable it once surmounted. Celtic stone. Off A923, Dundee–Coupar Angus, one and a quarter miles south-east of Coupar. Linked with Meigle. Sunday Service 11.30am

Open June to August, 1st Sunday 2pm-4pm

CHURCH OF SCOTLAND **B**

577 ST ANNE'S, DOWALLY

NO 001 480

Built in 1818 on the site of a 16th-century building, St Anne's is a small country church with a bright interior. The designer was probably John Stewart, although the church has been much altered since. Dates on the bell (which is still in use) and belfry suggest that they came from the earlier church. The chancel has carved screens which were originally in Dunkeld Cathedral. One of the memorials is to John Robb, a minister of the parish who perished in the shipwreck in which Grace Darling became a national heroine. The Church is situated on the right hand side of the A9, three and a half miles north of Dunkeld. Sunday Service 2pm, second, fourth and fifth Sundays of the month

Open by arrangement, telephone Mrs J Allan 01350 728995

CHURCH OF SCOTLAND **B**

578 DUNKELD CATHEDRAL

NO 024 426

Cathedral Street, Dunkeld

The Cathedral lies in a superb setting on the banks of the Tay. The restored choir, now used as the parish church, was completed in 1350. Chapter house 1469 adjacent to choir, contains a small museum. The tower, ruined nave and south porch are in the care of Historic Scotland. Just off A9, at west end of Dunkeld. Sunday Service, Easter to Remembrance Sunday, 11am

Open daily, summer 9.30am–7pm, winter 9.30am–4pm

CHURCH OF SCOTLAND **A**

579 FORTEVIOT PARISH CHURCH (ST ANDREW'S), FORTEVIOT

NO 050 174

In an area of historical importance – in the ninth century Kenneth MacAlpin had his palace here, and a basilica existed from the first half of the eighth century – this church, the third, was erected in 1778. It was remodelled in the mid 19th century. Celtic bell dated AD 900, one of five Scottish bronze bells. Medieval carved stones. The font is from the pre-Reformation church of Muckersie united with Forteviot in 1618. Organ by Hamilton of Edinburgh. Extensively renovated 1994. Linked with Aberdalgie and Dupplin. Sunday Service 10am

Open by arrangement, telephone Rev C Williamson 01738 625854

CHURCH OF SCOTLAND **C**

FORTEVIOT PARISH CHURCH (ST ANDREW'S), FORTEVIOT

FOWLIS WESTER PARISH CHURCH

580 FOWLIS WESTER PARISH CHURCH

NN 928 241

The church is a 13th-century building renovated in 1927 by Jeffrey Waddell of Glasgow with much Celtic ornament. It retains many of the original features including a 'lepers' squint'. The Pictish cross under the north wall is evidence of over 1000 years of Christian worship in the area. Turn off A85, five miles from Crieff to Fowlis Wester (signed). Sunday Service 11.30am for 2000, and at 10am for 2001

Open by arrangement, telephone Mrs McColl 01764 683205

CHURCH OF SCOTLAND B

581 ST MADOES AND KINFAUNS CHURCH, GLENCARSE

NO 167 223

Glencarse, near Perth

Built 1799 on the site of earlier churches and refurbished in 1923. T-plan church with laird's gallery. New vestry and entrance hall by David Murdoch of Methven 1996. Interesting historic graveyard with 18th-century gravestones of sculptural merit. Pictish St Madoes Stone now on display in Perth Museum and Art Gallery. Contemporary embroidered pulpit falls.

Sunday Service: September to May 11am; June to August 10am

Open 1st Sunday of month, June to September 1-4pm

CHURCH OF SCOTLAND WC B

ST MADOES AND KINFAUNS CHURCH, GLENCARSE

GLENDEVON PARISH CHURCH

582 GLENDEVON PARISH CHURCH

NN 979 051

west side of A823, 1 mile north of Tormaukin Hotel

Seventeenth-century church with large stained glass window by Webster of Glasgow, 1913, and small stained glass window in memory of Rev Alexander Taylor 1872-1949. Various memorial plaques. Pulpit and Communion table and chair carved by Mr Philips of Tormaukin. Large gravestone to Jane Rutherford. Sunday Service: 11.15am

Open at all times

CHURCH OF SCOTLAND WC **B**

583 ALL SOULS' CHURCH, INVERGOWRIE

NO 347 303

59 Main Street, Invergowrie

Red sandstone church with 140 ft spire, designed by Hippolyte Blanc 1890. High altar has beautiful Italian marble reredos and crucifix. Lady Chapel contains altar from Rossie Priory Chapel. Sculptured Stations of the Cross. Embroidered wallhanging to celebrate centenary of consecration 1996. Church hall used for community activities. Services: Sunday 10am Sung Eucharist; Wednesday Said Eucharist 10.15am

Open weekdays during school terms, 9am-4pm

SCOTTISH EPISCOPAL WC (only availble if Hall is in use) **A**

584 INVERGOWRIE PARISH CHURCH

NO 346 304

Main Street, Invergowrie

Building opened 1909. Architect John Robertson. Early Gothic with square tower and fine open timber roof. Pulpit and Communion Table of Austrian oak with carvings by local branch of YWCA. War memorial bell 1924. Stained glass window depicting Disruption minister Rev R S Walker conducting open-air Communion. Sunday Service 11am

Open July and August Wed 2pm–4pm. Keyholder Mr W Smith 01382 562759

CHURCH OF SCOTLAND WC B

585 KILMAVEONAIG CHURCH

NN 874 658

Kilmaveonaig, Blair Atholl

An Episcopal Chapel rebuilt in 1794 by John Stewart on the site of the old parish church of Kilmaveonaig 1591, and having belonged to the Episcopal Communion without a break since the Revolution. Enlarged 1899. Lorimer reredos added 1912. Old bell 1629, from Little Dunkeld church. Off A9 to Blair Atholl, opposite Tilt Hotel. Sunday Service 10am

Open by arrangement. Key available from Tilt Hotel

SCOTTISH EPISCOPAL B

KILMAVEONAIG CHURCH

586 KINCLAVEN PARISH CHURCH

NO 151 385

by Stanley, near Perth

Built 1848 on site of previous church. Mixed Romanesque and Tudor with a narthex at the west end and bellcote at the east end. Churchyard contains the war memorial lychgate, 1919, by Reginald Fairlie, and some table tombs of the 17th century and later. Built into the churchyard wall is the monument to Alexander Cabel (Campbell), Bishop of Brechin, 1608. Sunday Service 9.45am

Open by arrangement, telephone Mr Gordon 01738 710548,

CHURCH OF SCOTLAND WC WC B

587 THE OLD CHURCH OF RANNOCH, KINLOCH RANNOCH

NN 663 585

South Loch Road, Kinloch Rannoch

A Thomas Telford church of 1829, extensively altered and enlarged 1893. Wooden beamed roof, stained glass window, hour-glass by pulpit. B846 from Aberfeldy, B8019 from Pitlochry. Sunday Service 11.30am

Open daily 10am to dusk. Other times, key from Mrs D MacDonald, Bridgend Cottage, telephone 01882 632359

CHURCH OF SCOTLAND WC C

588 COLLACE PARISH CHURCH, KINROSSIE

NO 197 320

Kinrossie, by Perth

Early 19th century on site of an earlier church dedicated in 1242. Stained glass window 1919. Remains of medieval building. Important 17th- and 18th-century gravestones. A94 from Perth, signposted from village smithy.

Sunday Service 11.15am

Open Sunday 18 June, 2000 2pm-4pm.
Sunday 17 June 2001 2pm-4pm

CHURCH OF SCOTLAND

WC B

COLLACE PARISH CHURCH, KINROSSIE

589 LONGFORGAN PARISH CHURCH

NO 309 300

Main Street, Longforgan

Church of 1795 in traditional Scottish box shape. Tower 1690 with eight-sided steeple and unusual clock. Apse added 1900. Several stained glass windows. Wood carving by Sir Robert Lorimer and remains of medieval font. Unique pipe organ. Interesting tombstones preserved inside and graveyard with lychgate. Adjacent to A90, 16 miles from Perth and seven miles from Dundee. Sunday Service, summer months 9.15am. Winter 11.30am

Open Wednesdays 2-4pm, April to September. Or by arrangement, telephone Mrs Hulbert 01382 360294

CHURCH OF SCOTLAND WC B

LONGFORGAN PARISH CHURCH

590 MEIGLE PARISH CHURCH

NO 287 446

The Square, Meigle

Re built in 1870 by John Carver after fire destroyed the pre-Reformation stone church of 1431. Stands on the ancient site of a turf church erected by Columban missionaries around AD 606. Fine stone font. Interesting graveyard. Pictish stones in adjacent museum (Historic Scotland). Linked with Kettins. Sunday Service 10am

Open first Sunday, June to August 2-4pm

CHURCH OF SCOTLAND ♿ 👂 🚻 WC **B**

MEIGLE PARISH CHURCH

591 MORENISH CHAPEL

NO 607 356

by Killin

Built in 1902 by Aline White Todd in memory of her daughter Elvira who died in childbirth. The central piece of the chapel is the magnificent east window by Tiffany in heavily leaded tracery, and sumptuous stained glass showing Moses receiving the ten commandments on Mount Sinai. On A827 Killin–Kenmore. Served by Killin and Ardeonaig. Sunday Service 3pm, first Sunday of month during the summer

CHURCH OF SCOTLAND

592 MUTHILL PARISH CHURCH

NN 868 171

Station Road, Muthill, by Crieff

Replacing the twelfth-century church (still existing). Built in 1826 in Gothic style to a design by Gillespie Graham, nicknamed 'Pinnacle' Graham by those less enthusiastic for the sprockets of 19th-century Gothic. Pulpit canopy similarly sprocketed. A822, three miles south of Crieff. Buses from Stirling to Crieff. Sunday Service 11.30am (coffee 11am)

Open Sunday 1st August. Coincides with opening of nearby Drummond Castle Gardens (Scotland's Gardens Scheme)

CHURCH OF SCOTLAND ♿ 🚻 **B**

ST JAMES CHURCH, MUTHILL

593 ST JAMES CHURCH, MUTHILL

NN 869 170

Station Road, Muthill

Built 1836, designed by R & R Dickson of Edinburgh. Oldest Episcopal church in the area. Numerous family crests of historic interest and memorial tablets. Fifty yards from village centre opposite primary school. Linked with St Kessog's, Auchterarder. Sunday Service 9.30am.

Open by arrangement, telephone The Very Rev Randal MacAlister 01764 662525

SCOTTISH EPISCOPAL ♿ **B**

594 NORTH CHURCH, PERTH

NO 116 237

Mill Street, Perth

A pleasant city centre church built in 1880 by T L Watson of Glasgow in Italian Romanesque style. Sunday Services 9.30am, 11am and 6.30pm; Thursday lunchtime 1pm

Open by arrangement, telephone Mr G Weaks 01738 444033

CHURCH OF SCOTLAND WC **B**

595 ST LEONARD'S-IN-THE-FIELD & TRINITY, PERTH

NO 117 232

Marshall Place, Perth

Fine example of the late Gothic revival by John L Stevenson of London, opened in 1885. Outstanding architectural features are the crown tower and the heavy buttresses. The organ, which came from North Morningside Church in Edinburgh, was installed in the centenary year, 1985. Sunday Services: June to August 10am, September to May 11am

Open on Doors Open Day

CHURCH OF SCOTLAND **A**

596 ST JOHN'S EPISCOPAL, PERTH

NO 119 233

Princes Street, Perth

The present site has been used for worship since 1800. Present building designed by John Hay of Liverpool, 1850-51. Many stained glass windows, sculptures by Miss Mary Grant, chancel arch carved by Heiton. Fine Harrison & Harrison organ, 1971. Services: Sunday: Holy Communion 8am, Sung Eucharist 10.30am, Thursday: Holy Communion 11am

Open by arrangement telephone Mr T Mason 01738 627870

SCOTTISH EPISCOPAL WC B

ST JOHN'S EPISCOPAL, PERTH

597 ST JOHN'S KIRK OF PERTH

NO 119 235

St John Street, Perth

Burgh Church of Perth dedicated to John the Baptist and consecrated in 1242 on site of earlier church. Divided into three churches after the Reformation and restored 1923-26 by Sir Robert Lorimer. Good examples of modern stained glass including window of Knox Chapel by Douglas Strachan. Statue of John the Baptist by Indian sculptor Fanindra Bose and tapestry opposite Shrine (part of the 1926 restoration) by Archie Brennan of Dovecote Studios Edinburgh. Nave with barrel vaulting has carvings of events in the life of Christ. Glass screen at west door installed 1988. Sunday Services 9.30 and 11am

Open May to September, 10am-4pm weekdays, 12-2pm Sundays; October to April, when Church Officer is present, usually Wednesday to Saturday from 10am. Guided tours by arrangement, telephone Mrs M Howat 01738 626520

CHURCH OF SCOTLAND WC A

598 ST NINIAN'S CATHEDRAL, PERTH

NO 116 237

North Methven Street

First Cathedral to be built after the Reformation, being consecrated in 1850. The architect was William Butterfield. Baldachino in Cornish granite, fine wooden statue of the Risen Christ and interesting stained glass. Founder's window, the font and one of the banners by Sir Ninian Comper. Services: Sunday: Holy Communion 8 am, Sung Eucharist 11am, Monday to Friday Morning Prayer 9am, Wednesday Holy Communion 11am, Thursday Holy Communion 9am

Open Monday to Friday 9am-5pm

SCOTTISH EPISCOPAL WC B

PITLOCHRY CHURCH

599 PITLOCHRY CHURCH

NO 942 581

Church Road, Pitlochry

Built in 1884 by C L Ower, Dundee. The porch was added in 1995, built of stone from Pitlochry East Church, the East and West congregations having united in 1992. Seating arranged in a part circle around the communion table. Monument to Alexander Duff, 19th-century missionary. Identifiable as 'the church with the clock' 100 yards from main street. Sunday Services 9.30am All Age Worship, and 11am Traditional form of service

Open June to September, Monday to Friday 10am-12 noon and 2-4pm

CHURCH OF SCOTLAND **B**

600 PITLOCHRY BAPTIST CHURCH

NO 942 580

Atholl Road, next to Tourist Information Centre

Founded 1878 and originally meeting in a joiner's shop, the Pitlochry Fellowship built this church in 1884 to a design by Crombie of Edinburgh. Today's congregation welcomes visitors from across the world all year round. 'Through the Ages' Millennium exhibition in July during the annual Atholl Festival. Sunday Services: 11am and 6.30pm

Open by arrangement with Atholl Centre, a Christian holiday and conference centre, situated behind church, telephone 01796 473044

BAPTIST (Shop with Christian books and fair trade goods in adjoining Atholl Centre)

DUNDURN PARISH CHURCH, ST FILLANS

601 DUNDURN PARISH CHURCH, ST FILLANS

NN 697 241

St Fillans

Built 1879. Of particular interest is the medieval stone font. Oak panelling, pulpit and communion table with Celtic knotwork. Set in grounds with striking view across Loch Earn. Linked with Comrie and Strowan. Sunday Service 11.30am June to September; 12 noon October to May

Open daily, Easter to October

CHURCH OF SCOTLAND

602 SCONE OLD PARISH CHURCH

NO 134 256

Burnside, Scone

Church built in 1286 near to Scone Palace. Moved to present site in 1806 using stone from original building. Mansfield pew presented by Queen Anne of Denmark 1615. Memorial to David Douglas, botanist, in graveyard. A94 from Perth. Number 7 bus from Perth. Sunday Service 11am

Open Saturdays 8 March, 17 May, 16 August and 18 October 2000 10am–12 noon

CHURCH OF SCOTLAND WC **B**

603 ST ANDREW'S CHURCH, STRATHTAY

NN 910 534

Strathtay

The chancel was built in 1888 and the nave added in 1919. A vestibule and hall were added in 1982. Heavily carved woodwork on pulpit, lectern and priest's prayer desk. Lovely stained glass. A free-standing belfry was provided in 1995. In village, over River Tay from Grandtully on A827 between Ballinluig and Aberfeldy. Linked with St Mary's, Birnam. Sunday Service 11.30am

Open by arrangement. Key from village shop

SCOTTISH EPISCOPAL WC **A**

604 STANLEY PARISH CHURCH

NO 108 330

Stanley, Perthshire

Built in 1828 by local mill owners the Buchanan family for mill workers, the church seated 1000. It was adapted in 1962 and incorporated a new pew arrangement. The halls which are below the sanctuary were re-furbished in 1997. The vestibule houses the war memorial. The site is floodlit by night and the extensive church grounds hold an annual outdoor fete on the first Saturday of September. Sunday Service at 11.30am

CHURCH OF SCOTLAND **B**

STANLEY PARISH CHURCH

605 TENANDRY CHURCH

NN 911 615

Tenandry, Pitlochry

Small country church built in 1836 of stone and slate and of traditional design. Fine view of the Pass of Killiecrankie from the road above the church. Turn north from B8019 at Garry Bridge two miles north of Pitlochry (signed). Sunday Service 11am

Open daily

CHURCH OF SCOTLAND WC **B**

606 FOSS KIRK, TUMMEL BRIDGE

NN 790 581

South Loch Tummel Road, Foss

Founded AD 625 by St Chad and used until the Reformation. Fell into disrepair 1580, restored 1821. Perth bell 1824. Ancient graveyard behind the church with view of Loch Tummel. Linked with Braes of Rannoch and Rannoch. B8019 from Pitlochry to Tummel Bridge, then B846 to Foss or B846 from Aberfeldy to Foss. Sunday Services May to September first and third Sundays 7pm; October to April first Sunday 2.30pm

Open daily

CHURCH OF SCOTLAND **C**

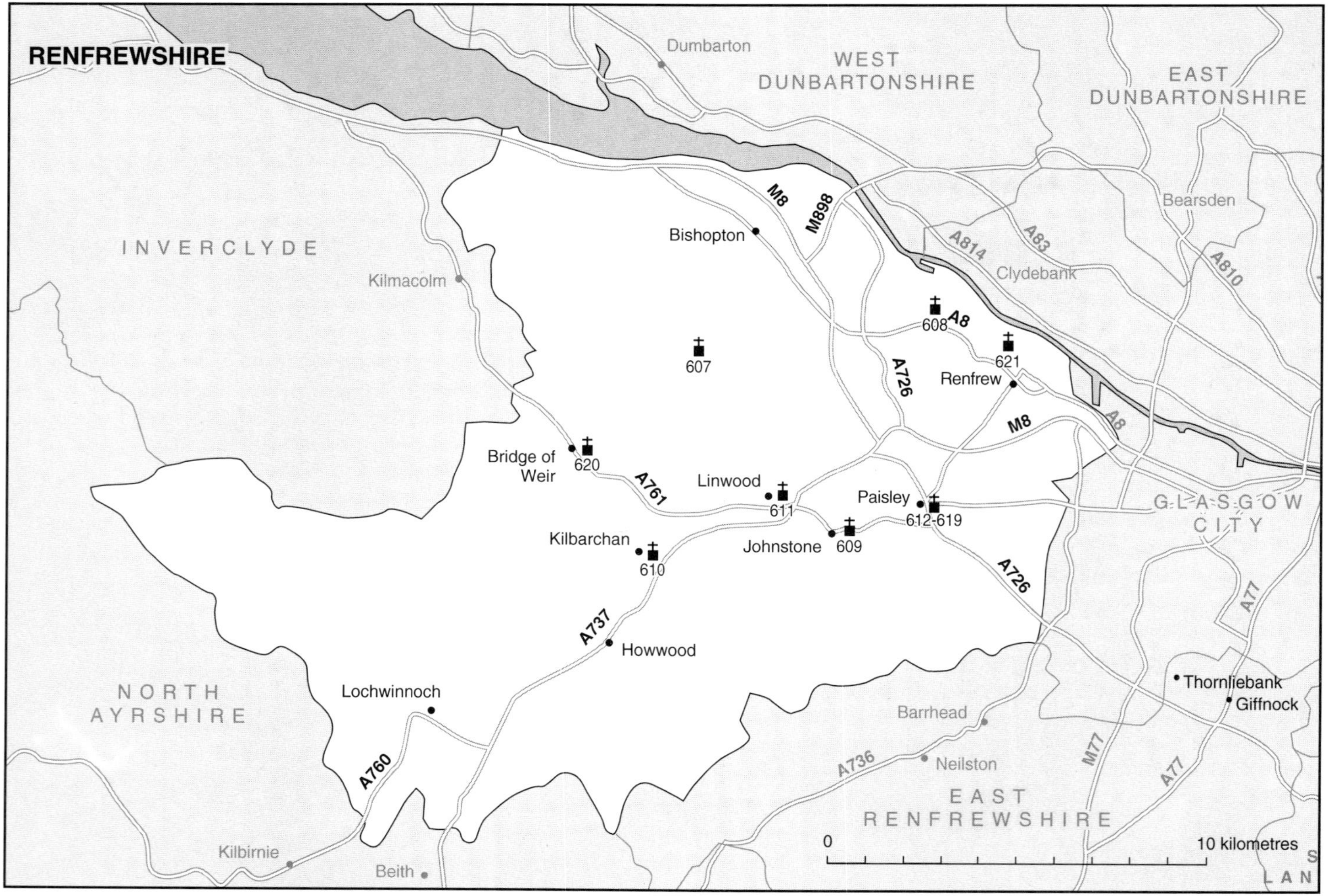
RENFREWSHIRE
Dumbarton
WEST DUNBARTONSHIRE
EAST DUNBARTONSHIRE
Bearsden
INVERCLYDE
Kilmacolm
Bishopton
M8
M898
A814
A83
A810
Clydebank
608
A8
621
607
A726
Renfrew
M8
A8
Bridge of Weir
620
A761
Linwood
611
Paisley
612-619
GLASGOW CITY
Kilbarchan
610
Johnstone
609
A726
A77
A737
Howwood
Thornliebank
Giffnock
NORTH AYRSHIRE
Lochwinnoch
Barrhead
A736
Neilston
M77
A77
A760
EAST RENFREWSHIRE
0
10 kilometres
Kilbirnie
Beith

RENFREWSHIRE

Local Representative: Mr Norman MacGilvray, 20 Well Street, West Kilbride, KA23 9EJ (*telephone* 01294 829221)

607 HOUSTON & KILLELLAN PARISH CHURCH

NS 410 671

Kirk Road, Houston

Gothic, 1874 by David Thomson, this building is the third on this ancient site. Very good stained glass. Interesting organ. Between Bridge of Weir and Inchinnan. Sunday Service 11am

Open Sundays 11am-1pm

CHURCH OF SCOTLAND **B**

608 INCHINNAN PARISH CHURCH (ST CONVAL'S KIRK)

NS 490 680

Old Greenock Road, Inchinnan

Sir R Rowand Anderson's Church of 1904 was razed to make way for Glasgow Airport, and the present building by Miller and Black, consecrated in 1968, incorporates much of interest and beauty from the earlier church. Foundation by St Conval in 597. King David I gave patronage of first stone church to Knights Templar, succeeded by Knights of St John. Celtic and medieval stones. Two miles west of Renfrew on A8. Sunday Service 10.45am

Open Thursday during term time, noon-1.30pm. Light lunches available

CHURCH OF SCOTLAND WC

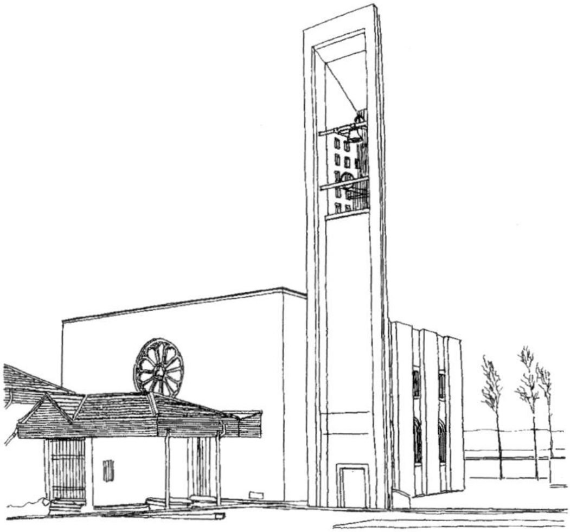

INCHINNAN PARISH CHURCH (ST CONVAL'S KIRK)

609 JOHNSTONE HIGH PARISH CHURCH

NS 426 630

Quarry Street, Johnstone

An octagonal building of grey sandstone built in 1792. Clock tower with spire. Stained glass. Historic graveyard. Town centre. Trains from Glasgow every 20 minutes. Sunday Service 11am; Songs of Praise 1st Sunday 6.30pm

Open Thursday to Saturday 10am-12 noon, all year. Tours by arrangement at church hall coffee shop

CHURCH OF SCOTLAND

B

JOHNSTONE HIGH PARISH CHURCH

610 KILBARCHAN WEST CHURCH

NS 401 632

Church Street, Kilbarchan

Hall built as the church in 1724 on the site of an earlier church. Present church completed 1901, architect W H Howie. Some fine stained glass resited from old church and glass from early 20th century. Three-manual organ built 1904 by William Hill & Sons. On A737 next to Weaver's Cottage. Sunday Services 11am; Wednesdays 10.30am, October to May

Open by arrangement 01505 342930

CHURCH OF SCOTLAND B

611 LINWOOD PARISH CHURCH

NS 432 645

Blackwood Avenue, Linwood

A spacious red brick building dating from 1965. An earlier church of 1860 existed on another site, demolished in 1976. The furniture and communion silver are from the earlier church. Contemporary art work includes a large aluminium cross presented by the former Rootes Vehicle Plant. Fine pipe organ 1957. Sunday Service 9.30am and 11am.

Open Friday 11.30am-1.30pm during school term, and by arrangement, telephone Mrs F Dooley 01505 331 065

CHURCH OF SCOTLAND

612 PAISLEY ABBEY

NS 4864

Founded in 1163. Early 20th-century restoration of the choir by P MacGregor Chalmers and Lorimer. Medieval architecture, royal tombs of Marjory Bruce and Robert III, the tenth-century Barochan Cross. Exceptionally fine woodwork by Lorimer, stained glass by Burne-Jones and others. M8, junction 27, follow signs to Paisley town centre. By train to Paisley, Gilmour Street.

Sunday Services 11am, 12.15pm (Holy Communion), 6.30pm

Open daily, Monday to Saturday 10am-3.30pm. Other details from Abbey Office, telephone 0141 889 7654

CHURCH OF SCOTLAND WC **A**

PAISLEY ABBEY

613 CASTLEHEAD PARISH CHURCH, PAISLEY

NS 486 640

Main Road, Castlehead, Paisley

Built 1781 as the first Relief church in Paisley. Interior renovated 1881. Bishop organ 1898. Graveyard has graves of Robert Tannahill (local poet), past ministers, merchants and the mass graves of the cholera epidemic. At west end of town, at junction of Castlehead Main Road and Canal Street.

Sunday Service 11am

Open May to September, Monday, Wednesday and Friday 2-4pm

CHURCH OF SCOTLAND WC **B**

614 GLASGOW INTERNATIONAL AIRPORT CHAPEL, PAISLEY

NS 478 663

Second Floor, Terminal Building, Glasgow Airport

A recent addition to Glasgow Airport, open to passengers and staff of all faiths and creeds. Christian Services are announced 30 minutes in advance by public address

Open at all times

NON-DENOMINATIONAL

615 MARTYRS' CHURCH, PAISLEY

NS 474 639

Broomlands Street, Paisley

The church is named after the Paisley martyrs who were executed in 1685. Built 1847 with additions and alterations, including tower and south front in neo-Norman style 1905, T G Abercrombie, architect. Inside are galleries on three sides on cast-iron colonnettes. The pulpit, 18 ft long, has been likened to the bridge of a ship. On A737 west of Paisley centre. Sunday Service 11am

Open Friday 10am-1pm

CHURCH OF SCOTLAND WC B

616 NEW JERUSALEM CHURCH, PAISLEY

NS 481 637

17 George Street, Paisley

Built for Wesleyan Methodists in 1810, and in use by Swedenborgians since 1860, this is an unusual building with halls on the ground floor and the church upstairs. Three striking stained glass windows by W & J J Kier, including one designed by Sir Noel Paton. Fine pulpit, communion table, and ceiling rose. Nearest railway stations Paisley Canal and Paisley Gilmour Street. Sunday Service 11am

NEW JERUSALEM CHURCH, PAISLEY

Open by arrangement, and on Doors Open Day, September, 11am-4pm, telephone Rev Robert Gill 0141 887 4119

SWEDENBORGIAN WC

617 ST JAMES'S CHURCH, PAISLEY

NS 477 644

Underwood Road, Paisley

Early French Gothic style to a design by Hippolyte Blanc, largely gifted by Sir Peter Coats 1884. Spire 200 ft. Full peal of bells, rung every Sunday. Father Willis pipe organ, rebuilt J Walker 1967. Stained glass windows 1904. Landscaped grounds. M8, junction 29, St James interchange. Sunday Service 11am

Open Monday, Wednesday and Friday, 10am-4pm. Also Doors Open Day, September, 10am-4pm. Contact day centre at rear of church for access

CHURCH OF SCOTLAND WC **B**

618 THOMAS COATS MEMORIAL BAPTIST CHURCH, PAISLEY

NS 478 640

High Street, Paisley

Built by the Coats Family as a memorial to Thomas Coats. Hippolyte Blanc Gothic, opened May 1894. Beautiful interior, 'by far the grandest of the Paisley churches' (Groome's Gazetteer) with carved marble and alabaster. Famous Hill four-manual pipe organ. On main street going west from Paisley Cross. Sunday Service 11am

Open May to September, Monday, Wednesday, Friday 2-4pm. Or by arrangement, telephone Church Secretary 0141 889 6690

BAPTIST WC **A**

THOMAS COATS MEMORIAL BAPTIST CHURCH, PAISLEY

619 WALLNEUK NORTH CHURCH, PAISLEY

NS 486 643

Abercorn Street, Paisley

Built 1915. Pipe organ by Abbott & Smith 1931, dedicated to Peter Coats, donor of this church. Its fine oak case was designed by Abercrombie & Maitland, Glasgow and carved and built by Wylie & Lochead, Glasgow. Near town centre. Sunday Service 11am; also first Sunday in Mossvale Hall 6.30pm; Wednesday 12.30pm

Open during Doors Open Day, September

CHURCH OF SCOTLAND A

620 ST MACHAR'S, RANFURLY

NS 386 653

Kilbarchan Road, Ranfurly, Bridge of Weir

Early Gothic 1878 by Lewis Shanks, brother of one of the local millowners. The chancel was added in 1910 by Alexander Hislop. Stained glass by J S Melville & J Stewart 1900, Herbert Hendrie 1931, William Wilson 1946, Gordon Webster 1956. Descriptive booklet by Maurice L Gaine 1996. A761 at east end of village. Sunday Service 11am (10.30am July and August)

Open Fridays 10am-12noon. Bridge of Weir Gala Week in June

CHURCH OF SCOTLAND WC

621 RENFREW OLD PARISH CHURCH

NS 509 676

26 High Street, Renfrew

The Church of Renfrew was bestowed by King David on the Cathedral Church of Glasgow in 1136. Within the present lancet Gothic 1862 sanctuary are two late medieval monuments, a hooded vault with recumbent effigies and an altar tomb. In Renfrew town centre. Regular bus services from Glasgow and Paisley. Sunday Services 11.15am and 6.30pm

Open during Doors Open Day, September

CHURCH OF SCOTLAND

WC B

RENFREW OLD PARISH CHURCH

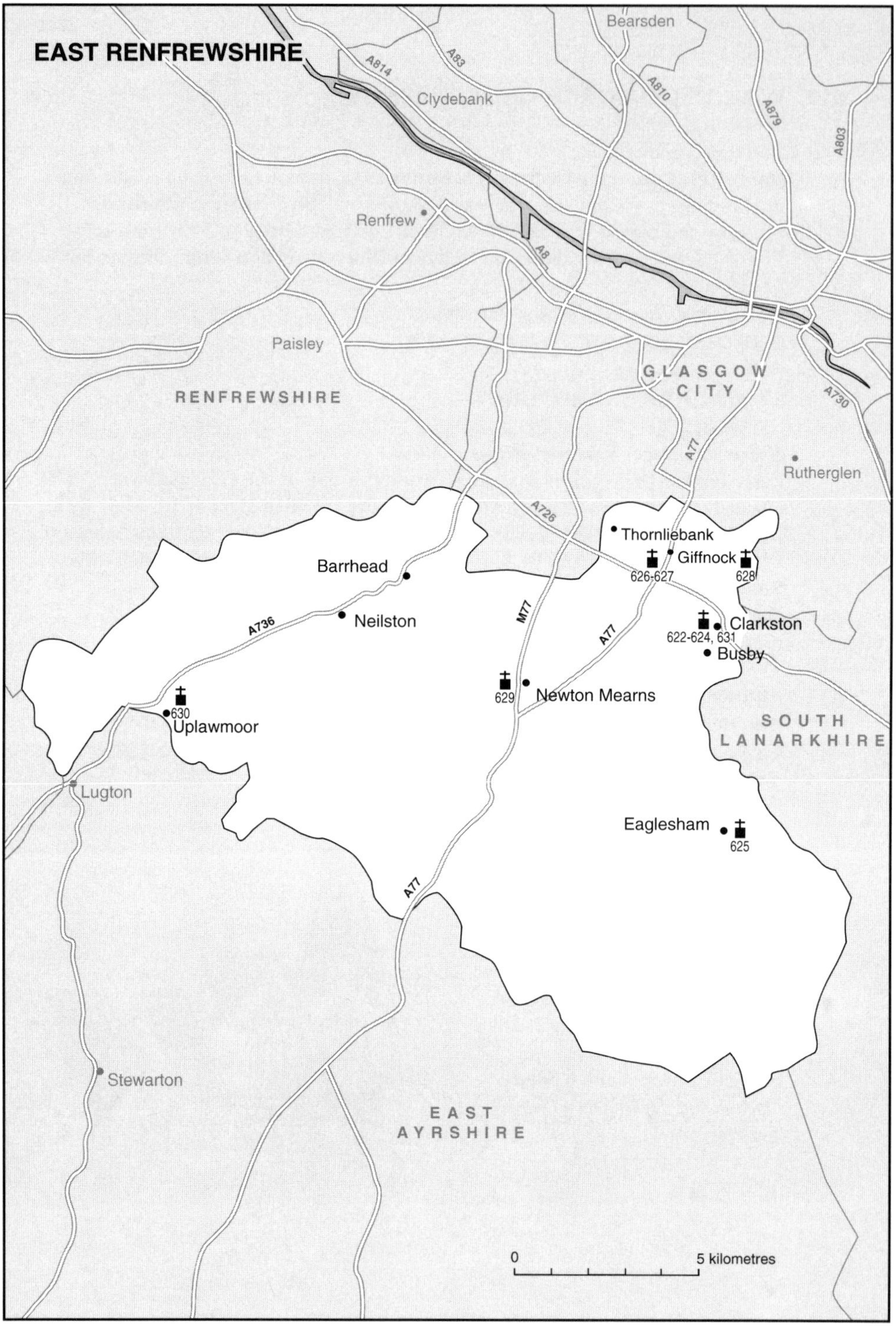

EAST RENFREWSHIRE
Bearsden
A814
A83
A810
A879
A803
Clydebank
Renfrew
A8
Paisley
RENFREWSHIRE
GLASGOW CITY
A730
A77
Rutherglen
A726
Thornliebank
Giffnock
626-627
628
Barrhead
Neilston
A736
M77
A77
Clarkston
622-624, 631
Busby
629
Newton Mearns
630
Uplawmoor
SOUTH LANARKHIRE
Lugton
Eaglesham
625
A77
Stewarton
EAST AYRSHIRE
0
5 kilometres

EAST RENFREWSHIRE

622 GREENBANK CHURCH, CLARKSTON

NS 574 568

Eaglesham Road, Clarkston

The Church designed by McKissack & Rowan was opened in 1884. The Chancel, furnishings and stained glass windows were added in 1937. A mural by Alistair Gray in the transept was completed in 1979. The Centenary Chapel was opened in 1984. Sunday Services 9.30am, 11.00am and 6.30pm

Open by arrangement, telephone Church Officer 0141 644 2839

CHURCH OF SCOTLAND

GREENBANK CHURCH, CLARKSTON

623 ST AIDAN'S, CLARKSTON

NS 573 574

Mearns Road, Clarkston

Hall Church built 1924 and present church 1951, architects Noad & Wallace. Building has a steel frame and brick interior. Red sandstone facing matches Hall. Stained glass including a pair of windows by Susan Bradbury 1998. Sunday Services: 8am Holy Communion, 10am Sung Eucharist, 6.30 Evensong first fourth and fifth Sundays

Open Wednesdays 9-11.30am

SCOTTISH EPISCOPAL

624 STAMPERLAND CHURCH, CLARKSTON

NS 576 581

Stamperland Gardens, Clarkston

Congregation's first service held in an air raid shelter of a local garage in 1940. Thereafter a local shop was occupied at 38 Stamperland Crescent before a hall church was built in 1941 (now hall of Church). Present modern building erected 1964, architect J Thompson King & Partners. Concrete bell tower. Three stained glass windows by Gordon Webster, previously in Woodside Parish Church. Pipe organ 1897 by Lewis & Co of Brixton and earlier in Regent Place UP Church, Dennistoun, Glasgow. Furnishings include items from 1938 Glasgow Empire Exhibition Church. Bas-relief of mythical pelican on outside wall. Sunday Services 10am and 11am

Open by arrangement, telephone Samuel Esler 0141 571 8451

CHURCH OF SCOTLAND

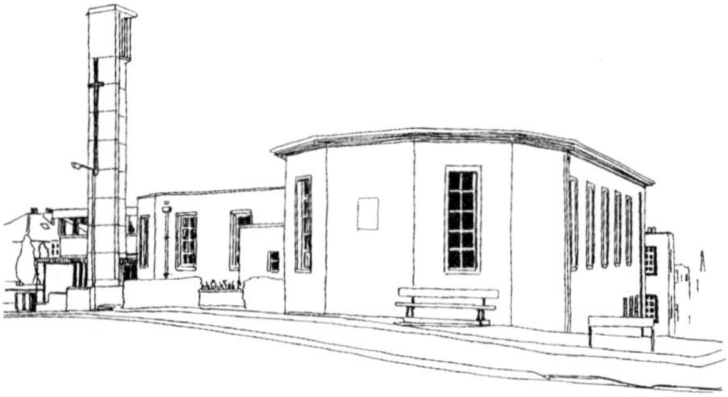

STAMPERLAND CHURCH, CLARKSTON

625 EAGLESHAM OLD & CARSWELL PARISH CHURCH, EAGLESHAM

NS 572 518

Montgomery Street, Eaglesham

The present attractive church with clock steeple was designed by Robert McLachlane and completed in 1790. It replaced churches on this site since early times. Former United Free Church is now the Church Halls and Carswell United Presbyterian Church refurbished as 'The Children's Church' (both located on Montgomery Street). 'Father Willis' organ and fine embroidered pulpit falls by Kathleen Whyte and Fiona Hamilton. Covenanter graves in churchyard. Sunday Services 9.45am and 11.15am *Open during Doors Open Day, September, and by arrangement, telephone the Beadle 01355 303411*

CHURCH OF SCOTLAND WC **B**

EAGLESHAM OLD & CARSWELL PARISH CHURCH, EAGLESHAM

626 GIFFNOCK SOUTH PARISH CHURCH

NS 559 582

Greenhill Avenue, Giffnock

A 'hall church' (now Eglinton Hall) was opened in 1914. The present church was begun in 1921 and dedicated in 1929. It is by Stewart & Paterson in late Gothic style with blonde sandstone. There is a fine collection of stained glass windows, including six by Gordon Webster. There are three recent windows, one by Sadie McLellan and two by Brian Hutchison. Sunday Service 11.15am.

CHURCH OF SCOTLAND WC **B**

GIFFNOCK SOUTH PARISH CHURCH

627 ORCHARDHILL PARISH CHURCH, GIFFNOCK

NS 563 587

Church Road, Giffnock

Church and hall built in Gothic Revival style, H E Clifford 1900. Centenary celebration year May 1999 to May 2000. Of local stone with a red tiled roof, squat tower with spiral wooden stair and roof turret. Extensions carried out in 1910 and 1935. Stained glass 1936-86 and wood panelling 1900-35. Two-manual pipe organ, Hill, Norman & Beard. Embroidered pulpit falls 1993. On east side of Fenwick Road, north of Eastwood Toll. Buses from Glasgow Buchanan and trains from Glasgow Central. Sunday Services: winter 11am and 6.30pm; summer 9.30am and 11am

Open by arrangement, telephone Church Officer 0141 620 3346/638 3604

CHURCH OF SCOTLAND B

ORCHARDHILL PARISH CHURCH, GIFFNOCK

NETHERLEE PARISH CHURCH

628 NETHERLEE PARISH CHURCH

NS 557 590

Ormonde Avenue, Netherlee

Built in neo-Gothic style of red Dumfries-shire sandstone by Stewart & Paterson 1934. Oak panelling and furnishings beautifully carved. Lovely stained glass. City buses via Clarkston Road. Sunday Services: September to May 11am and some at 6.30pm; June to August 9.30am and 11am

Open by arrangement, telephone Mr McVey 0141 637 6853

CHURCH OF SCOTLAND WC **B**

629 MEARNS PARISH CHURCH, NEWTON MEARNS

NS 551 556

Junction of Eaglesham Road and Mearns Road

Religious settlement and site since 800 AD, the present church dates from 1813 and was extensively renovated in 1932. Organ originally from Glasgow City Hall. Stained glass windows by Gordon Webster and James McPhie. South wall tapestry donated by the late Lord Goold. A phosphor-bronze weathercock weighing two and a half cwts atop the bell tower was erected in the late 1940s. Gate posts in the form of sentry boxes date from the era of the 'Resurrectionists'. Sunday Services: 9.30and 11am

Open by arrangement, telephone the Minister 0141 616 2410

CHURCH OF SCOTLAND WC **B**

MEARNS PARISH CHURCH, NEWTON MEARNS

630 CALDWELL PARISH CHURCH, UPLAWMOOR

NS 435 552

Neilston Road, Uplawmoor

Simple country church built 1889 William Ingram. Memorial glass sculpture depicting the Trinity by Ralph Cowan 1989. Garden of Remembrance dedicated 1997. Off B736 Barrhead–Irvine. On main street opposite village shop. Sunday Service 11am; Wednesday brief act of worship 12 noon

Open daily 11am-3pm. Soup lunch in hall adjacent October to March, Friday 12 noon-1.30pm

CHURCH OF SCOTLAND

631 WILLIAMWOOD PARISH CHURCH

NS 567 576

Seres Road, Williamwood

Built in 1937 as a church extension charge, the church is a fine example of mid-1930s church architecture. Original and somewhat austere interior upgraded and enriched. Historical and other information available. By rail from Glasgow Central to Williamwood or Clarkston, ten minutes walk from both stations. Bus services from Glasgow to Eaglesham, alight at Clarkston. Sunday Service 11am

Open February to June and September to December, weekdays, 9.45am-12 noon. Other information. telephone 0141 638 2091

CHURCH OF SCOTLAND

WILLIAMWOOD PARISH CHURCH

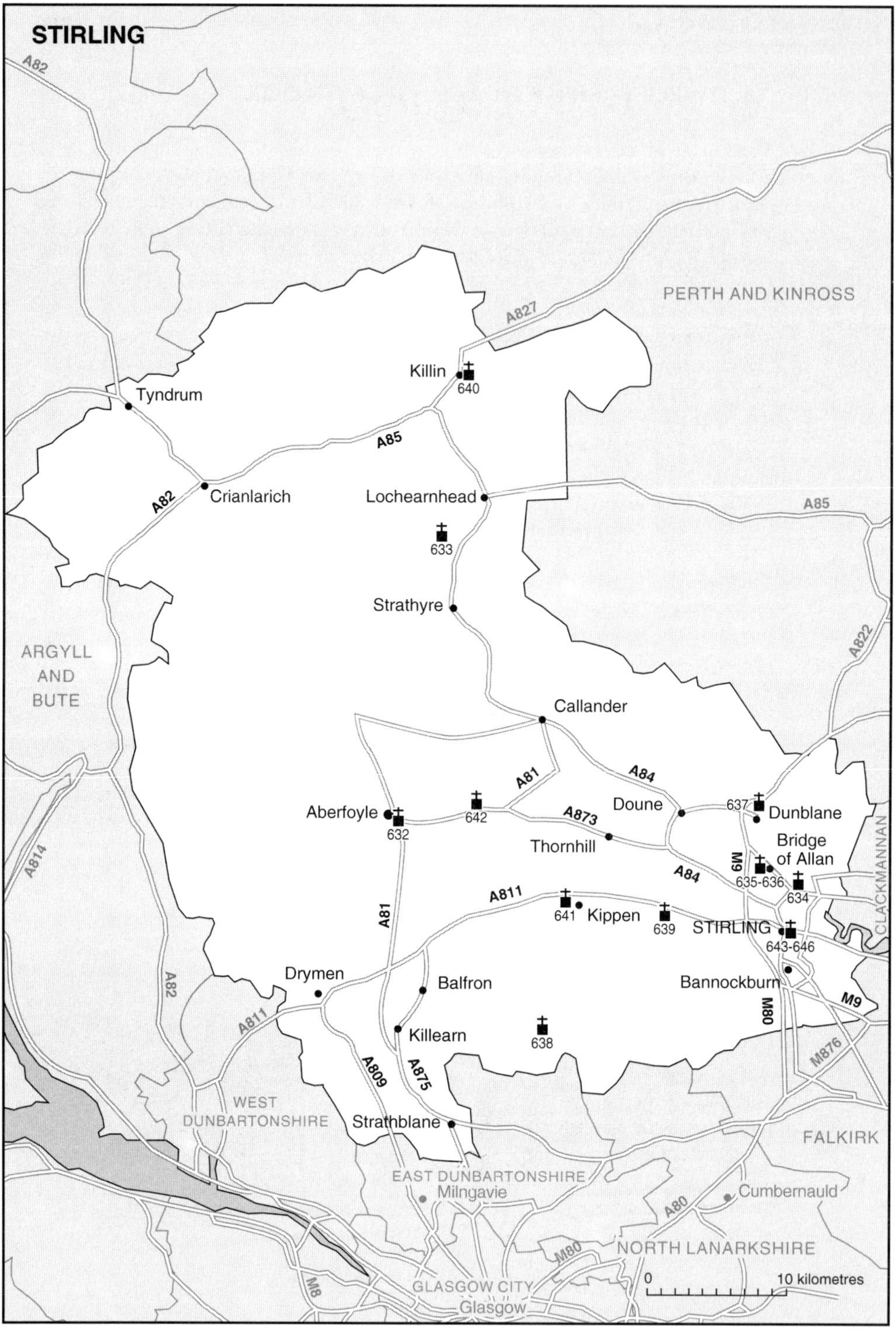
STIRLING
PERTH AND KINROSS
ARGYLL AND BUTE
WEST DUNBARTONSHIRE
EAST DUNBARTONSHIRE
NORTH LANARKSHIRE
GLASGOW CITY
FALKIRK
CLACKMANNAN
Tyndrum
Crianlarich
Killin
640
Lochearnhead
633
Strathyre
Callander
Aberfoyle
632
642
Doune
Thornhill
637
Dunblane
Bridge of Allan
635-636
634
641
Kippen
639
STIRLING
643-646
Bannockburn
Drymen
Balfron
Killearn
638
Strathblane
Milngavie
Cumbernauld
Glasgow
A82
A827
A85
A84
A81
A873
A811
A809
A875
A814
A822
A80
M9
M80
M876
M8
0
10 kilometres

STIRLING

Local Representative: Mr Louis Stott, Browsers' Bookshop, 25 High Street, Dunblane FK15 0EE (*telephone* 01786 824738)

632 ABERFOYLE PARISH CHURCH

NN 518 005

Loch Ard Road, Aberfoyle

John Honeyman designed this church which sits at the foot of Craigmore and on the banks of the River Forth. 1870, in early-Gothic style; it replaced the old kirk of Aberfoil on the south bank of the river reached by crossing the hump-backed bridge. The new church was enlarged in 1884 to include transepts. The interior is elegant with the minimum of ornamentation. Magnificent roof timbers. Stained glass, including a window by Gordon Webster, 1974. Two-manual pipe organ 1887 by Bryceson Brothers, London. On the B829. Linked with Port of Menteith. Sunday Service 11.15am

Open Saturday afternoon in August for church sale.
Other times, telephone Mr I Nicholson 01877 382337

CHURCH OF SCOTLAND WC **B**

633 BALQUHIDDER PARISH CHURCH

NN 536 209

Handsome parish church in dressed stone built in 1853 by David Bryce. Exhibition of the history of the church. Bell donated by Rev Robert Kirk (1644-92), a notable boulder font and the supposed gravestone of St Angus, possibly ninth-century. The ruins of the old parish church are in the graveyard where there are many intriguing carved stones, including that of Rob Roy MacGregor. A84 at Kinghouse. Linked with Killin. Sunday Service 12 noon

Open daily. Summer Music Sunday evenings during summer months

CHURCH OF SCOTLAND WC **B**

634 LOGIE KIRK, BY BLAIRLOGIE, STIRLING

NS 829 968

The tower, square and pedimented and surmounted by an octagonal belfry, was designed by William Stirling of Dunblane, 1805. The remainder of the church, an elegant whinstone box, by McLuckie & Walter of Stirling, 1901. Stained glass windows include one by C E Kempe and two modern windows by John Blyth. Fourteen oak panels depicting scenes from the Bible enclose the chancel and pulpit. The ruined Old Kirk of Logie, with its good selection of 17th- and 18th-century gravestones, is nearby. In idyllic rural setting at foot of Dumyat and in the shadow of the Wallace Monument. A91, four miles north-east of Stirling. Sunday Service 11.30am

Open Sundays, August 2-5pm

CHURCH OF SCOTLAND WC **B**

LOGIE KIRK, BLAIRLOGIE

635 HOLY TRINITY PARISH CHURCH, BRIDGE OF ALLAN

NS 791 974

Keir Street, Bridge of Allan

Built in 1860 and enlarged later, the church contains chancel furnishings designed in 1904 by the eminent Scottish architect, Charles Rennie Mackintosh. The church has an attractive timber roof and excellent stained glass windows. On corner with Fountain Road opposite Somerfield car park. Bus service from Stirling to Royal Hotel, one block. Rail service to Bridge of Allan Station, ten minutes walk. Sunday Service 11am

Open June to September, Saturdays 10am–4pm

CHURCH OF SCOTLAND ♿ WC **B**

636 ST SAVIOUR'S CHURCH, BRIDGE OF ALLAN

NS 792 973

Keir Street, Bridge of Allan

Built in 1857, and later enlarged, St Saviour's forms part of a group of Gothic revival buildings comprising church, hall and rectory by Alexander Ross. West window Stephen Adam. Pipe organ Forster & Andrews 1872. By road, bus and rail services from Stirling. On corner with Fountain Road.

Sunday Services: 8am Said Eucharist, first Sunday 10am Matins; remaining Sundays 10am Sung Eucharist and Sermon

Open during daylight hours. Other times, apply to the Rectory

SCOTTISH EPISCOPAL ♿ **B**

637 ST BLANE'S CHURCH, DUNBLANE

NN 783 014

High Street/Sinclairs Street Lane, Dunblane

Open 1854 as Free Church which through unions became East United Free Church and East Church of Scotland. United with former Leighton Church in 1952 to become St Blane's Church. Stained glass includes windows from Leighton Church, other windows by Roland Mitton. Interesting tapestries in vestibule including a reproduction of 'The Light of the World' by Holman Hunt. Pipe organ 1860 by Peter Conacher, perhaps the earliest example of his work in Scotland. Sunday Services: 11.15am (10.15am June to August), and 6.30pm

Open by arrangement, telephone the Minister 01786 822268 or Dr Duncan 01786 822657 or Mr Cattan 01786 822142

CHURCH OF SCOTLAND WC **B**

638 FINTRY KIRK

NS 627 862

Fintry Village

The present church, built in 1823, was constructed around the original kirk of 1642, and the congregation continued to worship in the old sanctuary while building went on around them! On completion, the inner church was demolished. The bell was transferred from old to new and is still in use today. Early 20th-century stained glass, including a First World War memorial window. Session House in the kirkyard added 1992. Linked with Balfron.

Sunday Service 10am

Open Easter Saturday, and first Saturday May to September, Saturday 2-4pm

CHURCH OF SCOTLAND WC **B**

639 GARGUNNOCK PARISH CHURCH

NS 707 943

Manse Brae, Gargunnock

Situated in very beautiful rural location. Village church 1650 on pre-Reformation foundation, renovated 1774 and 1891. Three individual outside stairs to three separate lairds' lofts. Two good 20th-century stained glass windows. War memorial by Lorimer. Mountain indicator. Graveyard. Five miles west of Stirling off A811. Sunday Service 11.30am

Open by arrangement, telephone Mr Brown 01786 860629

CHURCH OF SCOTLAND **B**

GARGUNNOCK PARISH CHURCH

640 KILLIN AND ARDEONAIG PARISH CHURCH

NN 571 330

Main Street, Killin

Distinctive white-harled octagonal classical church built in 1744 by the mason Thomas Clark to a design by John Douglas of Edinburgh. Inside it has been altered from a 'wide' church to a 'long' church. The Fillan Room, a small chapel for prayer in the tower, was created in 1990. In front of the church is a monument to Rev James Stewart (1701-96), minister of Killin who first translated the New Testament into Scots Gaelic (published 1763). At the eastern end of the village. Serves Morenish Chapel (see Perth & Kinross); linked with Balquhidder. Information about Services in Morenish Chapel from Tourist Information by Falls of Dochart in village. Sunday Service 10am

Open May to October during daylight hours

CHURCH OF SCOTLAND WC **B**

641 KIPPEN PARISH CHURCH

NS 652 849

Fore Road, Kippen

Built 1827 by William Stirling, extensively redesigned 1924-26 by Reginald Fairlie and Eric Bell. Exceptionally graceful, Latinate in style, and incorporating a splendid and perfectly combined display of (mainly) 20th-century Christian art, including works by Sir Alfred Gilbert, Alfred Hardiman, James Woodford and Henry Wilson as well as local craftsmen. Stained glass by Herbert Henrie. Sunday Service 11.30am

Open 9am-4.30pm (dusk in winter)

CHURCH OF SCOTLAND (ramp available for wheel chairs) WC **B**

KIPPEN PARISH CHURCH

642 PORT OF MENTEITH CHURCH

NS 583 011

On the shore of the Lake of Menteith, a church built in 1878 to designs by John Honeyman on a site of earlier churches with medieval connections. Simple rectangular plan, Gothic style, with square tower containing carillon of eight bells. Victorian pipe organ, probably by Brook. Surrounded by a graveyard and a few minutes walk from the ferry to Inchmahome where the ruined 13th-century Augustinian Priory may be visited. On B8034 beside the Lake Hotel. Linked with Aberfoyle. Sunday Service 10am

Open by arrangement, telephone Mr G Ellis 01877 385201

CHURCH OF SCOTLAND WC **B**

643 ALLAN PARK SOUTH CHURCH

NS 755 933

Dumbarton Road, Stirling

1886, Peddie & Kinnear with the interior modernised for the centenary in 1986 by Esmé Gordon. Radical change under consideration to bring interior and grounds to the requirements of the 21st century. Two large circular and three smaller stained glass windows to commemorate the fallen in the two World Wars, the ministry of the Rev Alan Johnston and members of the Kinross family. Sunday Service: 10am January to June, 11.30am July to December

Open by arrangement, telephone Mr Arthur Dawson 01786 475245

CHURCH OF SCOTLAND WC **B**

THE CHAPEL ROYAL, STIRLING CASTLE

644 THE CHAPEL ROYAL, STIRLING CASTLE

NS 790 941

There has been a Chapel in the Castle since at least 1117. It became the Chapel Royal of Scotland in the time of James IV in about 1500. The present building was built in 1594 by James VI for the baptism of Prince Henry. It was redecorated in 1629 in advance of the visit in 1633 of Charles I. After being subdivided to serve military uses there was a first phase of restoration in the 1930s, and the latest phase of work was completed in 1996. A large rectangular building with Renaissance windows and a central entrance framed by a triumphal arch along its south front. Notable features include decorative paintings of 1629 by Valentine Jenkin, a modern wagon ceiling reflecting the profile of the original, and modern furnishings, including a communion table cover designed by Malcolm Lochead. Services by arrangement

Open April to October, 9.30am–6pm; November to March, 9.30am–5pm

NON-DENOMINATIONAL (Castle Restaurant) **A**

645 CHURCH OF THE HOLY RUDE, STIRLING

NS 792 937

St John Street, Stirling

The original parish kirk of Stirling, used for the coronation in 1567 of James VI, at which John Knox preached. Largely built in 15th and 16th centuries. Medieval open-timbered oak roof in nave. Choir and apse added in 1555, the work of John Coutts, one of the greatest master masons of the later Middle Ages. Notable stained glass. Fine pipe organ, recently restored. Oak choir stalls and canopies 1965. Historic graveyard. Near to Stirling Castle. On Historic Stirling (open top) bus route. Sunday Service: time varies, see the church noticeboard

Open May to September, 10am-5pm. Venue for many concerts

CHURCH OF SCOTLAND **A**

646 HOLY TRINITY CHURCH, STIRLING

NS 793 934

Albert Place, Dumbarton Road, Stirling

One of Sir R Rowand Anderson's most distinctive churches 1878, close to Stirling Castle, old town and shops. Very close to town centre, on Historic Stirling (open top) bus route. Sunday Services: Eucharists 8.30 and 10.30am; Evening Prayer 6.30pm

Open mornings daily

SCOTTISH EPISCOPAL **B**

HOLY TRINITY CHURCH, STIRLING

CUMBRIA

647 THE CHURCH OF SCOTLAND IN CARLISLE

NY 3956

Chapel Street, Carlisle

Built 1834, altered 1979 and extended 1994. A city centre church, the interior is arranged over two floors with halls and kitchen on the ground floor and sanctuary on the first floor. The extension provides three floors housing ecumenical One World Centre, coffee lounge and Fair Trade shop. Two minutes from main 'Lanes' shopping area and civic centre, five minutes from the cathedral, castle and parks, ten minutes from Tullie House Museum. Two minutes from bus station in Lowther Street. Sunday Service 11am, also 6.30pm 1st Sunday (except January, July and August)

Open Monday to Friday 10am-2pm.

Coffee lounge and Fair Trade shop open Monday to Friday 10am-2pm

CHURCH OF SCOTLAND WC **A**

CHURCHES TO VISIT IN SCOTLAND

To:
The Director, Scotland's Churches Scheme,
Dunedin, Holehouse Road, Eaglesham, Glasgow
Telephone: 01355 302416
Fax: 01355 303181 *E-mail:* fraser@dunedin67.freeserve.co.uk
Website: http://churchnet.ucsm.ac.uk/scotchurch/

Please send me details and an application form for entry in the next Guidebook

Name

____

Address

____

____

Postcode

____

Name of Church

____

Address of Church

____

____

Postcode

____

Further copies of the current Guidebook are available from the above address at £10 hardback (£12 including p&p), £5.50 paperback (£7 including p&p); or contact Saint Andrew Press, 121 George Street, Edinburgh EH2 4YN (*Telephone:* 0131 225 5722. *Fax:* 0131 220 3113)

SCOTLAND'S CHURCHES SCHEME

ENCOURAGES CHURCHES TO:

- Open their doors with a welcoming presence
- Tell the story of the building, its purpose and the faith which inspired it
- Care for visitors in a sensitive and enriching way
- Work together with others to make the Church the focus of its community

SUPPORTS CHURCHES WITH:

- Thepublication of its comprehensive guidebook – *Churches to Visit in Scotland*
- Free advice on all aspects of visitor welcome, publicity, interpretation and exhibitions
- A network of local representatives in direct contact with headquarters
- Effective national publicity

SCOTLAND'S CHURCHES SCHEME GRATEFULLY ACKNOWLEDGES SUPPORT FROM:

THE SIR ALISTAIR BLAIR TRUST
THE CRUDEN FOUNDATION
THE DOUGLAS CHARITABLE TRUST
THE DULVERTON TRUST
THE EAST-WEST TRUST
THE INCHCAPE FOUNDATION
THE LLOYDS TSB FOUNDATION
THE McCORQUODALE TRUST
THE MANIFOLD TRUST
THE OPEN CHURCHES TRUST
THE P F CHARITABLE TRUST
THE PILGRIM TRUST

THE RUSSELL TRUST
SCOTTISH & NEWCASTLE PLC
THE PETER STORMONTH DARLING CHARITABLE TRUST
THE GARFIELD WESTON FOUNDATION

AND SEVERAL
ANONYMOUS PRIVATE BENEFACTORS

DONATIONS

Please consider making a donation to Scotland's Churches Scheme, either in an individual or corporate capacity, so that this guide may become an indispensable part of the Scottish calendar, and the permanent financial future of the Scheme is secured.

The options include [1] Donations and [2] Donations which generate additional monies through the reclaim of tax already paid by donors such as:

[a] A Deed of Covenant for a minimum of four years (see form overleaf)
[b] Gift Aid through donations of £250 or more
[c] Gifts through the Charities Aid Foundation
[d] Give As You Earn schemes operated by employers, and
[e] Bequests in a will, which are exempt from Inheritance Tax

Information and forms for [b] and [c] may be obtained from:

Scotland's Churches Scheme,
Dunedin, Holehouse Road,
Eaglesham,
Glasgow G76 0JF

Telephone: 01355 302416,
Fax: 01355 303181
E-mail: fraser@dunedin67.freeserve.co.uk

Donation Form

I enclose £ as a donation to Scotland's Churches Scheme

Name

Address

Postcode

Deed of Covenant Form

To: Scotland's Churches Scheme Charity No. SC 022868

I,

of [Address of Covenanter]

Postcode

promise to pay you for ___________ [1] years, or during my lifetime, if shorter, such a sum as, after deduction of income tax at the basic rate, amounts to

[2] £ ___________ each year

[3] from [*the date shown below*]

[4] Signed

Date

Witnessed by

Signature of Witness

Address of Witness

Postcode

NOTES

[1] Enter the period of the covenant which must be longer than three years

[2] Enter the amount you will be paying to the charity

[3] Delete as appropriate. If you chose to enter an actual date it must not be earlier than the date you sign the deed

[4] You should sign the deed and enter the date you actually sign it in the presence of a witness who should see you sign and then immediately sign as witness where shown

After completion, please send this form and remittance to: Scotland's Churches Scheme, Dunedin, Holehouse Road, Eaglesham, Glasgow G76 0JF. Tax reference ED729/94

THE OPEN CHURCHES TRUST

When Andrew Lloyd Webber in July 1994 launched The Open Churches Trust, he knew that the Trust could only hope to be a catalyst for something he felt needed to become a nation-wide crusade to return the best of our places of worship to the people.

The huge number of listed Grade I buildings, which had to be kept locked between services, meant that, initially at least, the Trust could only plant its corn-seed and hope that the culture of having these wonderful buildings open for the public to use and enjoy would spread.

The discovery of Scotland's Churches Scheme as a well-established and rapidly growing institution was like manna from Heaven. It is a perfect complement to The Open Churches Trust.

Our continued association has shown a marked and successful expansion throughout Scotland, England and Wales.

The arrival of 2000 AD has put much of the evolution of Christianity on a pedestal and through Simon Jenkins' wonderful book and articles a focus on opening churches is now publicly acknowledged. However well Scotland's Churches Scheme and this Trust do, we must not ever forget the Herculean effort being made by many institutions to achieve the same objectives. For Scots and English alike the Northumbria Christian Heritage project in 2000 is a wonderful example of the church, local government, tourist authorities and European regional funding working in concert.

Places of worship will continue to be the finest and most interesting monuments to man's ingenuity during the second millennium.

The National Trust
for Scotland
With over 100 varied properties in its care, The National Trust for Scotland is the conservation charity that protects and promotes Scotland's natural and cultural heritage for present and future generations to enjoy.
Explore Scotland's heritage and help to give our past a secure future by visiting our properties, becoming a member, or arranging a legacy.
For further information, please contact the Public Affairs Department, The National Trust for Scotland, 28 Charlotte Square, Edinburgh, EH2 4ET. Tel. (0131) 243 9300 or visit our web site at www.nts.org.uk.
WE CARE FOR SCOTLAND'S HERITAGE

LIFE & WORK
national and local news
lively features • strong opinions
plus...
interviews • profiles
readers' views
listings • competitions
LIFE & WORK
the magazine of the Church of Scotland
available on the first Sunday of the month
LIFE & WORK
DEBT CANCELLATION
YESTERDAY • TODAY • FOREVER • JESUS CHRIST
SPECIAL FEATURE:
OVER THE RAINBOW

INDEX OF ARTISTS

Number refers to church entry, not page

INDEX OF CHURCHES

Number refers to church entry, not page